THE MYSTERY BEHIND KNOWLEDGE:

Scepticism, Intentionality, and the Non-Conscious

Laurence Peddle

Paperback Print ISBN 978-1-8384289-0-7

Published by
Llyfrau Cambria Books, Wales, United Kingdom.
Cambria Books is a division of
Cambria Publishing Ltd.
Discover our other books at: www.cambriabooks.co.uk

Father

I saw him just once more
on that winter's night before
he left with the secret dead on Inver Hill
for one last October's long eclipse
wherein shadows all stand still.
Above dark Ireland's coast traced sea
it seemed he almost noticed me
and, for a moment, looked to say…
nothing. Raised a finger to his lips,
turned, and softly ebbed away.

Mike McNamara[1]

[1] Reprinted from the collection *Dialling a Starless Past* by kind permission of the author, Mike McNamara and the publishers Arenig Press. Available on Amazon and elsewhere.

Preface and Acknowledgements

The genesis of this book is not without interest, concerning as it does the world's longest railway station name. During a tutorial many years ago, a student mentioned that the station – Llanfairpwllgwyngyllgogerychwyrndrobwyllllantysiliogogogoch – was in Wales and that she had visited it. When I seemed to remember reading that the name was descriptive, she quipped that in any case no-one knew what it meant, for by the time one had read it to the end the beginning had been forgotten. "Perhaps one loses one's train of thought." another student, in so many words, piped up, and we laughed; but I was already, as it were, presenting my ticket.

For what had struck me with the full force, not of a train but of an epiphany, was that the uttering of a sentence is an event like any other, so that its understanding is conditional upon memory and expectation. What, then, of the implications for scepticism about induction and knowledge of the past? And if one such condition obtains, should there not be others, perhaps forming a system? From this point of departure via my PhD research at Cardiff University I worked out an anti-sceptical theory of knowledge, various parts of which were subjected to scrutiny by my peers at seminars and conferences over a period of several years. I benefited greatly from those discussions but the thesis about necessary conditions operating within a system over varying intervals of space and time has withstood criticism and has never hit the buffers. From departure to destination has taken twenty years, but this, I believe, has enabled the passengers to bond into a coherent group of arguments and themes.

Two decades is a long time to be stuck in an academic railway carriage, and the rushing past of so many years very nearly proved fatal to the project. In 2020 a serious illness came out of nowhere and a collision ensued, whereupon my former doctoral supervisor, Professor Christopher Norris, who happened to be passing, dragged me from the wreckage and took over the reins, not of the train, which I believe was powered by steam, but of anything that would effect a smooth transition from the train metaphor to one that involves horse-drawn conveyances of one kind or another. There must be something, but in the meantime I have Christopher and his wife, Valerie, to thank for finding a publisher who was able to turn typescript into print or into e-books in a matter of months rather than years. That person is Mr Chris Jones of Cambria Publishing, to whom I am very grateful. My thanks to Carolyn Michel of Design Elements for the book cover with its enchanting sylvan scene. The light filtering onto the woodland path from a hidden sun symbolises both insight to be gained and mystery to be contemplated.

Christopher Norris has given me so much support over all these months that the only way I can do it justice is to go into more detail. First, he restored my confidence, which was beginning to wane, in the book's academic worth, but also in my style of writing, with much in the way of humour as respite from close reasoning, and childhood reminiscence as respite from humour. And, too, he suggested to me, as has indeed proved to be the case, that the book would be better if there was less of it, in particular that the probability chapters, which consisted of numbers and mathematical symbols rather than words, would be immeasurably improved if removed altogether, and again the maxim about less being better, although taken to an extreme, still held good. I have, however, found a home for the expurgated chapters in my website at **www.laurencepeddle.com**, which is of general interest and not exclusively philosophical.

Speaking of which, the title of this book has also benefited from the knowledge Christopher has gained as the author of many academic works over a period of years, and although my original title was informative as to content, which it could hardly fail to be, given its length, he was able to convince me that there are important differences between the title of a book and an abstract of a book, the former working better if shorter than the latter, and again this turned out to be correct. The title we eventually agreed upon fits easily on the title page and even on the book spine. Christopher has, to sum up, been unwavering in his support and unsparing of the time that he has devoted to bringing the book up to standard and seeing it through to publication; and for this I shall always be grateful,

Next in line is my partner, Valerie Rogers, whom I love and

adore, and without whom, since a book needs an author, there would be neither; or at least I would be much thinner, rather like the book. Were it not for Val's daily struggle, in the early days of the illness, to find and prepare food that I could eat, I would have been reduced to eating food that I could drink. Fortunately, that problem has now been resolved, but she still has to work hard to support me, in particular to keep my spirits up and her worries hidden.

My thanks, too, to Professor Jonathan Webber of Cardiff University for his advice and encouragement, and to Professor Peter Lamarque of York University, again for the advice and encouragement I received but also for hinting, I seem to recall, that the book was overlong. A special thanks to Mike McNamara, about whom I shall wax lyrical, this being the first time for me to use that expression, not only in a book but also in my life, hence my barely contained excitement. Mike is a singer, songwriter, poet and leader of the Big Mac Wholly Soul Band based in Gwent.[2] Val and I became enamoured of Mike and the band several years ago, and I progressed very quickly from passive groupie to warm-up dance exhibitionist, though with Big Mac there was rarely any need to encourage dancers onto the floor. Interestingly, the less energetic I became with advancing years the more I blinged myself up, and if it had not been for the pandemic and lockdown, I quite probably would have ended up totally immobile in front of the stage but very sparkly and covered in hotfix crystals. I owe to Mike and the band the most thrilling Saturday nights out that one can readily conceive of, and my dream, now that the one about writing a book has been realised, is to dance once more to Mustang Sally, the ecstasy too much as it crescendoes to a climax and we suddenly stop, the music and I, with only the one starting up again, if this is the way that my life has to be.

I dedicate this book to Val, to Valerie, to Christopher, to

---

[2] Mike McNamara's published poetry collections are accessible via the Facebook Big Mac site at https://www.facebook.com/groups/21693080282

If you wish, you can read my reviews of Mike's poetry on my website. The collection titles are "Loose Canon", "This Transmission" and "Dialling a Starless Past". There are also my reports of Big Mac gigs .

Chris, Jonathan and Peter, to Mike and the other members of the band, whom I hope to meet once again one day, and to the clinical staff at Velindre, The Royal Glamorgan and Prince Charles hospitals, who took me straight from the crash to A&E, where my book needed umpteen stitches and some chapters amputated. Such a conceit, indeed the writing of this preface as a whole, is my way of letting off steam, the train standing at the platform once more, and in celebration of travels now completed and the discoveries that were made. One of them, concerning as it does the hidden reality of everyday consciousness, still has the power to unsettle me, the runaway train unstoppable at this point, and I believe that encountered for the first time its effects will be even more pronounced. Elsewhere, too, the view from each carriage is in parts very unfamiliar, and I trust that the new sights and insights will make the journey worthwhile.

CONTENTS

Introduction

I should perhaps begin with an account, albeit in barest outline, of what I hope to achieve. My aim is to refute the sceptic about induction, intention, perception, other minds and the past, but to that end I need also to solve a puzzle about the authority with which we self-ascribe sensations or beliefs and other intentional states and to resolve the more general problem of the underdetermination of theory by evidence. This programme can be carried through only if certain distinctions: between induction, other forms of factual inference and physical description, or between direct and indirect perception, or between knowledge of oneself and of others, are wrested away from the sceptic and re-examined in a more forgiving light. What is then revealed is that our reasoning about the world operates within a system characterised by the interconnectedness and interdependence of concepts and by necessary conditions of their application. In deploying this notion of a system, I hope to be able to confront the various issues in the same arena as that occupied by contemporary debate on them and thereby to contribute to it. Nothing if not venturesome, I shall also try to show that in trawling for solutions we bring to the surface the mysterious nature of the world.

For this to be achieved, we first need to solve the problems, one of my aims with regard to induction being to establish that radical inductive scepticism leads to epistemological solipsism, which is incoherent or self-refuting. Further to that aim, the basic conditions by which philosophical debate or discourse in general is made possible need to be exhibited, my concern being to demonstrate that they cannot be satisfied within the constraints of the solipsist's undermining of all that we think we know. To that end, one may ask what it is for indicative sentences to manifest semantic content, without which neither the sceptic and his opponents nor philosophy itself could exist. This leads us into a debate about the nature of intentionality, and in joining the fray I seek to exhibit the ways in which the intentional, insofar as its analysis is possible at all, may be analysed in terms of a system. I develop and defend that analysis by means of a critical examination of

Wittgenstein on meaning and understanding, together with a shorter critique of semantic non-factualism. Thus, it is that my treatment of the intentional precedes that of the epistemological problems.

Wittgenstein and the Intentional

In my discussion of Wittgenstein in the first and second chapters I take issue with his professed aim of dispelling philosophical perplexity about intentionality, for it seems to me that the problem of what it is that the intentional consists in is both genuine and profound. Wittgenstein, however, equates meaning and understanding with use, thereby rejecting the view that they are realised in subjective inner processes, with its implication that the first-person standpoint is prior to the third, and in ways to be determined. What I try to show is that his account of intentionality is vulnerable on two fronts, the first of which concerns the shortcomings of the thesis equating meaning with use. In what way does the concept of the past unfold along the lines of use and practice? My having had porridge this morning is an instance of a past event, but the connection with use is that I am using this present sentence to refer to my breakfast and to specify the main course. But also, I am using that sentence and this one to expose the absurdity of equating meaning with use, in relation both to the concept of the past and to the self-referential meaning of the present sentences. How should one even begin, it might be asked, to deconstruct this paragraph in terms of uses that do not just depend on its meaning but equate with it? Thus it is that we arrive at my own thesis, which owes much to Colin McGinn; namely, that the intentional is irreducible. In other words, and in line with common sense, that there are facts about meaning, understanding and so on and that they fall into a category of their own.

Along the second front we find Wittgenstein's defence of the third-person standpoint encapsulated in the slogan that inner processes stand in need of outward criteria. One might think that the converse would also have to hold, so that outward criteria need inner processes; but in fact I wish to take it further, for my contention, if common sense can be contentious, is that we can reason to ourselves, come to conclusions and solve problems, all without needing any third person light to filter into this inner cogitative sanctum. Consider my working out an *n*th term formula on the basis of the first few terms of a number sequence; and now ask yourself whether my opening the curtains a little by writing things down, perhaps those initial terms, is a necessary condition of my understanding, in other words of my working the answer out – or whether, on the contrary, it is merely a mnemonic device. We are within striking distance of the private-language argument, in defence of which it will perhaps be objected against us that, memory aids apart, it must be logically possible for me to share my reasoning with other people. But this is a truism and it need not detain us if the private language argument reduces to it: of course other people can in principle understand my internal monologue – they speak English, one assumes, and in any case it is conceivable that they could be in whatever brain state I am in when I work out, in any language, the *n*th term formula or whatever it may be.

The point to be made is that once we have established a position opposed to Wittgenstein's, as also to the semantic nonfactualism espoused by Saul Kripke, so that intentional concepts are no longer under siege, then we are free to explore them without having to keep away from the battlements. How, though, is the siege to be lifted? It is at this juncture that the notion of irreducibility comes to the rescue, the charge being led by Colin McGinn, the argument under his command running as follows. That intentional concepts have their own identity, such that the answer to the question of what it is to mean addition by plus is just that it is to mean addition by plus. Embracing this thesis and flying its colours, I now maintain that we are free to analyse intentional concepts rather than having to defend them. Thus liberated, we find that intentional states combine the occurrent and the dispositional, which therefore cannot conflict, the task of analysis being to tease out their interconnections. This requires the notion of a system, in terms of which the theory is outlined as follows, the reference being to understanding. First, we communicate with others only if we communicate with ourselves, so that communal understanding derives from that of the individual, which is therefore the basis on which the analysis proceeds. The elements to be

3

married up are the occurrent, the dispositional and the irreducible, together with conditions of discourse. If, to argue from a particular case, I understand the even number sequence, then my understanding is occurrent, for I must be suitably disposed, and if I now realise an appropriate disposition, perhaps by writing down the first few terms of the sequence, then again this is occurrent. Since understanding is irreducible, it cannot be defined in terms of dispositions; rather, one is disposed to understand in one way but not another, the possibility of misunderstanding also being accommodated.

But how, one might ask, is it possible from a first-person viewpoint to misunderstand a thing? This is not a rhetorical question on behalf of cognitive omniscience; on the contrary, it harks back to Kripke and his dismissal of the anti-sceptical appeal to dispositions, or further back to Wittgenstein's remark about whatever seems right being right. Seeking an answer, we note that the irreducibility thesis, insofar as we are obliged to accept its ramifications, determines the stance that we take on the associated issues. We know, if the notion of a system is brought into play, that misunderstanding is discoverable only within a framework of understanding; and, too, that it is quite easy to misunderstand, with complete cognitive failure requiring almost no effort. Take, for instance, a number sequence found in Wittgenstein's *Philosophical Investigations* and discussed in the first chapter of the present work. It is given by 1,5,11,19,29 as the first five terms, the aim being to work out an nth term formula. Suppose I assume that I need only consider the first two terms, perhaps now arriving at $2n^2 - 2n + 1$. I then realize my mistake when I substitute $n = 3$ into the formula. This involves a great deal of understanding on my part, without which the mistake could not have come to light. And if I had not bothered to check? Then I would not have discovered my mistake. Even on a verificationist view, this is not to imply that there is no mistake to discover. It makes perfect sense to speak of mistakes that I am unaware of making, just as it would in the case of my ignorance of other people's.

This is, indeed, unintentionally illustrated in the *Investigations* itself. Wittgenstein refers to a pupil taking his teacher to mean by an instruction to add 2 that he should ' "Add 2 up to

4

1000, 4 up to 2000, 6 up to 3000 and so on." ' (185); but there is no such sequence; for although we may arrive at 2000 from 1000 by the repeated addition of 4, it is not possible to then arrive at 3000 in increments of 6. Wittgenstein failed to check the sequence; but if we are unable to grasp his point, it is not because we have not noticed his mistake. What one does need to notice, that said, is that the section coheres only if a particular distinction is brought to bear: that between individual and interpersonal understanding, a separation that is not supportive of Wittgenstein's thesis. Thus it is that he conflates, and in a bad way, the separate sides.

Moving on from the intentional, we know that our findings have ramifications, for instance into the problem of avowals. According to Crispin Wright, the irreducibility thesis needs to be buttressed at the point where certainty attaches to avowals of intentional mental states, which he takes to be both occurrent and dispositional. How is it possible, he asks, to be authoritative about one's intentions if one is required to be suitably disposed, and in ways that go beyond the associated occurrent mental state? There is no such difficulty, he believes, in the case of avowed sensations, for one self-ascribes them on the basis of experiencing them. From these misgivings of his, the link between the avowals problem and the irreducibility thesis does not, in my view, emerge with much clarity; but what is independently apparent is that the problem is amenable to a system-based approach and the thesis to further investigation. This is the subject matter of the third chapter.

Embarking upon it, I argue that avowals of intentional states and of sensations are equally perplexing. Wright's mistake is to confuse avowed object with the avowal itself, this latter being intentional irrespective of whether its object is. Its dynamics belong within a system of conditions and connections; and these are such that an avowal obtains only if understood, with cognitive avowals themselves being subject to necessary conditions. I cannot doubt my own understanding in ways that threaten the doubt itself, this latter also being an avowable object, as are the beliefs by which I think that I understand or doubt that I do, all of which involves further understanding. The essential insight in relation to

5

the notion of a system or network is that the net may be cut or stretched at particular points only if intact elsewhere. The philosophical sceptic, held in its folds but oblivious of it or utterly unaware, narrows his myopic view until only particular interstices are in focus. Detecting a weak point, he then extrapolates from it as a general assumption, in which he may be joined by his opponents, who also fail to notice the incoherence. For the general case would equate with every node being cut, the philosopher's arguments having nothing to cling to. More succinctly: the sceptic refutes himself, as does his opponent in the assumptions that they share.

If this is correct, then the problem of avowals is that of analysis, by which it may be shown that avowals form a continuum with propositional attitudes or already include them—it hardly matters which— and that straightforward factual assertions, predicated of oneself as knowing the facts, are also epistemically continuous with avowals. That is, if I say that I feel afraid, this being unequivocally a mental-state avowal, or if I say that I am afraid that a lion will attack me, this being a propositional attitude, or if I say that I am afraid that the lion that attacked me will return, this being very obviously empirically indebted, then all of them are epistemically accountable, the differences between them being interesting but not important. For instance all three reports, even the first, are conditional upon the deliverances of memory and expectation, a fact from which much may be extracted, and will be in the body of the book. Speaking of which, the solution, I eventually conclude, is that avowals constitute a necessary condition of discourse, analysis of which has revealed that their authoritativeness is hedged about in a variety of ways, as also that within these bounds it is genuine. This latter clause germinates many seeds, showing as it does that analysis sheds light on concepts rather than uprooting them; hence the seedlings, but only if the growing conditions are right. I cannot authoritatively self-ascribe pain unless I can also say that I am not in pain or that I was in pain but no longer.

What, though, of the analysis of intentionality, given that it shares a double billing with avowals in chapter three. The billboard lights by which it is advertised illuminate the intentional as

6

a thing-in-itself, but showing its parts in any detail requires the spotlight of analysis. For Wittgenstein, to understand a numerical sequence is perhaps to feel that one traverses all the steps in advance; hence the perplexity he seeks to dispel. This is, if we are to make sense of it, a pointless trip to take; for the arithmetical reconnaissance person would have to understand the numbers thus anticipated. For us, in any case, it is a problem that challenges us to find a resolution, its difficulty also apparent in the case of recollective memory; and, too, in that of linguistic as well as arithmetical understanding. Recalling a childhood picnic in the hills above my home, it is as if I re-live the past at the same time as my memory reduces to mental images, feelings of nostalgia and other flotsam in the flow of consciousness. And these words I write are squiggles invested with meaning, its character unknown, except that it goes beyond them. What is needed is a theory of the intentional that accounts for its particular paradoxicality and, as we shall see, turns out to belong to a larger theory: that of consciousness as the bright star in a firmament of dark matter, the latter manifested in the gravitational pull of the non-conscious. This global theory will rise above the horizon from one chapter to the next until it reaches its zenith and completes the present work.

Perception and the Problem of Induction

With that in mind, I now turn to perception and take issue with perceptual scepticism, again by deploying the notion of a system, my target this time being the theories of indirect realism and phenomenalism. My aim is to defend direct realism, to which end I first point out that the phenomena exploited by the sceptic, such as those of illusion and perspectival relativity, in other words change of appearance according to perspective, are particular forms of what I refer to as perceptual variability, defined in terms of the relation between perceiver and object being such that the appearance of the latter, as indeed of both, will vary with perceptual conditions. My thesis is that variability of this kind is fundamental to what it is to perceive, a corollary of which is that it must be compatible with direct realism within a system, so that the sceptic cannot make legitimate use of it. Similarly, I argue that perception is intrinsically intentional, where this includes its being inferential, again to the detriment of the sceptical agenda.

If this is correct, then the insights gained are transformative, for we know that the intentional does not reduce, as also that our thesis, or one of them, is that it thereby acquires a mystique. One of the constructions upon these pages is that of ultimate intentional mystery, its foundations in the non-conscious, the structure arising from one chapter to the next. It follows that the material world is itself a thing of concealment, its appearances presenting a united perceptual front. Not even the slightest stone, after all, can be chipped at until it cracks open, its essence laid bare, for new sensory surfaces instantly close over, the stone's hidden truth now dispersed among its flakes.

This brings us to the problem of induction, a salient feature of which is that knowledge of the past and present is assumed to be exempt from sceptical threat, this being reserved for one's apparent knowledge of future events. Pointing this out, I now argue from perception being intrinsically predictive and memory-belief being non-demonstrative to the conclusion that the radical inductive sceptic is obliged to reject knowledge of the present and the past. This is epistemological solipsism, which is easily shown to be self-refuting, this form of scepticism thereby being fatally undermined.

The sceptic's arguments, however, their sting removed, continue to pose a threat, if not to knowledge then to understanding. If empirical inference—my thesis will be that inference of a narrowly inductive kind is unimportant—lacks the force of logic, and if it can be justified only by begging the question, as Hume would have it, then how can we know anything at all? The answer, if room is left for the mysterious and perplexing, is that Hume was correct in one sense but not another. It is false that empirical inference lacks the force of logic; for the *a priori* enters into it via necessary conditions. It is true that any justificatory appeal to, for instance, probability theory, pre-supposes the validity of induction; but it does not follow that the sceptic on the bridge can congratulate the crew. On the contrary, he is now becalmed, and the forces closing in on him are those by which the notion of a system will emerge as victor. *All* empirical belief

8

belongs within a system in which the truth of a myriad other beliefs is presupposed. Pressing this key, I expect the upper case "P" to appear on the screen, as indeed it does, and again for good measure. And now try to make a list of all the enabling beliefs by which that action, expectation and confirmation was made possible. Progress, if you like, to imagining an ancient age when there were no keys, except for doors, and Hume was obliged to use a quill when he wrote that "complete unpredictability attaches to all future events", or words to that effect: how did he know that the quill would work? Or that the written sentence would end with "events"? The source of our continuing perplexity is that there is no escape from the system.

Applied Mathematics

That being the case, I now propose that Hume and his critics should be taken to ask not whether we can justify our empirical beliefs but how this is to be achieved. This is moderate scepticism in connection with analysis and I now treat of it by examining the various ways in which applied mathematics has been enlisted to the cause of justifying empirical belief. Since my contention is that these recruits have logical force if suitably trained, I try to show that deductive relations may carry over into physical-world application. But what I mean by this is that the propositions of mathematics belong within a system, one which also accommodates empirical reasoning, so that all cognition operates within it. A defining property of that system, I now claim, is that our discourse about both concrete and abstract features of the world is governed by necessary conditions. This framing within a network, it will become apparent, is one in which the difference between empirical and deductive inference is not such as to bring them into strict opposition.

Since this is all in urgent need of elucidation, I now focus in detail on applied geometry, the probability calculus and the theory of arrangements. Consider the theorem of Pythagoras, which states that the sum of the squares on the sides of a right triangle equals the square on the hypotenuse. If, for instance, a right triangle of sides three and four inches is drawn, then by Pythagoras the hypotenuse is five inches. This, according to the empiricists,

9

is a contingent fact, which Hume, no doubt, would file under induction, the logical force of the Pythagoras theorem then being confined to the pure mathematics which drives it, and this in its turn perhaps being dismissed as analytic. As a filing system it all works very well, but one's conviction that the hypotenuse *must* be five inches long would seem to have fallen out of the in-tray. Picking it up, the rationalist places it in the tray marked "*a priori* knowledge" or "synthetic *a priori* truth", where its existence is at least acknowledged. How, though, to resolve the perplexity we may feel? It is not unknown for appeal to be made to the fact of different possible geometries, but I fail to see how this can bring any cognitive relief. All that is needed is to specify that our concern is with planar geometry, whereupon the baffled face of lines, angles and areas re-appears.

Similarly with arrangement theory, which again has deductive impetus when applied to, for instance, the number of ways in which heads and tails may be combined when r from n coins are selected, that number derived from the theory. Try as one might, one will never find an additional way, and standing the coins on edge would be a futile form of cheating. Note, too, that in this case, unlike the geometrical, nothing counts as an alternative axiomatic scheme that also has application. So far, then, the notion of applied logical force has been visited but not penetrated, and little has been said about closing the gap between logic and fact.

We do, however, have a plan, concerning which the epistemological analysis of memory in terms of necessary conditions should now prove instructive, at least if our aim is to break the deadlock between rationalist and empiricist. Note, to begin with, that all reasoning at every moment depends on memory, and that such reasoning cannot be more certain than the memories that enter into it. How, then, is memory to be justified? The answer I give is that the question of justification can arise only in particular cases, for the process of doubting, verifying or disconfirming particular memories must always be informed by others, the veridicality of which cannot itself be in question, or only at the cost of an infinite regress opening up. Taking memory in general to be veridical is a necessary condition of cognitive processes and is fundamental within a system. This is also true, and in the same way, of expectation and recognition, and likewise of meaning and understanding. If we consider what it is to understand, it is only in particular cases or in relation to particular categories that I can doubt whether I understand or believe that I do not, for doubting involves understanding, which illuminates all belief. To argue in this way is to appeal to an epistemological anthropic principle.

Keeping this in mind, let us ask again about the logical status of geometry. Re-visiting Pythagoras, we know that the theorem about right triangles may be established in several ways, for instance in the form of Euclid's proof, which depends axiomatically on such notions as that of line, area, angle and similarity. Given that the axioms are satisfied, the theorem logically follows, so that our concern is with the axioms. What, then, of their enabling conditions and the logical status of the proposition that the axioms are satisfied? Is it a contingent fact that — to simplify matters — straight lines exist or can always be constructed? But now, it is doubtful whether one can conceive of a strictly non-linear physical world; and this hardens into certainty if such a world is required to accommodate philosophical debate about the logical status of geometrical applications. But this is indeed a requirement, and we do have that debate; therefore ours is not such a world. Arguments of this type are one of the key elements in the approach taken in this book. Since we know that there are straight lines, the intersection of any two of them is always possible, at which point, so to speak, it is easily proved that they form opposite angles that are equal, as also that the lines can be perpendicular; and the proof of other properties, including Pythagorean ones, will follow if a third line is added to form a triangle. Generalising to the whole of geometry, this is to say that the possibility of geometrical application is a necessary condition of the existence of a physical world in which the question of logical status can arise.

If to this it is objected that even if necessary conditions guard the door to applied maths they do not provide a key, then that, suitably contextualised, is one of the lessons to be learned: that the fact of such application exposes the limits of human understanding. The context is that in which necessary and contingent may be shown to be more intimate than they seem, in which case everyday empirical inference also has its imperatives. Examples abound if only I can think of one, for instance my belief that this matchstick triangle in front of me will not spontaneously combust within the next minute. Or, if that is deemed unsuitable, perhaps because a sudden burning event is just one of a myriad possibilities, all negligible, then replace it with my belief that the triangle will be physically stable for at least that length of time. These two examples are connected, but we shall set that aside, and in order to make a more pertinent point: that the compelling character of my faith in time-limited matchstick stability is in every way the equal of my certainty that the hypotenuse of this right triangle, given sides of three and four inches, is of length five inches. The crucial point, established in the body of the work, is that the two certainties are interdependent vis a vis enabling conditions.

Problem Resolution and Mystery

Once the sceptical problems under consideration have been dealt with, our attention should turn, in my opinion, to the metaphysical implications of that notion of a system which has been instrumental in resolving them. If perception is intrinsically inferential and intentional and thereby belongs within a system, as opposed to the deliverances of our senses never going beyond immediately given perceptual data, then it shares this property with knowledge of the past via memory and with empirical and deductive knowledge in general. My claim is that the sceptic deludes himself when he believes that from an external vantage point he is able to critically examine that system; for nothing counts as being outside it, and this is just as true for the non-sceptic as for the sceptic, so that there really is no escape, neither in philosophy nor in the sciences.

What follows, with regard to metaphysical implication, is that the existence of a closed system is inherently mysterious; and also, as I then try to show, that the philosophical problems that concern us, when all of them are solved, transmute individually into mystery, this being manifested in conceptual discontinuities which overlap with those from which the problems originally derived. Since these discontinuities together constitute a place of fundamental darkness, of such depth that it is uncontacted by

12

illumination nearer the surface, only the notion of ultimate mystery can do justice to this metaphysical subduction zone. That said, we may ask what the surface consists in, and this will give us a reference point for the mystery itself. Hence the discussion, over two chapters, of mystery as a philosophical topic, or mysterianism in the case of Colin McGinn, those chapters also being used as a platform for my own views on the nature of the mystery in question. If these are correct, then the surface referred to, if we continue the analogy, is consciousness itself, and the mystery resides in the non-conscious, which is connected with the conscious via intentionality.

Thus it is that I claim to have devised a new theory of mind: one that connects the conscious, the non-conscious, the intentional and the mysterious. Since the newcomer here is the notion of the non-conscious, the metaphysical counterpart of the unconscious mind in psychological theory, I put some effort into establishing its credentials; and, too, I suggest reasons why the existence of such a realm would seem to have been overlooked. These feature in my discussion of what I refer to as the myth of conscious adequacy. Another of the threads running through these two chapters is again that of mystery

How is it, to retrace our steps a little, that perplexity remains after the individual problem has been solved, and that it finds its objective justification in what seems to be a mystery inseparable from the solution? Since the answer depends on the particular problem, let us first of all take our bearings from paradox and discontinuity relating to perception, the philosophical study of which we may imagine ourselves embarking upon for the first time. Having waded out from the shallows of naive realism, we quickly discover that we are not so buoyant in these deeper waters, the old assumptions being dragged under by the sceptic, and that the objective reality of the external world is under threat. We learn that the bent appearance of a partially immersed stick has sinister implications, and we worry about our own immersion in the problem, our thoughts dangling in sceptic-infested waters; and, too, we are disturbed to discover that the subjective component of perceptual experience looms larger than we had assumed, because, for instance, the transparency of visual experience turns

13

out to be an artefact of the phenomenology involved. Already obvious, at least upon reflection, is that the other senses are deeply subjective, audition being a case in point: how can it be, with regard to hearing a sound, that it is both a subjective experience and an instance of the auditory perception of objects and events in the world?

Still, at least there is something out there, however far distant on the horizon, that we discern through this fog of subjectivity and doubt, except that it may now occur to us, though it is often overlooked, that if we query whether the physical world is real, then the existence of our sense-organs and body must also be in question, and therefore the nature of the perceptions from which we started. Reflection along these lines is not just difficult but also disorientating and leaves us all at sea, though we always have to act, as Hume would say. But in the meantime we may pause in our struggles, ear flat against the water, and listen for aftershocks as new theories displace old certainties.[3]

If one such theory, the one I have sketched in this introduction, is correct, then it is partly by appeal to the inferential and variable characteristics of perception that the sceptic about direct realism may be refuted if the notion of a system is deployed – but these are among the very properties that form the basis for perceptual scepticism itself. Hence the persistence of the perplexity by which the arguments of the sceptic gain purchase. How is it, for instance, that this table-top in front of me can vary in colour, or apparent colour, according to conditions of observation? The system-based answer is that perceptual variability pervades the whole of what it is to perceive, as with the varying colour appearances of a table, only one of which is deemed to be its real colour. Thus, the real colour of the table, or of any object with a fixed colour, has basic ontological parity with its other apparent colours and in that sense is not privileged in relation to them. The distinction between real and apparent colour obtains within a system in which colour variation enters into both terms of the dis-

---

[3] The first draft had "ears", not "ear", but then I realized that this is anatomically impossible

14

tinction and into the criteria by which it is applied. Thus it is that the sceptic loses purchase when perceptual variability is shown to be fundamental. But now, although this answer has to be accepted, given the truth of the theory, it is itself a source of perplexity — or, if preferred, of ontological disquiet akin to a sense of existential mystery. When I look at this table, after all, I see it as a solid, stable object despite its visual variability. It is at this point that the notion of perceptual intentionality will throw light on the matter, but only by deepening the darkness that remains; for it is possible to show that intentionality, both perceptual and in general, itself constitutes a mystery, or even that all that is mysterious derives from it. This will be revealed when we arrive at a detailed theory of consciousness, only the outline of which will be sketched in this introduction.

Mystery and the Past

If perception is intrinsically inferential, and intentional in other ways, too, then it necessarily involves the passage of time and the memory of past events. That being the case, the idea of the past is itself mired in paradox, so that once again we find ourselves manifesting perplexity via the posing of rhetorical questions, similar in tone to those about perceptual intentionality. How is it, for instance, that a mental image can seem to be the kind of thing that the memory of a past event consists in? This question, less rhetorical when elevated into a philosophical problem, at that level may receive an answer in which the question's presuppositions, about memory being reducible to mental images and suchlike, are rejected in favour of the concept of the past being irreducible in its intentionality. This, as far as it goes, resolves the conceptual problem, and the epistemological problem capsizes in its wake. How can there be any reason to trust one's memory, the sceptic asks, given that the past affords no direct epistemic access? The answer is that the impossibility involved is fundamental and applies to all memory, including that by which the sceptical question conveys the sceptic's argument, so that self-refutation follows from the question itself. Within a system the embracing of memories by which others are kept at arm's length for purposes of scrutiny is a necessary condition of memory, as also of the ex-

15

pectation integral to it.

That said, the perplexity re-invents itself and perhaps deepens, so that it is quiescent only for a time, the reason for which is that to lose one's grip on memory as philosophical problem is to fall back into a sea in which the metaphysics of the concept of memory is unaffected by solutions at the surface. Beginning to descend, suppose I actively consult my recollections when describing my childhood home. The back door opened into a scullery; on the right a net-curtained window above a sink with a metal draining board. Against the wall opposite the door a boiler, mainly for the washing of my father's working clothes. And now I see with such ghostly vividness, as if beholding an apparition, my mother using a stick to push trousers and shirts into the boiling water. But how can it be, I ask myself, more out of surrender than hope, that I remember all this as if communing with the past? I know that memory is irreducible, its intentionality a thing in itself, but the same question keeps knocking at the door: how can my memories of my mother leaning over the rail of the boiler, of the scalding water churning and foaming, of swollen clothes breaking the surface like whales in a storm, be both real and ethereal, as if here, now, and yet so far from home? It is as if a ghostly leviathan of memory rises up from the past into a turbulent present, events from one's childhood vividly illuminated in its phosphorescent wake.

In what way, one might ask, is the notion of memory related to that of the past? This quickens the descent, for when I recall so vividly my mother in the danger zone of the boiler, the fury barely contained, I see myself tremulously observing her, and I wonder what she and I were thinking. In reality, of course, I could not see myself, and if on that basis my memory is deemed to be false or distorted, then this is to assume, perhaps, that it bears an intimate causal relation to remembered objects or events, in some sense as if it were a copy of them. But in what sense, exactly? How can my memory-copy of my mother doing the washing, which took an hour or two, itself last only a minute or two? And how, in any case, might a fleeting, ghostly mental image, devoid of numerical identity, be a copy of a physical object? And not just a physical object, as if static, but my mother washing clothes, dragging them out of the boiler, then perhaps feeding them through the wringer, and carrying them out to the washing line.

But now, if this is correct then it points to a remarkable fact: that the intentionality of memory goes beyond the conscious experience of it, and in such a way that we mistake this latter for the whole, so that not only non-conscious memory but the fact of its existence, until we reflect on it, is hidden from view. Memory is intentional and so is the declarative use of language; hence the close link between the recollection of a past event and its description. Just as my memory of my mother involves memory images and other conscious phenomena, so it is that these words I am writing, which are about her, resemble her not at all. And nor, in other words, do the memory images. This should be obvious once pointed out, but we may have to ponder the matter in the case of my referring to marks on paper themselves, again including the present sentence. And in both cases the intentionality involved is on the one hand undeniable, insofar as it is conscious, and on the other hand completely opaque, insofar as it is not. Hence the remarkable fact: that I do not know what the past consists in, nor do I understand language as a form of the intentional. This is mysterious and shocking, even more so if we note that these paragraphs, about the opacity of memory and language, themselves instantiate it. To repeat: I have no grasp of the concept of the past, or if I do then it must reside in the non-conscious, which in a quite peculiar sense is a prohibited area.

Speaking of which, the perplexity about the past that we rationalise as mystery also manifests itself in relation to very recent memory as it merges into awareness of the present. If the lived reality of present experience falls away into the past in the very act of coming into existence, thereby conflicting with our impression of that reality as existing in, as it were, the continuous present tense, then a similar discontinuity must obtain in the particular case of present physical reality. To exhibit its nature, note first that we are never more at home with our sense of the physically real than when examining a medium-sized solid object of stable appearance, preferably one that we can handle, such as a pebble. A presently examined pebble, then, fits snugly against the ontological benchmark by which we judge the reality of the contents of this world, whereas those belonging to the past fall short in a way that may be hidden from us. Thus, I say that yesterday I plucked this pebble from the beach, and I thereby refer to an event which was real at the time, just as my now licking the pebble, having washed it first, is presently real; but my memory of this pebble found then, perhaps experienced as affording direct access to that past event, might be the same even if entirely false; for it is a present process of recall, whereas there is no ontological sense in which the past at present exists, or the present in the past, and therefore no direct access. Hence the discontinuity, for the impression we may have is of such access, and yet the past may seem unreal compared with the present, or a presently observed object or event, despite our grip on the felt reality of the present itself being uncertain, given that it is instantly swept away into the past. The only way to ease the associated cognitive disorientation, in my view, is to spin the other way, thereby accepting that there are intrinsic limits to what it is to understand, beyond which it yields to contemplation when the spinning stops; not mystically, except as mood music, but straightforwardly.

Thus it is that I gaze at this pebble, the same as countless others all around me, and I take its perfect smoothness to be living proof, as it were, of the persistence of physical identity through time. I fully grasp the process by which a myriad daily tides have turned rough stone into smooth pebble on a sandy beach, the sand itself being testimony to millions of years of weathering. And yet, I have not the slightest inkling of what it is that the cognitively intentional consists in, the mystery being absolute, its smooth surface to be contemplated but only in that sense to be understood, and in a way that seeks to transcend everyday familiarity. And so it is that I watch as the swelling sea lifts and carries a crowd of smaller pebbles farther up the sloping sand, and I listen to their click and clatter as they slide back down on the tide's inward breath. I know nothing of what passes between them, or of the wider discourse of the sea, the sky and the land.

The Mystery of Empirical Knowledge

Since our present concern is with mystery, we are taking the relevant problems to be resolved, including that of induction, so that we are left with analysis in terms of a system and its revealing of epistemic limits. That empirical knowledge, which includes induction, is at least perplexing is obvious from the ways in which temporal concepts and those of perception, empirical belief or inference, memory and intentionality in general all interact within a system and enter into, for instance, a belief of mine that a wood pigeon will raid the garden bird table today, my evidence for which is that it has done so every day for several months. Hume when radically interpreted would dispute the validity of this inference, and my thesis in the text is that his arguments are self-refuting. But even with empirical belief securely moored in this way, albeit in mud, the sea of uncertainty having retreated far out, it threatens to rush back in, this time with the force of a more radical unsettling of the epistemic status quo.

To begin with, we know that the exercise of inductive or empirical belief is always conditional upon other things being equal. Returning to our example, if I believe that the pigeon will reappear today, then I discount the possibility that it has been taken by a peregrine falcon; also, I consider not at all the barely conceivable, for instance that it has been trained to make a limited number of visits, yesterday's being the last one. That said, let us now elevate that possibility to the status of rival hypothesis, to the effect that, other things being equal, the pigeon has been trained in such a way that it will not appear in my garden again. To take this hypothesis at all seriously would, quite clearly, be irrational, for there is no reason to believe that the pigeon has been trained, and other things are far from equal, since they include the probability that the pigeon will visit today, as it has done for many months.

But why exactly do we prefer the one hypothesis to the other or entertain only the one, given that they are both consistent with the basic fact of the pigeon's visits to my garden? This is an example of the problem of the underdetermination of belief by evidence, my system-based solution to which, transposed to the present case, runs as follows. Try to imagine a world in which any empirical belief obtains only if the possibilities that might falsify it are actively eliminated rather than ignored. Forming the hypothesis, on the basis of previous daily visits, that the pigeon will visit my garden today, I now begin the process of elimination by asking my neighbour whether she is, or knows anyone who is, a trainer of wild wood pigeons, to which she replies 'No, I am not such a person, nor do I know of anyone who is.' Given the nature of my enquiries, I must now form the hypothesis that her words have their usual meaning, which in its turn requires investigation, as does this latter, which in turn.... But this is both incoherent and regressive. We are back, then, with necessary conditions, and again we find that they provide a solution and inform our perplexity but without resolving it; for we may still ask why it is that we have one belief rather than another. What I am hinting at, given the context, is that there is a level at which no answer is possible, the reason for which, when we arrive at it, will involve intentionality and the non-conscious.

But surely in the present instance, it will be said, we know the answer, for it is given that the pigeon has paid a daily visit for several months, on which basis it is likely to turn up again today. This, however, is to ignore the point just made or implied: that induction is possible in any particular case only if it plays no part, except notionally, in at least some of the predictions involved in taking other things to be equal. Perhaps I expect the pigeon to re-appear partly because I have ascertained that peregrines are rarely seen in this area, but this, again, has the ceteris paribus clause attached, for I predict that other things being equal no peregrines will come hurtling out of the sun. Thus it is that in considering not at all the possibility that the pigeon has been trained, I would say, if asked, that I had no reason to consult it. But this equates, in terms of necessary conditions, with having a reason to ignore it. That is, it is not as if I do not know whether the pigeon has been trained, so that I need to make enquiries; rather, I do not need to make them, perhaps because I implicitly predict that no evidence of training will be found. This, however, cannot be quite correct, overlooking as it does the necessary conditions in place, such that I cannot coherently make the enquiry. What is true of pigeons is also true of zebras if the corresponding possibility is that they are painted mules, this being the stock example that we shall also discuss.

Continuing in our attempt to remove induction from high epistemic office, the sun rising as the inductivist has claimed that every day it will, except that this time it shields us as we close in on him, suppose that by sheer coincidence my neighbour now acknowledges, or so it seems, that she has trained the pigeon to never again visit my garden. In this case a nominal possibility now begins to acquire evidential weight against my expecting the pigeon to turn up today. Making enquiries, I am told by my neighbour that in her garden shed I will find the cage in which she administered electric shocks to the pigeon, together with the device that she used. Finding the cage and the device, as I fully expected to, and trying to decide whether to believe her, I ask myself would it really be possible to train a pigeon by means of an electrically operated cattle prod, the pigeon being so much frailer than a cow? And could it, by any method, be conditioned to perform an action only a certain number of times? One does not need that number of seconds, even without knowing it, to work out the answer, which is a resounding no, the point being that it may not seem to me, if I reflect on it, that inference from past frequency weighs heavily in the balance when the scales tip so decisively against the woman's claim. It lands very lightly, too, on my expecting, on the basis of the woman's testimony, to find a cage in the shed, my justification for which is that very likely she would not make a false claim that she knew was about to be exposed. Justification of this kind, based as it is on my present interaction with the woman, belongs within a system of connections and conditions, for instance in relation to dispositions, reference to which involves counterfactuals. Thus: if she were known to me to be mendacious, then other things being equal I would be less confident about finding a cage in the shed; or, if she were known to be a stickler for speaking truly, I would be even more confident than I now am.

What I actually say, as I just did, is that very likely she would not make a false claim that she knew was about to be exposed. In all three instances an inferential connection to past frequency is easily made; but this is true in all circumstances, even those in which I say that I believed the woman because my intuition told me that she was being truthful. The connection here, or so an inductivist would claim, is with most of my past intuitions turning out to be veridical, for if they had not, then I would be less than confident, other things being equal, about the present one. It is all too easy, I now submit, to shape evidential pieces to this pattern of inference — hence my remark just now about prediction of a kind that is only notionally inductive. That notion is, indeed, so easy to apply that even logical or mathematical pieces could be made to fit the pattern, at least until put to the test. Thus it is that in the discussion of the logical status of applied Pythagoras I make the case, in order to show how easy it is to make it before demolishing it, that we are certain that the theorem will hold in a particular instance because it always has in the past; and then I demolish it. If, after all, the theorem has deductive force, then one may guarantee that it has always held in the past; but this is not an argument for its inductive status, the same being true of necessary conditions, which again may help to explain, perhaps in terms of natural kinds, the fact of repeated instantiation of particular physical features or events. That is, it is a necessary condition of empirical knowledge, as also of the possibility of physical-object description, that repetition of such instances obtain. Concomitantly, we are misled, or philosophers of some persuasions are, into taking inductive inference to be epistemically fundamental, thereby blinding ourselves to the crucial role of necessary conditions within a system.

We are now in a position, having shown that induction is not fundamental, to go deeper in search of what is, perhaps by descent below the level of necessary conditions, even, and into the unconscious. I shall continue to refer to this latter, by the way, pending introduction of the concept of the non-conscious. Returning to the pigeon-training example, recall that I expect to see a cage because my neighbour told me it would be in the shed. Suppose I say that I believed her because she looked truthful. Here, as always, one might invoke past frequency, and in a variety of ways, a fact which I again suggest should give us pause. I might say, if told that her looking directly at me with wide eyes is not good enough, that I trust her because in my experience habitual liars usually look shifty, or do not usually tell easily exposed lies, or not about cages in sheds, or objects of any kind in domestic outbuildings, or that most of my neighbours have been truthful, or have not lied on a Tuesday, and so on. What in fact I should say is that my favourable impression of her is good enough, or if it falls short this is not because it fails to gain further support, in particular from past frequency in one form or another. The reason, I go on to say, is that the appeal to frequency itself goes beyond inductive inference, the onus now being on me to explain what I mean.

To that end, suppose I rack my brains trying to recall other occasions on which I have had an expectation based on the testimony of a person who looked trustworthy. If I succeed, which is to say that I acquire a memory-belief, how am I to justify it? In the main text I argue that it is no use appealing to past occasions of correct remembering, for I would have to remember them, such memory-belief in its turn needing to be justified....It follows that there is no such requirement, and this, I believe, will resonate with our everyday recollection of past events and with experience of belief in general, such as my present predictive belief about what will resonate. I just *have* that belief, this being another way of putting it, and this is true of all belief, however closely it is based on evidence. Since the extreme case here would be that of logical implication, let us examine an instance of modus tollens: if A, then B. Not B; therefore, not A, which we may suppose that I say to myself out loud. And now it occurs to what I assume to be the sceptic in me that by the time I arrive at the consequent, in this case the contrapositive of the antecedent, then this latter has fallen away into the past as if it had never been. How, my assumed inner sceptic asks rhetorically, can the consequent obtain? If the question is about the conditional statement as a sentence consisting of sounds in the air, then this removes any semantic or logical content, as if the sentence were in a foreign language, and it makes no difference whether the whole or only part of it is considered. But the sentence does have such content, so let us take the question to be non-sceptical and to concern itself with the analysis of the intentionality of logical reasoning. How, then, is it to be answered? Intentionality is irreducible, or so I argue in the text, and this is to say that it is a thing in itself — but what kind of thing? The theory I shall now outline is that the intentional is both conscious and non-conscious.

23

Theory of Consciousness

Consider again my understanding of "Not B; therefore, not A", this time as a statement in its own right. Let us try, in order to fail, to account in purely conscious terms for its intentionality. We might first appeal to the phenomenal difference between grasping the proposition and not even recognising it as a sentence in English; and this is indeed relevant. But what could it mean, one must ask, to say that the whole of that difference is phenomenological? If it were, then our theory of intentional irreducibility would be false, but the arguments in its favour are compelling, and they themselves indicate the existence of the non-conscious, which we shall now dissociate from the unconscious. Secondly, intentionality is partly dispositional, and I have argued, in the text, that dispositional properties are not reducible to their manifestations but derive from, as it were, a categorical source. Again, then, this argument points beyond consciousness. Thirdly, and this time if we consider the whole of the modus tollens argument, in other words both antecedent and consequent, is it really possible, with only the tools of consciousness at our disposal, to relate the former to the latter by way of entailment? A state of consciousness, this being a thesis I seek to establish in the text, cannot logically dictate, or indeed in any way determine, another state of consciousness, and the same for conscious events.

Thus it is, to go back a little, that I just *have* a belief or that I reason in a particular way, this being how it consciously appears to me: not gratuitously, as if irrational, but on the surface of a deeper scheme of things, or so I may suspect. And rightly, if our theory is correct, not only in the case of memory and expectation but also in that of belief in general, the taking for granted of which, in the system-referenced sense, is a necessary condition of discourse. It is within this framework that standards of rational belief and sound reasoning have their application, which is to say that it is not as if anything epistemically goes. Expecting to see a cage, so that I just *have* that expectation, I can give a reason, which is that I was told it would be there. And my memory of being told? I just have it. Expecting to see my hand when I remove my glove, donned because I anticipated finding a dead

24

pigeon in the cage, again because of what I was told, I just *have* that expectation, for which I can give any of a variety of reasons, all of them superfluous as justification. Otherwise, one might as well require me to justify expecting to be able to lift my arm to remove the glove, in which case one should first of all justify the memories and expectations that enter into the stating of what it is that one requires, and those that enter into the justification....The upshot, again in terms of memory, is that if I just *have* a particular one, perhaps feeling, even, that it bobs to the surface unannounced, or perhaps not, then in either case it plumbs the depths of the non-conscious, the secret nature of which we shall now investigate.

If we start by recapitulating the odd point or two, I have tried to show, albeit by oversimplification, this being an introduction, that conscious experience depends on the workings of the non-conscious. In making that case, I refer to the non-conscious rather than the unconscious, one reason for which is that the notion of the unconscious evokes that of brain processes. But the theory of consciousness I am proposing, I say, belongs to metaphysics and thereby transcends one's knowledge of the psychophysical, which belongs to neuroscience or philosophy of science, not to a theory of what must ultimately be the case. That said, one of my concerns is to exhibit the theory not only as pointing to ultimate mystery, non-conscious intentionality being by definition unknowable, but also as a product of analysis that elucidates much that would otherwise remain puzzling. It can, in other words, be put to work, for instance in explaining, insofar as this is possible, how it is that "Not B; therefore, not A" , which we treated as a statement in its own right, acquires logical status and the role of consequent in the inference from "If A, then B" to "Not B; therefore, not A". My understanding of this inference at the conscious level is a process in space and time, hence our difficulty with the disappearance of the first part from consciousness in order for the second part to be ushered in. The implication here, I then go on to say, is that "If A, then B", as an utterance, cannot deliver its logical force to the end of the sentence by which the inference is conveyed, such that it transforms "Not B; therefore, not A" into a consequent. Clearly, there is no logical force to be had, or not between utterances, for they are sounds in the air, whereas logic and meaning are intentional. These come into play when the notion of non-conscious intentionality is introduced; but it cannot apply to only part of the inference, say its latter part, for this would not be consequent upon the first part. Thus it is that the inference as a whole reaches down into the non-conscious.

If we reason in this vein, it soon expands into an artery and then, rather aptly, into a full-blown circulatory system, the evidence for the existence of the non-conscious being found across all conscious processes, as is easily shown by targeting their temporality and narrowing it virtually to a point. If, for instance, I am counting up to 10, having just said "5", then an instant later there is, well, a silence and, at the conscious level, an epistemic void, the first five numbers no longer obtaining in any conscious form. How do I know, this being metaphysics, that the next number is 6? I cannot see it or hear it and I cannot remember the last number in an intentional void. A mental image of "5" would be just that: a shape, the same as if the "5" were upside down, and the same if the "5" shape or the "6" shape physically appeared, perhaps on a screen. The "6" shape, for example, would be the content of an instant of consciousness, but intentionally it would be lifeless, like the electrocuted pigeon. Point made, we can zoom back out to encompass the whole process from 1 to 10, which again would be devoid of numerical meaning, this time from beginning to end.

What else can be said, one wonders, about the link between the conscious and the non-conscious? The answer, insofar as it obtains, is again of everyday interest; for if I have a belief, say a memory-belief, then it stands on its own, as already mentioned, the puzzle being that very often I cannot evidentially support it in its particularity, for instance if it is a childhood memory, and yet I am confident that the basic recollection, if not the minutiae of what stood where and when, is veridical. The reason, it may now be seen, is that my conscious memory is the surface of the sea of the non-conscious, the same as the conscious experiences by which I registered, all those years ago, the events I now remember. It is in the depths of the non-conscious that the connections are made between past and present, as we say at the surface, and memories formed.

Since the metaphysical account just given, if correct, holds universally in the sphere of the intentional, we should now find it less puzzling that we just *have* our beliefs, in support of which we just *have* other beliefs, with all that this implies about necessary conditions within a system in which the non-conscious is fundamental to what it is to be conscious. This is a system that we may now understand in terms of conscious processes, by definition always at the surface, connecting deep into the realm of the non-conscious, the essential nature of which is at the core of that which presents itself as impenetrable mystery. These are the bare bones of the theory of the conscious, the non-conscious, the intentional and the mysterious that I flesh out in the body of the text.

Perhaps mention should now be made of the epistemological problem of other minds, such that a radical other-mind sceptic, if we suppose her to be genuinely convinced that other people do not exist, is not on that account incoherent or self-refuting, and neither is conceiving of such an individual at all difficult. She would need a teddy bear on which to project her emotional needs through the bars of her isolation, and perhaps she would attempt to engage it in philosophical debate. The point to be made is that all the main discontinuities with which we are concerned challenge our understanding of other people, together with sources of perplexity that are particular to such understanding. All too often, indeed, we experience cognitive frustration when faced, as it were, with people in corporeal form, the human body itself constituting a discontinuity. Taking this further, imagine that our sceptic renounces her apostasy, this being a double renunciation, and meets full-blown other people for the first time since back in the fold. Such an experience, if she still hopes to be able to communicate with them after failing with soft toys, is like landing on an alien planet the surface of which one begins to explore, perhaps without noticing that the process is just that of familiarisation, which may be hostile to a deeper grasp of what it is to be another person.

This brings us to the last chapter of the book, most of which takes the form of a revised version of the article "The Meaning and the Mystery of Life", which concerns itself not with the chimera of ultimate reality but with mystery and with what it is for human life to have meaning, both in a religious and in a secular context. With regard to the former, I critically examine the universal assumption by which life's meaning is equated with the truth of religion. It is conceivable, I argue, that the eternal hereafter could turn out to be something of an anti-climax, for not even in Heaven can the excitement of making a new start in life or death last forever. On our present planet, I say, there are bright colours and much that is of beauty to behold, and bodily pleasures to be savoured, the sensuous and the sensual combining in the last sentence of this last chapter, which is meant to be the final word.

That apart, it is better, perhaps, to pin one's hopes not on life after death but on science and technology, with mortality treated epidemiologically, the ultimate aim being to find a cure for death; and there are many problems that the scientist believes can in principle be resolved. An exception is perhaps the Hard Problem, so-called, of how it is that consciousness can exist at all, a mystery that some theorists believe to be irresolvable. Since neuropsychology, the science of the relation between brain and mind, is a relatively new discipline, many of its practitioners disagree, excited as they are at the prospect, as they see it, of finding all the answers. But theirs is the study of correlations between mental and brain states, and if these are distinct then the Hard Problem will not be solved to the satisfaction of those philosophers who cleave to it. In my view the mystery of intentionality overwhelms that distinction and is genuinely ultimate and irresolvable in the metaphysical sphere. That leaves theoretical physics and its theory of everything, which will present itself as a self-consistent set of equations by which all physical phenomena may be accounted for. But this will be in principle as opposed to practice, the "everything" not inclusive of predicting the winner at Ascot or human as well as equine behaviour in any detail. It is arguable, indeed, that the theory will be as much descriptive as explanatory, the same as at present, and that in any case there will always be a perplexity of philosophers, this being the collective noun, who, hopefully, will continue to be puzzled by the simplest of

28

things.

That said, science as religion captivates us all, and it might seem to hold out the prospect, however nebulous, of revolutionary insights or discoveries such as to elevate our understanding of the world and reveal a hitherto unobservable reality transformative of the human spirit. This, however, is a delusion, as attested by the discovery of the sub-atomic in all its esoteric otherness; and it is no good, either, expecting technologically superior extraterrestrials to be able to rescue us from our benighted state. According to astronomers, there may be billions of Earth-like planets in our galaxy, which is to say that terrestrial philosophy departments may not be alone in the universe. But our counterparts on these exoplanets will face the same epistemological and conceptual problems as we do, and will speculate in the same way, and to no avail, about hidden reality. Or, there again, they may accept their limitations and speak instead of that which is ultimately mysterious. The galaxy may be teeming with philosophers, not one of whom, really, has any idea what in the Milky Way is going on. Here on Earth, meanwhile, I should like to propose a solution to some interesting philosophical problems, which at least will serve as a distraction from unanswerable questions concerning the transcendent mystery thus revealed.

Chapter 1: Intentionality

My aim in these first chapters is to develop a theory of the intentional by which the main philosophical difficulties besetting the concepts of meaning and understanding may be resolved. The point of the exercise, apart from its intrinsic interest, is to pave the way to a solution of traditional problems: not only those by which this book gains its title but also others, for instance Goodman's Paradox. The general connection here is with philosophy necessarily involving the use of language, without which there could be no university philosophy departments, any would-be philosophers, if wordlessly prescient, having to wait in caves and rock shelters for language to evolve.

My procedure will be to elucidate the nature of meaning and understanding by critically examining other people's views, in this chapter mainly those of Wittgenstein, whose *Philosophical Investigations* will be our primary source. This will involve the detailed analysis of key passages, one advantage of which is that we can make our own exegetical mistakes rather than relying on other people's. This close attention to the text is to some extent imposed on us by the difficulty, not so much of summing up the author's views, which are opposed to scepticism and to the very notion of a genuine philosophical problem, as of distilling his arguments from the flow of gnomic utterances by which he conveys them. Sometimes, however, the task will prove too much for us, and then we shall seek enlightenment from his commentators.

Perhaps we may begin with Wittgenstein on understanding. He supposes that there are two people, A and B, and that B watches A write down the numbers 1, 5, 11, 19, 29 as the initial terms of a sequence, at which point he says that he knows how to go on. Wittgenstein now asks what it is that B's understanding consists in, and he suggests several possible answers. Perhaps B tried the nth term formula $a_n = n^2 + n - 1$ after A had written the number 19, so that the next number confirmed his hypothesis.

Wittgenstein points out, however, that the formula could occur to B without his understanding it:

> For it is perfectly imaginable that the formula should occur to him and that he should nevertheless not understand. "He understands" must have more in it than: the formula occurs to him. And equally, more than any of those more or less characteristic *accompaniments* or manifestations of understanding. (152)

And again: 'If there has to be anything "behind the utterance of the formula" it is *particular circumstances* which justify me in saying I can go on – when the formula occurs to me'. (154)

Let us consider the thrust of Wittgenstein's argument. He has yet to specify what the particular circumstances might be, though he promises to shed light on them when he investigates the concept of reading, this being the task that he sets himself next. In the meantime, the following comments may help to fill the gap. Suppose that several nth term formulas, including $a_n = n^2 + n - 1$ occur to B as flotsam in his stream of consciousness, so that he barely glances at them as they drift past. Then if he is now told the formula or otherwise comes to know it, and if he remembers it passing through his mind earlier, he does not claim that at that earlier time the understanding of the sequence came to him, despite the fact that the formula did. There is a distinct difference between this earlier occurrence of the formula in his mind and the way in which he now recognises it as the formula for the sequence – or at least there *seems* to be. The point about this difference is that it concerns an occurrent mental event; what also has to be said, however, is that such an event could not in itself constitute understanding the formula, since we need only think that we understand it for that event to occur, and also for the reason that to understand anything at all is to have the appropriate dispositions. We should keep in mind, perhaps, that Wittgenstein has yet to mention them. Note, too, that to think that we understand the formula, or to doubt whether we do, is indeed to understand something, and that this form of understanding cannot be gainsaid, since to doubt it is to manifest it.

1.1: Reasoning as Mental Process

Clearly, we can agree with Wittgenstein that there are interesting questions about what it is to understand an item, if that is what he would say. In the present case, for instance, one should not, strictly speaking, refer to *the* formula rather than the conventional formula, this latter derived from the regular pattern of increase between terms. The definite article misleadingly implies that the given number sequence uniquely determines the formula $a_n = n^2 + n - 1$. Nor should we say, as I did, that if we correctly predict that the next number written down after 19 will be 29, then this confirms that the formula is the right one. Strictly, one should not speak of confirmation, for a finite sequence is, in itself, consistent with an unlimited range of continuations. Since we do speak of it, the conventions must be understood or perhaps unselfconsciously adhered to. This brings us to another point, and it concerns the apparent fact that although the given sequence does not determine any particular formula, a formula has to fit it, and in any case a formula does uniquely determine a sequence— unless, that is, it does not. There is only one ascending order prime number sequence such that for each term a unique successor exists; but this latter is false for the sequence formed by adding 2 up to 1000, 2+x up to 2000, 2+2x up to 3000..., 2+(n-1)x up to 1000n...For there is no such sequence for $x > 0$, this being a fact to which we shall return. The present point is that although Wittgenstein may be understood as holding this notion of determination up to scrutiny, one suspects that a clear articulation of his misgivings would remove them, their place taken by appreciation of complexity. Enough has already been said, after all, to indicate that the links between a formula and a sequence, or what seems to be one, form a network involving necessary conditions—one to which the understanding of those links also belongs. Dispositions play a crucial role, but so far there is no reason to think that they are incompatible with occurrent intentionality.

Since there is little prospect of clarity of the kind mentioned, we must continue, noting first that in the same breath as he speaks of a formula coming to mind, he also mentions trying out different ones and using them to predict the next term. But now, this is very dissimilar to the case in which a formula is merely glanced at, and the main difference is that in trying out formulas we engage in a process of constructing and testing hypotheses, to which end we use inference and calculation. Perhaps, then, I may venture even at this early stage to re-assert received wisdom lest the obstacles to overturning it fail to impress. Wittgenstein's aim, albeit never clearly stated, is generally taken to be that of showing that the cognitive is the communal, where this is to imply that the grasp of a formula, for instance, is not self-contained—rather, it involves the practice of the community at large. This is obscure, but at least it enables purchase on the central role of overt manifestation of understanding and meaning, except that one's grip on it immediately slips away. For if common sense is our guide there is no such role, or not if one distinguishes between individual understanding and interpersonal communication.

Since it is this distinction that I wish to emphasise, let us reconsider the example of A inviting B to find "the" formula for the sequence of numbers. I claimed earlier that there is no unique formula, and presently we shall establish that this is indeed the case. If in the meantime we assume it for the sake of argument, then on the face of it B cannot hope to succeed, or not unless there are factors involved by which the range of possible formulas is very severely restricted. Clearly there are, for conventions exist by which, for the present class of cases, the correct formula will always be the simplest, which is to say linear rather than quadratic, or this latter rather than cubic, and so on. A clarifying comparison here would be with intelligence tests in which the subject is presented with different shapes, say, and asked to pick the odd one out, which he is able to do only because of the shared understanding by which one oddity stands out from the many others also on offer.

There is no denying, then, that linguistic and other conditions of a suitable kind must be satisfied if interpersonal communication is to obtain; but also that the interplay of language between people, far from precluding the possibility of self-contained individual understanding, would seem to depend on it. This is the received wisdom the strength of which was emphasized earlier, my present purpose being to reinforce it even further by focussing on an individual's grasp of, in the present case, number theory. Modifying the example to suit that aim, suppose, if the mathematics is to be kept within bounds, that there are only three initial terms to contend with, so that the sequence is given by 1, 5, 11....Now consider not B, who is trying to guess the formula or number pattern that A has in mind, but A himself, who has no need to guess. Suppose further that A is not presenting B with a puzzle or testing him, so that he is not limited by the usual problem-setting constraints; in particular by having to use the simplest formula, in the present case given by $a_n = n^2 + n - 1$. Then A is free to find a higher algebraic polynomial, say of cubic form given by $an^3 + bn^2 + cn + d$. Using linear equation maths, we arrive at $a_n = an^3 + (1 - 6a)n^2 + (1 + 11a)n - 6a - 1$ for all positive rational values of a. This reduces to the original quadratic formula if $a = 0$ and to a simple cubic if $a = \frac{1}{6}$, in which case

$$a_n = \frac{n^3 + 17n - 12}{6} = 1, 5 \text{ and } 11 \text{ for } n = 1, 2 \text{ and } 3 \text{ respectively.}$$

There are, then, an indefinitely large number of nth term formulas for sequences with initial terms 1, 5 and 11, each of them continuing in a different way beyond $n = 3$, and the same for the original sequence beyond $n = 5$. Such facts are concealed, not from view but from scrutiny, for Wittgenstein insists on taking a third-person standpoint, the emphasis being on B's grasp of A's construal of the sequence and formula, not on A's itself. We, however, have placed A centre stage, the spotlight being on his own ratiocination, and what is thereby declaimed is that his overt act of writing the five numbers down, convention and simplicity apart, tells the audience nothing at all about the next number in the sequence or about any formula by which it is determined. Hence the reference to a rather large obstacle.

An exactly parallel case is that in which I read an English text, for instance this one, and understand it as I read it, so that my understanding is immediate. I may be wrong, of course, about my grasp of particular words, just as I may have calculated incorrectly in the numerical case; but the point being made concerns all the ways in which understanding enters into reading, even when my grasp of a particular word is at variance with its public meaning. Besides, I cannot later come to doubt, except in the most bizarre circumstances, that I understood most of what I had read, or that I manifested understanding in working out the formula. And if, bizarrely, I did question myself in that way, my reasons could not be such as to apply to the cognitive processes involved in entertaining the doubt. The same is true of particular thoughts rather than prolonged reasoning, as when I wake at night and worry about whether the front door has been left unlocked. The thought that I may not be able to get back in can perhaps be put to rest only if I try the door, but I cannot doubt my understanding of the thought itself, for this would be to doubt the thought, in other words to replace one thought with another.

We shall have to see how such facts about authoritative self-knowledge and occurrent understanding impinge on Wittgenstein's thesis equating meaning with use or on his claim that inner thought processes stand in need of outward criteria, with its implications not only for meaning and understanding but also for the evidential aspect of our knowledge of other minds. Much of this work will be carried out in the third chapter, on avowals, by which point I hope to be able to outline a solution to the problem of intentionality, insofar as this is possible. In the meantime, there is what seems to be the significant fact that inner thoughts are self-contained and that one's understanding may be exhibited to oneself in one's reasoning, as in the case of working out a formula, a process the grasp of which seems immediate and occurrent, so that it is this that we should focus on rather than on seeing or imagining a formula in isolation. To sum up our findings thus far: outward criteria require inner processes.

1.2: Wittgenstein on Reading

Let us now turn to Wittgenstein's investigation of the particular circumstances attaching to the ability to read. By "reading" he primarily means reading aloud but without necessarily understanding the words, since one may know how to pronounce them without knowing what they mean. As far as one can tell, he is sceptical of the assumption that reading is a special conscious activity of mind, such that 'the one real criterion for anybody's *reading* is the conscious act of reading, the act of reading the sounds off from the letters.' (159) Thus he asks us to imagine that A, in order to deceive B, learns a Russian sentence by heart and says it out loud while pretending to read it. And then the sensations he has are characteristic not of reading but of pretending to read, in other words of cheating, so that he knows that this is what he is doing..

Perhaps the first step in glossing this passage is for us to query Wittgenstein's use of the word "sensation", which does not seem entirely apposite in the context of its being said that there can be a sensation of hesitating, looking closer or misreading, or of saying something by heart, rather than that one is aware of them or that they are conscious acts or states. It may be that his use of this word, apart from the ironic reference to cheating, betrays a particular bias, a possibility to which we shall presently return. It seems odd, too, to suggest that A knows that he is reading on the basis of what is characteristic of that activity. If, in my own case, it is on that basis, then part of my evidence that I am reading is that I hesitate, correct myself, lose my place, look at the words at the same time as I say them, and so on. But this makes it sound as if on the basis of the evidence I think it probable that I am reading. The fact is that even when I say aloud only a single, short sentence, so that the hypothesis that I am reading would be only weakly confirmed, it never occurs to me to doubt that I am reading the words, as indeed is the case when I say the first of them. Clearly, this talk of evidence and confirmation is very ill-suited from a first-person point of view to the concept of reading, and it would be more accurate to say not that it seems to me that I am reading but that I am in reading mode, as always when I look at words and understand them. What does this indicate, it may be asked, about the nature of the intentional? And that of avowals?

We shall answer as best we can in this chapter and elsewhere, with more light shed on it when the notion of the non-conscious is introduced; but our present concern is with the analysis of a concept, in this case not even of reading in the usual sense but of reading aloud without understanding. In reading aloud one is not required to exhibit any great skill, in the sense of correctly matching the spoken to the written word, and it is easy to imagine a foreign student of English reading aloud in a halting manner in which every word is mispronounced. Indeed, the essence of what is involved may be illustrated in many other ways, for instance in the case of drawing balls from a bag with a view to naming the colour of each ball as it is drawn. What is essential here is that naming the colour derives from recognising it, and if the process of deriving is generalised to encompass reading, naming and direct physical description, then arguably it is fundamental to the connecting of language with the world. This, however, is what Wittgenstein now goes on to say:

> But imagine the following case: We give someone who can read fluently a text that he never saw before. He reads it to us – but with the sensation of saying something he has learnt by heart (this might be the effect of some drug). Should we say in such a case that he was not really reading the passage? Should we here allow his sensations to count as the criterion for his reading or not reading? (160)

These remarks at least indicate what it is that Wittgenstein is trying to show. He is not denying that the person may have sensations, or reducing them behaviouristically; rather, such remarks perhaps again prefigure his thesis that inner processes stand in need of outward criteria. If, however, one examines this particular case, then it is impossible to imagine having the sensations of reciting by heart at the same time as one reads aloud from an unfamiliar text. If this is not immediately apparent, then perhaps the reason is that it is obscured by Wittgenstein's use of the word "sensation", as if introspection when reading aloud or reciting by heart reveals only a sequence of sensations as the conscious content of that process. The truth is rather that I derive the spoken from the written word as part of the perceptual experience of reading aloud, so that the reference should be not to my sensations of reading but to my awareness that I am thus engaged. By the same token, the reference should be to my awareness of reciting by heart. What Wittgenstein is really inviting us to imagine is that I read the text aloud at the same time as I think that I am reciting it from memory. But how could that be possible? All I need do is close my eyes and, lo and behold, I cease to say the words! I am no longer able to see them, whereas if I knew them by heart I could continue with the charade, at least until it was noticed that I was reading with my eyes shut.

In making these criticisms, and in the earlier paragraph, I have cited what is arguably the main defining property of the concept of reading aloud: that of deriving the spoken from the written word. Wittgenstein, however, asks of a person we have taught to read, 'But why do we say that he has *derived* the spoken from the written words? Do we know anything more than that we taught him how each letter should be pronounced, and that he then read the words out loud?' (162) The obvious answer here is that we know that in other people reading involves deriving, as it does in ourselves, and that we have as much reason to attribute this process to others as we have to ascribe pain to them in suitable circumstances. When discussing the use of a psychological term, Wittgenstein always wishes us to take a third-person point of view; but we should not acquiesce in this if it leads to distortion of the facts. The answer should, as I said, be obvious, but the obvious is not to Wittgenstein's taste, for he now suggests that the uses of the verb "to derive" exhibit family resemblances, to which he adds 'And in the same way we also use the word "to read" for a family of cases. And in different circumstances we apply different criteria for a person's reading.' (164)

What this indicates is that Wittgenstein finds it significant that there are family resemblances rather than essential similarities between different cases of deriving, which he suggests is also true of reading. The fact is, however, that the use of the verb "to derive" is the same in similar cases. Thus, if I read aloud a line of unfamiliar text, which is to say that I derive each spoken word from a corresponding written word, then this is what I do for each word in the line and each line in the text, a fact which raises a question as to the relevance of dissimilar cases of deriving. Perhaps Wittgenstein appeals to them in order to show that the use of "to derive" or "to read" will depend on the particular circumstances. I suspect, however, that he would take exception to the following as an instance of the circumstances attending a particular case. Suppose that I read aloud from a text with which I am unacquainted, so that I derive the spoken from the written word. This means that as my eyes track across the page then for the most part I do not know exactly which words are coming next, so that it is only when I see them that I am able to say them, the shape of the particular words I utter being in that sense uniquely determined by my reading of them. When, on the other hand, I cannot read but only pretend, having memorised a spoken script, then I do not derive what I say from what I see.

The indication here is that there is indeed a conscious activity of reading aloud, essential to which is the process of deriving the spoken from the written word. Even if we agree that on a wider view there is no essence of reading, such as to transcend the different senses of "to read", we may still ask whether the fact that there are different kinds of reading has anything to contribute to a discussion of any particular one of them. There is, as all shoppers know, the kind of reading in which an electronic device scans the bar code on a plastic strip, unless it is short-sighted, and here there is no conscious activity at all, let alone a conscious process of deriving one thing from another. Clearly, this tells us little about a person reading aloud, so perhaps we should consider a more similar form of reading. We have yet to mention vocalised Braille reading, for instance, which differs from visually derived reading aloud only in that the spoken word takes its cue from the felt shape of the inscribed word. But now we seem to have the opposite problem, for it is this very similarity which militates against any difference, such as it is, illuminating the connection between inner and outer aspects of reading aloud.

To criticise Wittgenstein in this way is to take a common-sense approach to the consciousness of other people, as also to what it is to derive the spoken from the written word; but it is this approach that Wittgenstein continues to call into question. Focussing on the phenomenal aspects of the process of reading, he now asks, 'But when we read don't we feel the word-shapes somehow causing our utterance?' (169) He now invites us to read a sentence aloud and then to say it at the same time as we look along a line of symbols in arbitrary sequence. In the first case, he says, one may feel that uttering the words is causally connected with seeing them, a connection that is absent in the second case. He goes on:

> But why do you say that we felt a causal connexion? Causation is surely something established by experiments, by observing a regular concomitance of events for example. So how could I say that I *felt* something which is established by experiment? (169)

This is a spurious argument, and on all counts, for we do not need to feel, as if sensations were involved, the causal connection, and awareness of it does not depend on experiment or frequency of instantiation. If we speak from a script it does not occur to us to deny that in reading aloud we are aware of deriving the spoken from the written word, where this is to imply causation, all of which is also true of reading silently. In my view it is better, harking back to a point already made, if we speak of being in reading mode, and if we then go on to tease out the implications.

Pressing home that point, suppose that a monolingual foreign student to whom we are teaching English phonetics is looking at a text we have given him and that we speak his language, so that there is verbal communication between us. Then our evidence that he is reading to himself, albeit without understanding, would have to go beyond his looking at the text, this being only a necessary condition of his reading it. Still, we might combine it with already knowing that he is able to read English aloud, from which we infer that he is now reading to himself. This could be checked by asking him to memorise a few sentences and repeat them back to us without looking. According to Wittgenstein, however, when a person reads aloud all that we know is that he is pronouncing each word of a text, rather than that he is deriving the spoken from the written word. If that is correct, then the student being able to read aloud provides no evidence at all that he is now reading silently to himself, an activity with no unmistakeable outward sign. This, however, is counter-intuitive, for we all know what it is to read silently to ourselves, an activity in which I am now engaged as I write these English words, knowing that I understand them, and in which I was once engaged, initially without understanding, when learning French. When it comes to his reading aloud, we may check that he is by following the text as he

40

reads from it, but this itself is an inner mental process on our part, one in which we associate the written with the spoken word. Again it has no outward sign, apart from our looking over his shoulder as he speaks, an action to which a variety of interpretations may be attached.

If this reasoning is along the right lines, then the concept of non-cognitive reading, whether silent or spoken, may be such as to depend on inner processes as truth conditions. If, the student now having started to utter the words, I look over his shoulder and claim that he is reading aloud, and if I do not thereby ascribe to him the inner process of deriving the spoken from the written word, then all that happens is that I associate the words he speaks with those I read, a correspondence which on its own makes no sense of its being said that he is reading, or that I am checking that he is. What, in any case, would the distinction between reading aloud and reciting by heart amount to if it picked out only behavioural differences? In this connection it is true that Wittgenstein is not a strict behaviourist, for his view is that inner processes require outward criteria, as with his remark that a formula coming to mind betokens understanding only if particular circumstances arise, presumably those in which it is publicly exhibited. But he also says that when a person reads aloud we know nothing of any inner process of deriving, rather than that such a process must be manifested in behaviour. In this matter our wish to accommodate Wittgenstein may conflict with everyday intuition, all the more so if it is applied to silent reading, the attendant difficulties also thrown into relief if we consider a point of view from which they are absent: that in which appeal is made to the notion of an explanatory system.

On that view the correspondence between the words spoken by the student and those read by me as I look over his shoulder is explained by his also reading them, so that his inner processes come into play just as mine do. Similarly, that the two of us both see and hear the words he speaks is also part of the explanation; for how else is it to be explained that the words he speaks are the same as the ones I read? Well, perhaps it is a coincidence —uh, no. It is worth suggesting, then, even at this early stage of our critique of Wittgenstein, that we should think not of outward criteria but of a system of reasoning and language use in which inferential and explanatory connections obtain between the inner life and overt behaviour of ourselves and other people. If this is correct our task should be that of analysis, not that of dissolving misconceptions.

1.3: Return to Wittgenstein on Understanding

What I propose is that we set a course for that analysis by ascertaining the extent to which it diverges from Wittgenstein's approach. He now returns to his discussion of a pupil learning the sequence of even numbers, and he supposes that the pupil has been taught to write the sequence as far as 1000, at which point he disconcerts his teacher by writing 1004, 1008, 1012....When the pupil insists, despite the teacher's efforts to correct him, that he is going on in the same way as before, Wittgenstein remarks 'In such a case we might say, perhaps: It comes natural to this person to understand our order with our explanations as *we* should understand the order: "Add 2 up to 1000, 4 up to 2000, 6 up to 3000 and so on."' (185) There then follows a dialogue in which Wittgenstein agrees that the teacher meant the pupil to write 2002 after 2000 at the time he gave the instruction, even though he may not have been consciously thinking of those numbers. To mean it is to be suitably disposed, for instance to say "2002" if asked for the successor to 2000. Wittgenstein suspects, however, that the teacher reads more into it than that, misled as he is by the grammar of the words "know" and "mean". He goes on: 'Here I should first of all like to say: your idea was that that act of meaning the order had in its own way already traversed all those steps: that when you meant it your mind as it were flew ahead and took all the steps before you physically arrived at this or that one.'(188)

Reading this passage, it is clear that Wittgenstein takes himself to be challenging the usual view of what it is to give meaning to a word, this also being his approach to the usual view of what it is to understand, which we may correctly conceive of as being in some sense immediate. But there is, or so we may be tempted to say, a more direct sense, about which Wittgenstein asks 'But have you a model for this? No. It is just that this expression sug-

42

gests itself to us. As the result of the crossing of different pictures.' (191) What these passages indicate is that Wittgenstein's concern is with the problem of reconciling what seem to be conflicting notions of what it is to understand or to mean. On the one hand it seems that we cannot grasp in an instant the whole use of an expression, since that use is extended in time; on the other, it is as if in some sense we do, the use being both present and not present. But this is taken to be incoherent, hence Wittgenstein's claim that we have no model for it. What he himself would say, according to some commentators, is that there is nothing problematic about the notion of grasping the whole use of a word in an instant, provided that the sense we give to it is consistent with a particular view of what it is to mean and to understand. On that view, we grasp the meaning of a word when we become proficient at applying it in the same way as other people.

This is food for thought, but while it is being digested let us ask whether we are misled as to what it is to mean and to understand. According to Wittgenstein, when we mean one sequence rather than another it is as if the act of meaning traverses all the steps in advance, this being the distorted picture we have or the incoherent idea to which we are in thrall. And in the same spirit, it is as if we grasp the whole sequence in a flash. A problem here is that Wittgenstein relies heavily on the use of metaphor, and it is not of a kind that can be easily paraphrased, except by its further use. Perhaps, then, we should look for guidance in the following: 'Thus you were inclined to use such expressions as: "The steps are *really* already taken, even before I take them in writing or orally or in thought." And it seemed as if they were in some *unique* way predetermined, anticipated – as only the act of meaning can anticipate reality.'(188) But now, the first sentence is just a variant of its being said that the steps are traversed in advance. If we turn to the second sentence, then a dictionary may be useful here, and mine defines "predetermined" as "decided or established in advance". This is a skeletal definition which in a particular case it is left to the context to flesh out. In the present case the reading it would be natural to make is that the steps are predetermined in the sense of being determined by criteria of correctness already established. But since they *are* determined in this way, we would not be wrong to think that they are; therefore, it cannot be what Wittgenstein has in mind when he speaks of our being misled. Since we are no further forward, let us turn to Wittgenstein's emphasis on the steps being uniquely predetermined. If this refers to there being only one correct step at each stage, then again this is in fact the case given the conventional meaning of "add 2". Perhaps, then, the sense of "uniquely" is given by "only the act of meaning", so that it refers to the special way in which such acts anticipate reality. Unfortunately, we are still running on the spot, for it is just this special kind of anticipation that needs to be explained.

Finding an explanation is, however, no easy task, not only because of the use of the kind of metaphor for which there is no clarificatory paraphrase but also for other reasons. One such is that since Wittgenstein would agree that we may grasp in an instant the meaning of a word, it is not as if we are free to interpret him as denying that this is possible, thereby giving definition to what he says. Rather, it is what we imply by such a possibility that Wittgenstein finds problematic, except that he does not really tell us what it is that we imply. If we seek enlightenment indirectly, perhaps consulting the thesis equating meaning with use, then we come away empty-handed; and the reason, apart from that thesis being obscure in its own peculiar way, is that although it merges with the claim that we mislead ourselves as to what it is to mean and to understand, it is because of our misconceptions, or so I believe that Wittgenstein would say, that we fail to appreciate that the meaning of an expression lies in its use. But that thesis, despite what he says, does appear to challenge the conviction we have that understanding occurs at an "instant". I use the scare quotes because one's concern should be with occurrent, not instant, understanding; and in the normal way of things the conviction we have, or the belief whose correctness we take for granted, is that we understand an instruction at the time that we receive it, the cognitive propensity already in place, and that we continue to understand it in implementing it, if that is what we do. Or, there again, that we think we understand it, which itself is a form of understanding. To speak in this way is, however, to flirt with system-based analysis, which will be fully embraced in due course. Showing a little more bare flesh, note the following: that it is a necessary condition of discourse, both with others and with oneself, that we take for granted that we understand when we think that we do, this being the framework in which particular cognitive doubt may obtain. Clearly, there is much more to be said along these lines; but in the meantime we have Wittgenstein to deal with, in particular his claim about the ways in which we are misled, the nature of which continues to elude us.

Nothing for it, then, but to try to ascertain for ourselves where, if anywhere, we go wrong. Suppose that I instruct you to write down the first few terms of the arithmetical progression with initial term 7 and constant difference 17. If you are able to oblige, does this mean that you have a picture, however muddled, of your mind traversing all the steps in advance? But here are the first four terms: 7, 24, 41, 58 ..., after which, if you are like me, you have to pause your pen, as it were, between them. So much, then, for your mind traversing all the steps in advance and antici- pating them in a way that is peculiar to meaning. Very well, but you immediately wrote down the initial term and perhaps the second, in which case it may be said that you anticipated them. But in what way, however vaguely or elusively, were you thereby misled? Perhaps all that it amounts to at the conscious level is that you feel confident about being able to continue the series. But this brings us to another questionable assumption of Wittgen- stein's: he seems to take it that to understand the instruction is to be able to carry it out. But it is quite possible, if you do not have a grounding in sequences and series, that you do not understand the expression "arithmetical progression", but would be able to carry out the instruction if differently phrased; or that you are semi-numerate and in any case unable to continue the sequence after the first few terms. That said, this distinction between un- derstanding and implementation illuminates not at all the nature of our misconceptions according to Wittgenstein; nor does the example just discussed point to their existence or indicate in any way that we are misled. If we learn the meaning of "arithmetical progression", perhaps by being told it, then we may feel confi- dent about being able to apply it correctly, so that in this way we anticipate its application. But this is not the same as feeling that in some ineffable sense our understanding leaps ahead of itself. One might as well maintain, if I announce that I plan to cartwheel from Cape Town to Casablanca, that it is as if I traverse the African continent in advance, rather than that I am confident that my unique mode of locomotion will deter predators.

How, then, should we interpret these passages? Perhaps the only way to give content to them is to take the interlocutor to believe that acts of meaning and understanding are such as to have purely categorical truth conditions. That said, this is to portray him as a quite idiotic Watson to Wittgenstein's Holmes, one who seems forced into the view that to mean a particular sequence, say, is to consciously represent each term of it in the act of meaning. Anxious to escape this absurdity, he clutches at metaphor and declares that the steps are traversed in advance, really already taken, and so on. That for Wittgenstein we are thus misled is a proposition to which many commentators assent. For instance, in *Meaning, Understanding, and Practice* Barry Stroud takes Wittgenstein's target to be the notion of understanding as a mental state, where this is to imply that we should be able to introspect it. What we thereby encounter, however, are non-intentionally describable mental phenomena, as when we read and understand a sentence, a process which may nevertheless be described as that of looking at marks on paper or screen. Although this experience of understanding a text may be very different from when one has no idea what the sentence means, such a difference cannot be that which separates understanding from the absence of it, and for the simple reason that understanding is intimately connected with application and use. Stroud's Wittgenstein then cautions us against appealing to the existence of an occult cognitive realm in which understanding has its being and generates its own application. Rather, we should identify understanding with application itself, or with use, custom and practice in the public domain. But this, to anticipate, is where the chasm between Wittgenstein and my own approach is at its widest and deepest, for the existence of an "occult" intentional realm is just what the turning of these pages will reveal.

If we return to the present, common sense would suggest that understanding is both occurrent and dispositional, these being

46

happily married up and easily able to accommodate use, so that again we may ask whether it is really true that we are mired in the difficulties from which Wittgenstein professes to be able to extricate us. Take, for example, an extreme case of imparting meaning to a word: that in which at midday I answer a question by saying that Scott is in Spain, followed immediately by my saying that Scott is on the moon, where these are replies to two different individuals asking 'Where is Scott?' If the possibility of superluminal travel is discounted, then I must be referring to two different people named Scott, in response to what I understand to be the different references made by my interlocutors, one of whom is an astronaut's husband. But this is to say that at midday I imparted a particular meaning to "Scott", followed immediately by a change of meaning, one which corresponded to differences in conscious awareness and, or so I shall now begin to argue, to non-conscious differences. But in what way do I mislead myself when I reflect on this change of meaning? Do I believe that it occurred at a particular time? But it did occur at a particular time. Very well, but am I under the impression that my mind flew ahead to the answers I was about to give, or to the moon, and in a way peculiar to meaning and peculiar *tout court*? I knew what I had said or was about to say, but in this I was not mistaken, whereas I would be if I denied that dispositions were involved. Clearly they were, and I was not misled into denying that this is compatible with instant change of meaning. The difficulties, in other words, are those of analysis, about which more will presently be said.

Now consider not meaning but understanding, for instance if you are asked 'When did you last see your mother?' Note that your mind does not fly ahead of itself and alight on the necessary conditions by which you may be said to understand the question, one of which is that you be able to use the word "mother" in a variety of sentential contexts. This is an instance of your being suitably disposed, but the thought that you are need not be in your head. Now take the further step of actually answering that question in your thoughts, so that you are presently recalling to yourself the last time you saw your mother. Does it seem to you that introspection reveals only mental images, including word images, as if they were cognitively and semantically inert sensations? Then either you never had a mother or this time you really are misleading yourself.

If this critique of Wittgenstein is along the right lines, then his imaginary interlocutor seems to lack verisimilitude, depending on whether real people and philosophers view meaning and understanding as having the anticipatory mystique that the interlocutor claims to discern in it. Mystique is one thing, mystery another, and irreducibility another again. Since the whole point about words and symbols is that they partake of intentionality, we need to ask whether Wittgenstein in the passages under review has at least managed to pinpoint the main source of our perplexity about the intentional, to which the answer, in my opinion, is that he has not. He seeks to straighten, as it were, the confused picture we have of the steps being taken in advance, or of the cognitive in some other way running ahead of itself. But to depict it thus is to shunt into a siding the role of the dispositional, such that in the present case I grasp the sequence if I would know, at least in theory, how to calculate the successor to any given term, and if in other ways, too, I am suitably disposed. This is understanding as ability, and it clashes with the picture that according to Wittgenstein we have of it. But is it really true that we overlook the cognitive role of dispositions? There is no reason, after all, why understanding should not be both occurrent and dispositional, given the intimate connections between them.

There is, or so I shall claim in the chapter on meaning as use, a clear sense in which meaning and application are connected. That is, to mean one thing rather than another by an expression, which necessarily involves understanding it, is to apply it or be disposed to apply it in a particular way, all of which involves further meaning and understanding. This is the crucial point: that occurrent understanding depends on cognitive dispositions, which determine not only whether we understand but *what* we understand. None of this is to imply that the meaning of an expression equates with its use. On the contrary, it indicates that Wittgenstein is disabusing us of misconceptions we do not have—but also that they do not matter, for what counts is analysis.

48

Expanding this a little, the equating of meaning with use follows not at all from the fact, if that is what it is, of my entertaining a distorted picture of traversing all the steps in advance. It is, after all, only a picture. What counts is whether any views I have on the nature of the intentional are mistaken, presumably the view or assumption that understanding, for instance, is known by its introspectible mental glow, such that the cognitive object lights up, this being what the understanding of it consists in. No point, then, in testing one's grasp of number theory, the issue being only that of whether the light is on, which one is able to authoritatively avow to be the case. As for treating other people— but enough has been said if we wish to avoid turning satire into farce. Clearly, no self-respecting chimpanzee, even, would subscribe to such nonsense.

This returns us to Wittgenstein, who as we know would disagree; and by his account it is only in virtue of the shared public use of an expression that an individual can impart meaning to it. But this is at odds with his own arithmetical example. He supposes that the pupil understands the order "add 2" 'as *we* should understand the order: "Add 2 up to 1000, 4 up to 2000, 6 up to 3000 and so on."' But this, or so it seems, is an example of interpersonal mis-communication such that '*we* should understand' implies that the teacher has in mind the conventional meaning of "add 2". Note the rather sneaky use of "*we*" to subliminally personify community practice in the form of the teacher, who in fact is an individual the same as the pupil. That being the case, it is at the same cognitive level that the teacher and the pupil have a different understanding of the instruction, about which, presumably, the teacher believes, judging by the "and so on", that she knows what it is that the pupil understands by it. She does not, but we shall come to that in a moment. The point at present is that as I see it nothing in this passage supports the thesis that shared public use is necessary to individual meaning and understanding. On the contrary, teacher and pupil impart a different meaning to the instruction, in line with their divergent construal of it.

And now, taking the above to be correct, let us take advantage of Wittgenstein's error and resolve it as best we can. I argued earlier that for a positive integer x there is no such sequence as that which starts with 2 up to 1000, $2+x$ up to 2000, and so on, this being the present apparent sequence if $x=2$. Since it is a mistake to think that one can arrive at 3000 from 2000 in increments of 6, we must suppose that the pupil writes 2, 4, ..., 1004, 1008, ..., 2000, 2006, ..., 2996, 3004, 3012 ... (or 2996, 3002, 3010, ...), the teacher not being able to anticipate which it will be, not only on this occasion but when the next arbitrary choice is made, and the one after that, and so on .... She thereby thoughtfully illustrates a distinction between the orthodox and idiosyncratic use of language. The teacher's use of "add 2" is conventional, the pupil's not, but with no hint of either of them being cognitively disadvantaged. With regard to communication, however, they fail utterly, the teacher not even being aware of the extent of that failure, or not if we assume, absurdly, that the aforementioned error is hers, not Wittgenstein's. Thus it is that section 185 is about interpersonal communication, as are the implied necessary conditions. People communicate through language only if they manifest a shared linguistic understanding, otherwise one might as well announce to a surprised world that the French and the English communicate when they both use the word "pain", the one eating and the other groaning.

There is, too, another insight to be gained, which also is about seeming to traverse all the steps in advance. The pupil himself may not realise that there is a problem with the sequence rule, or not until he encounters it; and yet he might say beforehand that he will add 2 up to 1000, 4 up to 2000, 6 up to 3000, 8 up to 4000..., this last also impossible if he adds 6 up to 3002. The point is that seeming to incorporate all future steps into knowing in advance how to go on does not favour Wittgenstein's thesis if the role of dispositions is recognised. If I wish to carry out the instruction "add 2", which in order to avoid being subtly influenced by Wittgensteinian mood music I shall envisage as a note to self, then clearly there are dispositions involved, even in the case of my foolishly denying it, a necessary condition of which is that I am disposed to repeat if required or silently remember the denial, other things being equal.

Further to this, it seems to me that the present interpretation is exegetically the only coherent one, the rejoinder to which, I am

sure, will be that the different sections have to be compared together and treated as parts of the wider thesis if justice is to be
done to them. Very true, but the point is as follows: suppose, as I
claim to be the case, that section 185 on its own is capable of only a single coherent construal, such that individual understanding
is presented as being necessary to interpersonal communication.
Suppose further that it is re-visited via the lens of another section,
in which the opposite thesis is presented, in particular number
258, which we shall discuss in connection with private language.
Then the claim that it supports this later thesis or prefigures the
argument of that section is an unwitting misrepresentation. The
reader sways to it because that is the tune that Wittgenstein plays,
with section 185 clearly intended to support his thesis; and to
keep one's balance, or to try to, is to return to that section with
hands over ears, one to each, and to read what is written and as it
stands. In practice, however, one reads it when predisposed to
register it as the argument that Wittgenstein intends it to promote—hence the risk of misrepresenting it, both to oneself and to
others. This brings us, complete with our own preconceptions, to
the private language argument.

1.4: The Private Language Argument

Let us begin by pointing out that the private language argument
presents formidable difficulties of interpretation. This is in part
connected with the fact that it cannot be a condition of referring
to one's own sensations that others happen to understand the reference, for they may not; therefore, what is required is that in
principle they could. This is vexingly obscure, not least because
much of one's inner life is apparently exhibited to others, and
through the words by which it is described, as with dreams and
thoughts and sensations and indeed with much of what we experience; and yet we are told that for such description to be meaningful, even to ourselves, it has to be conformable to outward criteria of correct use. If description falls into this category, then in
what way is it an outward criterion? I can, after all, silently describe my sensations to myself; and this, far from being an outward criterion, is claimed to be the kind of experience that needs
one. It is observations of this kind, in my opinion, that should be

the starting point for any debate about the private language argument, its proponents being asked to respond to them.

If we now turn to the argument, Wittgenstein sets it out in concentrated form in section 258, where we are asked to imagine that in a diary one writes a sign, say "E", whenever one feels a certain sensation, which we may suppose to have no characteristic outward expression. Perhaps one concentrates on the sensation when writing the sign, in order to make it a sign for the sensation. But Wittgenstein claims that in this case there is no criterion of correct use for the sign, so that, 'One would like to say: whatever is going to seem right to me is right. And that only means that here we can't talk about "right".'

Might it not be, however, that such criteria are provided by one's recall of the sensation? Rejecting this possibility, Wittgenstein says that it would be like trying to check one's memory of the departure time of a train by calling to mind an image of the timetable, his point being that this mental image would itself have to be tested for correctness if it were to serve as confirmation of the memory. There are, of course, methods of verification in such cases, but these consist not in conjuring up a mental image but in consulting the timetable or in some other form of interaction with the world.

A rebuttal of this argument is given by A.J.Ayer, who maintains that such methods are themselves based on what he refers to as acts of primary recognition, the same as with recognising a sensation, and that all facts and memories depend for their confirmation on memory itself. Referring to Wittgenstein's example, he claims that there is no crucial difference between relying on one's memory of a timetable and actually consulting it, for even when the figures are in black and white one still has to recognise them. Even if these are checked in their turn, giving rise to further checking, and so on, then, 'unless there is something that one is allowed to recognise, no test can ever be completed: there will be no justification for the use of any sign at all.' (1973: p.41)

Let us look into this, noting first that it assumes a distinction between the identifying act and the steps that lead up to it, such that they are grounded in the act. Suppose, then, that I return to a timetable to check my memory of my previous reading of it, my concern being with a particular train time, which I have not been sure that I remember correctly, and that my expectation of the timetable turns out to be correct. This is very strong confirmation, as always in such cases, but what we need to ask is whether Ayer's distinction can do the work required of it. Looking at the timetable on the second occasion, I see words and numbers, this being the identifying act. But thus described it serves not at all as confirmation of memory, or indeed of anything else, and what is missing is the intentional context, with all that this implies about my registering what I see as not just squiggles but train times. And, too, all that is implied about my remembering and understanding the steps by which I have arrived at this point with the intention of confirming my memory, also remembered, and with the expectation of what I will find if my memory is correct. In some of this the reference should, if one insists, be to awareness rather than to memory, but it would make no difference, the point being that the memory, expectation and understanding involved in checking cannot itself be checked except as a separate process, about which the same applies. It follows that at this micro level Ayer's implicit distinction is invalid: one distinguishes, rather, and on another level, between confirming and disconfirming the particular memory. So much, then, for the whole idea of a self-contained or independent act of primary recognition on which a process of checking depends if everything is not to "hang in the air".

That idea, or so I believe, is incoherent, as is the further idea, the two being related, of a sensation imprinting meaning onto a word, so that it stands for the sensation. We are asked to imagine that we focus on the sensation when pronouncing or writing the letter "E"—a semantic incantation—and that the representational essence of the sensation transfers itself to the sign. If we substitute "pain" for "E", it becomes obvious that we invest it with meaning only if we are able to separate it from the sensation and refer to this latter in its absence. Otherwise, we are limited to such locutions as "pain, now", which lack in elegance what they also, or so it seems, lack in sense. Ayer (p. 38) takes Rudolph Carnap in *The Unity of Science* to refer to such expressions as belonging to a "protocol language", Carnap's claim being that they constitute a direct report of immediately given conscious items. But also, according to some, they may be understood only by the subject, which is to say the item's owner, this being an extension of the claim.

Since, however, Ayer's Carnap disagrees, believing as he does that other people can understand one's protocol statements, he feels obliged to give a behaviouristic interpretation of them in their third-person use. This is problematic on all fronts, not least because the notion of grammatical person has no application to such word pairs as "pain now" or "now pain", this latter being more lyrical, indeed quite poignant. In fact, such locutions are soon jettisoned when people embark on a discussion of private language, so we shall follow suit. A difficulty with behaviourism, which gives every impression of being fatal, is that psychological statements would have two distinct meanings, depending on grammatical person. But the theory entails that when A ascribes pain to B the reference is to pain behaviour; and to ascribing behaviour when A notes that B is ascribing pain to himself. Though not really, for nothing would count as B ascribing anything to anyone. A, then, would be a psychological solipsist. Since, however, A would be the only human being, A would have to be myself, in which case I should believe that I am a psychological solipsist, and thereby unable to ascribe consciousness to other people. I am not that person, therefore the theory is incorrect, which in any case it would have to be; for one cannot state it without distinguishing between a person and an automaton, for instance in saying that B is not a person, which the theory prohibits being said. The theory specifies that B is a person, which is to say an automaton, and also it denies that B is a person, since B is an automaton. This is incoherent and need not detain us.

If, on the other hand, a behaviourist seeks to avoid such entanglement, to which end he resorts to full-blown physicalism, so that even his description of his own mental states is behaviouristic, then one cannot do better, by way of dismissing absurdity, than to quote from *The Meaning of Meaning*. (1989) Its authors, Ogden and Richards, famously remarked that a physicalist, anxious to appear consistent, would have to 'feign anaesthesia'.

Where, then, does this leave the private language argument?

It is clear that similarities obtain between that which the argument opposes and Carnap's theory of protocol language, testimony to which is the following passage from *The Investigations*. Speaking of the possibility of a private language, Wittgenstein writes, 'The individual words of this language are to refer to what can only be known to the person speaking; to his immediate private sensations. So another person cannot understand the language.'(243)

There are, on the other hand, differences, one of which, as Ayer points out, is that for Wittgenstein such a language is not even intelligible to the subject himself. In this, it seems to me, Wittgenstein displays more insight, though we have seen that his argument about memory has to be rejected. Even without it one may still maintain, with regard to the disputed semi-metaphysical account of meaning acquisition in the case of inner consciousness, that focussing on a sensation while incanting a word, say "pain", is neither necessary nor sufficient. It is not necessary because the question of how we learn sensation words is contingent; and for the most part we do not know exactly how we learnt a particular word or expression, the comparison with learning a foreign language being one that we should perhaps avoid making. And it is not sufficient because nothing follows from it. It may be, as often happens, that we have severe toothache at the same time as we repeat the word "pain", with its English pronunciation, while badly learning the French word for bread. What counts is that one should be suitably disposed in one's self-ascriptive or other-ascriptive use of "pain" in sentences, the details of which come under the heading of conceptual analysis. We shall delve into them in the chapter on avowals and elsewhere, our findings perhaps being of interest in themselves as well as in their implications for the wider issues with which we are concerned.

What matters now is that the semi-metaphysical account is wholly misconceived even on its own terms, given the incoherent claim that a subject, when he focusses on a sensation while naming it, confers on that name a meaning that only he can understand. It is this that is incoherent, for it implies, or would if it made any sense, that the actual immediate sensation, in all its individual identity as belonging to the subject, is what the word captures in its meaning. This is magical thinking and we should not linger over it, all the more so when it is pointed out that in this context the word "immediate" has no application. That is, we focus on the sensation while uttering the word "pain", but in the moments taken to utter the word, however quickly we speak, the original sensation has extinguished itself in the first of them, so that by the time the "n" sound is uttered it is too late. This is analysis taken to a temporal extreme, in other words it is micro-analysis, but it is none the worse for that, and what it shows is that the assimilating of one sensation to another through time is presupposed in the claim that only the subject can understand his word for the immediate sensation. So much, then, for protocol statements and their intimations of the primitive, and also for the basic nature of Ayer's acts of recognition of sensations and time-tables. They are primitive in one way, hence the aside about magical thinking, but that is not what our protagonists mean.

So far, then, we can agree with Wittgenstein in his repudiation of the very idea of a private language intelligible only to the subject; but obstacles to any further agreement will now be rolled onto the road if we compare him with Carnap. According to this latter, such a language is possible, in which case other people cannot refer to it, their apparent such reference having overt sensation behaviour as its object, notwithstanding the fact that quite often there is none. That, however, is incidental, given the major hurdles by which any distinction of meaning according to grammatical person may be opposed. Put another way, the language of mental states is univocal, so that "I am in pain" and "you are in pain" mean the same through all the various combinations of interpersonal reference, such as A quoting B about A or B, and so on. For Wittgenstein, inner ostensive definition of mental states does not have the magical naming properties that Carnap is able, presumably, to introspect, this being that about which we agree with him.

But Wittgenstein, perhaps rather puzzlingly, prefers not to take this demystifying of the process of inner naming to indicate that we should look to some other inner process, no doubt involving dispositions and the ability to refer to sensations in their ab-

56

sence. What it does indicate to him, as to Carnap, is that there must be outward criteria by which inner processes make themselves publicly known. This, however, presents insuperable difficulties, one of which, as already mentioned, is that in many cases mental states have no natural outward expression, relying instead on the use of description to make themselves known to others. But in what sense is the self-ascription of sensations, say, criterial? For instance, it is not as if, when I say that I have tinnitus, other people respond appropriately to the sounds I make. They respond to what I say when I speak English, just as others might respond in the same way to the same statement in a foreign language. They respond, in other words, to what I *say*, which is that I have tinnitus, and the only criteria in play are linguistic, concerning as they do the various conditions of understanding as applied to the statements that I make.

If, on the other hand, there are outward criteria to be had, as with pain, then they correlate only very loosely with inner mental states. Basically, I may react to my pain in such a way as to indicate where it is felt and how severe it is, and visible injury may also provide a further indication, as also the causal context. But these are one thing and my pain is quite another. What it all points to, one might think, is that there is much more than this to knowledge of pain in oneself and in other people. Indeed, I shall argue later that discourse about oneself and others belongs within a cognitive and semantic system driven by the interplay between language, experience and the world. Wittgenstein does, it has to be said, refer to the need for 'stage-setting' (257) if the naming of a sensation is to make sense, and this would seem to be in accord with the idea of a system. But it is not the case that inner processes must have natural outward expression if they are to be understood.

1.5: Counter-Example to the Argument

Time, then, for a convincing counter-example to the private language argument. Suppose that I am treated by a doctor for not going out enough, the pills having the interesting side effect of washing away colours from what I see, so that my visual screen, as it were, becomes monochrome, showing only black and white.

Then I am still able to assure myself that my errors of public application do not betray a lack of understanding of the words for the colours that remain to me. Looking at a particular swan, I say to other people that it is white, which is what I remember, only to be told that it is black, which makes it an Australian swan or a painted Mute swan; and it may be that the swan appears black to me, or that it appears white, but in either case I am able to differentiate between the two.

All the same, if my experience of which objects appear white and which black differs markedly from other people's, then I may give the impression of not even knowing the meaning of "black" and "white", let alone the words for chromatic colours. We could go even further and devise a hypothetical situation in which this impression was reinforced, for instance by specifying that the medication affected not only my perception of colour but also the apparent colour stability of physical objects. The colours would be stable for other people, other things being equal, but for myself they would fluctuate between black and white quite haphazardly on different occasions. If this is correct, then the problem for Wittgenstein is that an individual may give meaning to colour words even when external criteria for their correct use are unfulfilled. A possible objection here is that in this example my colour words derive from the public language of colours, my grasp of which was already established before I took the medication. But this is a contingent fact about colour concept acquisition, the point at issue being that of whether my use of colour words depends on public criteria; and it would, I think, be easy enough to modify the thought experiment so that I acquired the concept in some other way. I conclude that it is not the case that words have meaning only if their use is conformable to public criteria of correctness.

Let us now recapitulate the main points of this chapter and prepare for the next. I have tried to show that we are not in thrall, as Wittgenstein suggests that we are, to misleading and conflicting pictures of what it is to mean and to understand. Rather, our concern should be with questions of analysis, and there is no reason to believe that they have to be dissolved instead of answered, or that only the sceptic about meaning and understanding is able to answer them. That, at least, is the thesis I am trying to establish, to which end I propose in the next chapter to critically examine not only the equating of meaning and understanding with use but also the sceptical view of them taken by Kripke. This is all as a preliminary to a modest proposal of my own, already prefigured in this chapter: that it is only within the context of a system that an adequate account can be given of what it is to mean and to understand. This itself is part of a more ambitious plan by which a theory of intentionality and consciousness will take shape as the various problems yield to a system-based treatment. The upshot will be that although the intentional may not be "occult"—unless in scare quotes—its essence is not in custom or practice either, since it makes prior entrance into both of them. Rather, the key concepts are those of the conscious and the non-conscious, the terms of discourse being metaphysical.

With all that in mind, I have emphasised the first-person view of understanding and the fact that it is not only occurrent but also dispositional. Crucial to the difference this makes is the fact that understanding is governed by assertibility conditions, which I take to be in line with common sense. If I claim at time t, as much to myself as to others, that I am able to mathematically derive the impossibly beautiful $e^{i\pi} + 1 = 0$, and in that sense to understand it, there are circumstances in which I may fail in that attempt at time $t+1$ without having to forfeit the claim, for instance if I suffer a stroke in the meantime or go blind or sleep not at all or…or abducted by aliens who confiscate my pen. Back on Earth meanwhile, much remains to be done if the theory now emerging is to be brought to fruition, and if an answer to scepticism is to be plucked from it. As in this chapter, my aim in the next will be to cultivate a particular account of what it is to mean and to understand, but with more emphasis on the ways in which inference enters into language use. The method, as before, will be to clear the ground currently occupied by Wittgenstein, and also, in this next chapter, by Kripke. It will then be easier to unearth the hidden connections between language and the world.

Chapter 2: Meaning as Use

Continuing our critique of Wittgenstein, let us now return to what he says about use, custom and technique. With regard to this latter, there is considerable overlap between the notion of ability or technique and that of understanding or meaning, the verbal expressions of which are in many cases interchangeable. It matters little whether we say that we understand the even number sequence or that we are able to expand it; this is also true of our saying that we know how to ride a bike or that we are able to ride it. It is undeniable, then, that to exhibit understanding is to display ability or technique, though this does invite a question as to the significance of that fact. In seeking an answer, we should perhaps begin by considering physical rather than mental ability, a difference which the following detour into traffic will illustrate.

Imagine that a robot has been programmed to learn to cycle, a skill which it quickly masters as it becomes adept at weaving between vehicles and ignoring traffic lights on red. There are circumstances in which it would not be misleading to say that the robot knows how to ride a bike, though we should perhaps have to stop short of describing it as being angry and disappointed when it fails its cycling proficiency test. This is all from an external point of view, the robot not being credited with an inner life, and what it shows is that criteria of cycling ability are behavioural, as in some ways are criteria of understanding. The point here is that I am not being inconsistent in everyday life if, with regard to appraising a student's understanding of an item, I focus on her cognitive behaviour, which is to say her grasp of the item above water, rather than on her stream of consciousness. This may also be the case if the stream deepens into intense cogitation, the student's frown more concentrated, my concern still being with overt performance rather than the flow of hidden mental processes. Similarly, if I ask for apples in a greengrocer's my interest is in whether the assistant understands my request in the sense of being able to carry it out, his mental processes being no concern of mine in any other way.

In fact, this pragmatic behaviourism or functionalism is even more pronounced in our epistemic approach to other species to which we attribute understanding, for instance in the case of dogs and bats. Some dogs are highly intelligent and quick to learn, at least according to their owners, who would probably concede, that said, that the grasp of arithmetical sequences would seem to have eluded them thus far. This is probable rather than certain because human beings, especially dog lovers, are notoriously anthropomorphic, even if they stop short of similarly characterising other species, perhaps with the exception of their anthropomorphic pets; and it is arguable, indeed, that we have no genuine insight into the cognitive processes of a dog fetching its lead or of a bat hanging very cleverly upside down. All that we can say, on the present account, is that understanding, even if it requires consciousness, manifests itself in overt behaviour, particular inner processes being unknowable in the case of other animals and inessential in the case of other people.

There is, as already acknowledged, some truth in this, provided that it is qualified in terms of the distinction between first- and third-person points of view and their interrelations within a system. The difference this makes is that when interpersonal exchange is characterised by pragmatic behaviourism this detracts not at all from the fact of inner processes of understanding. If the student is deep in thought, perhaps mentally working out the fourth term of the sequence with initial term 7 and constant difference 17, then irrespective of whether she gives the correct answer her mental processes are cognitive, which is to say that reasoning and understanding define them, her denial of which would itself involve them. This is to say that from her own perspective her thought processes necessarily manifest understanding, as do mine from mine. But also, there is my perspective on her, and it may well be that I am aware of her being deep in thought, or even that in principle she could describe in detail her calculations, just as I can describe my own processes of reasoning.

Inescapably, we are drawn back to the first-person point of view, from which vantage point there is no harm in saying that understanding involves technique, or is exhibited as a technique, or not outwardly exhibited at all, as when I re-read these words or read other text or register what other people say. Wittgenstein, however, would disagree, citing as he does the case of a shop-keeper who responds to the request for five red apples by opening the drawer in which they are kept and consulting a colour chart, whereupon he counts out five red apples. Wittgenstein now goes on 'But what is the meaning of the word "five"? – No such thing was in question here, only how the word "five" is used. (1)

Here we can at least catch a glimpse of what Wittgenstein has in mind when he equates meaning with use. The shopkeeper is depicted as having to take a circuitous route to the understanding of English, or of particular instructions, and we have to imagine, I suppose, that he is not able to take the shortcut of translation into a language he already knows. The emphasis is on what he does, and this is meant to show that in a wider context any question as to the nature of meaning can be answered in terms of use. This is not to imply that there is no such thing as meaning, for in English "meaning" and "to mean" have a use, the whole of which forms a practice, or, as Wittgenstein would say, a language-game.

The problem is to try to distinguish this thesis from the com-mon-sense view that use of language involves technique, and one place to start is with the actions of the shopkeeper. We saw that he carries out the instruction by breaking it down into simple steps and matching words against colours and objects, so that the meaning of the words lies in the use he makes of them. The im-plication here is that this is also true of actual linguistic under-standing and practice, so that, for instance, the shopkeeper would quickly learn to understand English in the way that we all do and would be able to dispense with elaborate reminders and carry out the order without more ado. That is, he would read the order and immediately place five red apples in a bag, handing them to the customer in exchange for payment. This is what would normally happen, and again it illustrates what could be meant by the use that the shopkeeper makes of words. At this level, indeed, it is easy to imagine replacing them with pictorial signs, in the present case a colour picture of five red apples on a slip of paper. But now, this immediately invites a question as to whether more so-phisticated functions of language to convey meaning are amena-ble to the same interpretation in terms of use. Statements about the past come to mind, as also any statement that is abstract rather than concrete in meaning.

2.1: Assertibility Conditions and the Past

If we consider the thesis in connection with statements about the past, then our first step, however odd this may seem, is to remind ourselves of the reality of past events, to which end we may conduct an experiment. Place a clock and a Ming vase on the worktop in your kitchen. At midday push the vase over the edge and note that it smashes into pieces on the ceramic tiles and raises a cloud of ash dust, the last remains of your cremated parents. The time is now 12.01 p.m. and the result of the experiment is conclusive: a minute ago you really did smash that vase; also, your parents were once alive and really did exist, as did your childhood. It is also the case that although your spouse is out at the moment, you know that he or she exists and is going to be annoyed and then start worrying about your mental state, all of which involves memories of past events.

It has been argued that those who equate statements about the past with their use are not denying the reality of past events; but it needs to be asked what they could mean, apart from the entirely uninteresting fact that such statements are used to refer to past events. For instance, we have quoted Wittgenstein as claiming, with regard to the meaning of the word "five", that this equates with its use. Now try to imagine a similar claim about the statement that a moment ago I placed five apples in a bag or sacrificed a precious vase to philosophical enquiry. No doubt you soon gave up, but if you are now asked to make the same imaginative effort a propos the semantic content of this paragraph, or any in this book, then quite likely you will have even less idea how to proceed. So much, then, for abstract meaning as use, irrespective of tense, and including the abstractions involved in the thesis itself: that about meaning as use. Not that concrete meaning is any less resistant to the thesis, nor the concept of the past with which we started. The fact is that if the thesis equating meaning with use calls into question the reality of the past, then it must be wrong, for each of us knows that events in his or her history were real, just as present events are real. If, on the other hand, the thesis does not threaten reality in this way, then again we have to ask what could be meant by it, with one eye on the possibility that it means very little beyond the truism that language has its uses.

With the other eye, however, we need to widen our purview so that the question of meaning as use may be considered in terms of its connection with truth conditions. A difficulty here is that of separating the truth conditions of a declarative sentence from its meaning, one approach to which is to distinguish them from assertibility conditions. In many cases there is a clear distinction between the truth of a proposition and the grounds for asserting it. For instance, the truth condition of "he is in pain" is that he is in pain, to which we could also appeal when giving the meaning of the sentence, as when we say that what we mean by it is that he is in pain. Hence the difficulty of separating the truth conditions of a statement from its meaning. The assertibility condition, on the other hand, is that which warrants our asserting that he is in pain, in this case the man's pain behaviour and attendant circumstances.

The difference between the two conditions is clear and distinct, but there is nothing perspicuous in the proposal by some philosophers to substitute assertibility conditions for truth conditions. To appreciate their reasons we need to consider a particular class of statements, namely those whose objective meaning is in some sense problematic. Belonging to this class are the value judgements which are the subject matter of ethics and aesthetics. If I say that sunsets are beautiful, ugly or a little on the plain side or that it is morally good to kill carpet mites provided that it is outside the mating season, then a question arises as to the reality of the abstract qualities of beauty and goodness or their opposites to which I appeal. With regard to truth conditions is there an actual state of affairs which, if it obtains, makes it true that sunsets are beautiful? Is there anything in the world, in some sense independent of my beliefs, which makes it true or false that certain actions are morally good? Concomitantly, what in any case does it mean to speak of the beautiful or the good? To such questions philosophers have provided a variety of answers, some of which, if correct, clearly preserve the truth-conditionality of this class of statements, either by interpreting them naturalistically or by taking them to be irreducible in meaning. Set against this are

64

projectivist or expressivist theories, according to which value-judgements are essentially expressive of attitude or emotion, despite being cast in the form of declarative sentences in assertoric mode. What projectivism is usually taken to imply is that the statements in question misrepresent reality, since they project upon objects and actions the non-existent qualities of beauty and goodness. This raises a difficult question as to whether such statements are truth-conditional, one answer to which is to argue that if they are misleading or wrong then they must assert something and therefore be governed by truth conditions; but it would have to be that these are incapable of being satisfied, given that beauty and goodness are not objective qualities.

The point is that these issues can arise only because they are circumscribed within a framework in which truth-conditionality is in general taken for granted, which is to say that propositions about assertibility conditions are themselves taken to be true or false in the usual way, incoherence thereby being avoided. Since all propositions, including these, necessarily depend on the ordinary concept of the past, the equating of truth-conditions with assertibility conditions would be incoherent. This dependence arises from the fact that to propose that something is the case is necessarily to imply that one remembers the proposition one has advanced, at least from one moment to the next, where this includes remembering that one has advanced it.

One reason for this critique of the assertibility thesis is that I wish to dissociate this latter from the system-based analysis of intentionality developed later and already making itself felt. Another reason is that the assertibility thesis ramifies into the equating of meaning with use, at least on one interpretation, for if there is no fact of the matter as to what we mean, then it seems to follow that there are no truth conditions, their place being taken by conditions of assertibility. This is in line with Kripke's reading of Wittgenstein, and it connects with the emphasis on criteria in the *Investigations*. What I have tried to show is that the assertibility thesis is untenable, as also the thesis equating meaning with use. That this latter thesis should be rejected may also be shown in terms of the deductive character of mathematical inference.

Suppose that I try to work out an nth term formula for the finite sequence 1, 5, 11, 19, 29, 41. Looking at these terms, I would guess – perhaps from experience – that a suitable formula would be quadratic. So let us try $n^2 + n + 1$. No, the first term is wrong, so make it $n^2 - n + 1$. No, this time the second term is wrong, so try $n^2 + n - 1$. Yes, it works for each term. Clearly, this process of reasoning is heuristic, my discoveries determining the inferences that I make. That said, if I find that for $n = 2$, $n^2 - n + 1 = 3$, whereas the second term of the sequence is 5, then the formula $a_n = n^2 - n + 1$ *cannot* be correct. But now, if this reasoning is informed by deductive inference, so that it involves mathematical relations between signs, then what could it mean to say that such inferences are a matter of use or practice? If this is to deprive them of their logical force, then instead of explaining them it vitiates them; and if it is not, then it says nothing at all about them.

2.2: Critique of Kripke on Rule-Following

That, at least, is what common sense would suggest, and if this is to be our guide then the foregoing criticisms have general application to the thesis equating meaning with use. Another approach to them is to ask whether the thesis implies that the use of an expression is unconstrained except by habit or custom. An affirmative answer would again be counter-intuitive, regardless of whether the use in question is that of the individual or the community; and it is not clear that Wittgenstein would subscribe to it. Nonetheless, it is an answer given by some commentators, notably Kripke, whose radical interpretation of the *Investigations* must now be considered. He is of the view, repudiated by Baker and Hacker (1984), that for Wittgenstein the character of rule-following is so extremely paradoxical as to compel the sceptical conclusion that meaning and understanding are non-factual. Setting aside the question of whether it is faithful to Wittgenstein's views, the sceptical thesis propounded by Kripke has been taken to merit examination on its own account, and the place to start is with his argument about what it is to give meaning to an arithmetical sign. Suppose that I denote by the symbol "+" the addition function, the sum of only two terms being considered, and that I have never summed any terms greater than 56, apart from the present one, which takes the form 57+68 =125. Then we may imagine a sceptic asking how I know that in my previous use of "+" I meant addition, such that this past meaning determines the answer 125. Perhaps I meant "quaddition" such that $x + y = 5$ if x, y >56. The intention here is not to call into question my memory; rather, it is to cast doubt on the whole idea of what it is to follow a rule or give meaning to a word.

One way to try to meet this challenge would be to appeal to some inner sense-determining experience accompanying my previous use of "plus", a move which the sceptic anticipates by treating such experience phenomenologically. How could a mental state attending one's previous use of "plus" determine its present use? he asks. In the same way the sceptic about the concept of the past may insist on treating memory processes as a succession of mental images, these being all that the memory of a past event seems to amount to, in which case it is no more than the sum of its parts. The concept of memory, however, is commonly taken to be that of a special kind of temporal awareness of events as having occurred, whereas a mental state is just an item of experience like any other, so that the only awareness would seem to be of the mental state itself.

At this point we may try to answer the sceptic by turning to the dispositional element in rule-following. For instance, if I have grasped the addition rule then I am disposed to give to each addition sum a particular unique answer. But now Kripke in the role of sceptic argues that rule-following cannot be equated with an individual's actual dispositions, for then it would not be possible to distinguish between correct and incorrect applications of a rule. The reason is that there cannot be a rule without standards of correctness, so that the concept of a rule is normative. Besides, dispositions are always finite, whereas addition over integers may take any of an unlimited range of values. Since we appear to be unable to answer the sceptic, the only conclusion, according to Kripke, is that 'there can be no such thing as meaning anything by any word.' (1982: 55)

That is what he says and presumably means, despite the paradox implicit in his meaning what he says, and he now turns to what he calls the sceptical solution to the problem, by which he means a solution that acknowledges that there is no fact of the matter as to what it is for an individual to follow a rule. What is wrong, says Kripke, is the assumption that an individual considered in isolation may follow a rule, the truth being that it is possible only if one is regarded as a member of a community, the rule being constituted by communal practice itself rather than the practice complying with a separately identifiable rule. The problem here, however, is that such a solution gives every indication of being inchoate, as I shall now try to show.

According to Kripke, if I have never summed any terms greater than 56, apart from the present sum, which takes the form 57+68=125, then nothing in my previous use of "plus", including my accompanying mental states and processes, determines its present use and yields 125 as the answer. That is Kripke's argument, his conclusion being that the sentences of mathematics and language in general are devoid of sense. If that is what they are, there can be no objection to my grouping sequences of letters, numerals and other linguistic marks into genuinely non-semantic sentences. The point of them is that they will not be tainted by association with mental states normally described as those of linguistic understanding. Here is an example:
"Fi xe sulp owt yhw slauqe net, dna owt sulp yhw slauqe nevele, neht ex slauqe 4 dna yhw slauqe 3." This means nothing, as required, and when scanning it we are not in a mental state that we misconstrue, according to Kripke, as that of understanding. Rather, we are in a mental bubble of incomprehension. Gently blowing that bubble along, reverse the nonsensical sequences just given and let the bubble settle onto them: "If ex plus two why equals ten, and two ex plus why equals eleven, then ex equals 4 and why equals 3." Using the more usual notation: if $x + 2y = 10$ and $2x + y = 11$, then $x = 4$ and $y = 3$. Very likely, if you are like me, the bubble immediately burst on contact with sense, this being the point of the exercise; for if Kripke is right then the simultaneous equation and its solutions, which we are wholly mistaken in thinking that we understand, are just as nonsensical as their reverse counterparts, which clearly are devoid of sense. This is not only incoherent but also self-refuting, for if it were valid then

nothing would count as Kripke being correct or as my agreeing or disagreeing with him.

This may be summed up as follows, and in *reductio ad absurdum* form. If the sceptic starts from the collision of there being no fact of the matter as to what words mean, and if he attempts to salvage from the wreckage the notion of communal practice, then this notion is nothing if not expressed in words, which thereby become self-referential. We read sense into them only by construing the thesis of communal practice to be true or false; but in taking it to be truth-conditional the sceptic refutes himself. Put another way, if the thesis of semantic non-factualism were correct, the notion of similar communal use would have no application, the linguistic landscape being littered with the uncoordinated utterances of individuals talking nonsense.

Let us now try to work out where Kripke has gone wrong, noting first that he has a reason for targeting previous applications of a rule. His reason is that the sceptical problem can be formulated only if one's present practice is not itself open to question. For instance, if I now say that 57+68 =125, the sceptic will agree that by "+" I now mean addition, and that all my words and his have their usual meaning. This has to be conceded, says Kripke, but he adds that once the problem has been stated it poses a difficulty for one's present use of words considered at a later stage. What this overlooks is that the sceptic's words are no sooner uttered than they recede into the past. The fact that it is the immediate past makes no difference — the sceptic still has to question what was meant by them, that question having to be challenged in its turn, and so on into an endless regress. Relatedly, the concept of the past is essential to Kripke's approach; but if there is no fact of the matter as to what we mean, how can it be possible to refer to previous linguistic use?

Why is it, then, that Kripke's radical semantic scepticism does not meet with outright rejection? It is partly because he addresses a genuine problem: that of the perplexing character of intentionality. But in particular it is because he claims that the sceptical problem can be stated only if the sceptical conclusion is not unleashed until after the statement has been made. I have argued that there can be no such period of grace, but the present point is that because the problem stated is that of giving meaning to an arithmetical sum, the sceptical conclusion being retrospectively that there is no fact as to what is meant, we fail to notice that the same would be true of any statements, including those by which the conclusion itself is found to have meaning. In short: the arguments in support of the thesis of semantic non-factualism are incoherent and the thesis refutes itself.

What, though, of the difficulties about intentionality that remain after the sceptic has been refuted? The point to be made, which by its very nature is a pivotal one, is that we must now turn from scepticism to analysis, knowing as we do that the fact of intentionality cannot be gainsaid, however outlandish the form that it may take. Thus it is that the notion of a system is brought into play, as also that of the irreducibility of intentional concepts, which at a later stage we shall connect with the theory of consciousness already remarked upon.

2.3: The Irreducibility Thesis

One advocate of the thesis that meaning and understanding are irreducible is Colin McGinn, who argues that if the candidates for meaning examined by Kripke all fail to qualify, where these include mental states assimilated to sensations, then what follows is not that there is no fact of the matter as to meaning — and understanding — but that it stands on its own, a thing in itself, in the sense of not being reducible to anything else. Thus it is that for McGinn the crucial question, in connection with the sentence "he means addition when he uses the plus sign "is that of why we cannot specify its truth conditions by *'re-using* that sentence, frankly admitting that no other specification of truth conditions is available – precisely because semantic statements cannot be *reduced* to non-semantic ones.' (1987: p.151)

This approach, it seems to me, is correct; for it is indeed the case that the fact of meaning obtains and that it cannot be reduced to sensations or dispositions; therefore it is irreducible. This is corroborated by our everyday experience of intentionality and even, in a sense, by the perplexity it engenders when, as it were, we look for the engine. Consider what it is for me to grasp a number sequence, say the one with initial term 7 and constant difference 17. I manifest that understanding by reasoning about the sequence or, if reading and writing are involved, by merging together thought, perception and action to yield the inferential steps by which I proceed. Characteristic of engaging with the sequence in this way is that I extend particular segments of it, work out the harder terms or successors in its higher reaches, check that I am right and perhaps correct any slips or errors I may discover, and so on, all of which are instances of cognitive processes.

Let us now consider the ways in which the rejection of semantic scepticism and adoption of the irreducibility thesis illuminates afresh the sceptic's arguments, in particular the thesis that meaning and understanding cannot be reduced to dispositions about mental states phenomenologically construed. This is undeniable, since they cannot be reduced at all, in which context analysis reveals that they are both occurrent and dispositional, this latter in the sense that occurrent understanding depends on one's being disposed to understand, such dispositions being actualised in the form of further occurrent understanding, itself dependent on ..., and so on. As already remarked upon, one's dispositions do not determine whether one understands; rather, their particular character determines what it is that one understands.

Next in line is Kripke's claim that the individual cannot distinguish between his actual dispositions in relation to a rule and those that the rule requires him to have. Certainly, I may misapply a rule, fail in my efforts to grasp it, or even altogether misconstrue it. Since, however, this is to imply awareness on my part of the cognitive shortcomings involved, which itself is to presuppose that the distinction can be made, it presents itself as a counter-argument to Kripke's thesis. To this he would rejoin, presumably, that no distinction can be made between one's actual dispositions with regard to checking one's grasp of a rule and those that such checking requires one, or would require one, to have. The short way with such radical scepticism about intentional concepts is, as we have seen, to impose a condition of our own: that the sceptical thesis should be self-applying without lapsing into incoherence or refuting itself. This is a test that it easily fails, for the sceptic cannot state his case without standards of correctness coming into play. If to this it is objected that these are communal standards, indistinguishable from community practice, then the rejoinder should be that to speak of such a practice is to imply the possibility of deviating from it, otherwise anything would go, and clearly it does not. It should also be that to speak of such a practice, thereby giving meaning to one's words, is to refute oneself. How is the sceptic to distinguish between his actual dispositions with regard to what he means by semantic nonfactualism and those that the relevant meaning rules require him to have?

This is more than enough to make the point, but I cannot resist one more nail, to the effect that Kripke's indistinguishability thesis would apply to all forms of the intentional in which standards of correctness would seem to play a part, including those that enter into perception and therefore perceptual inference. Looking at this table edge in front of me and seeing it as having a particular appearance, I expect it to appear slightly, and suitably, different if I incline my head a little to one side, and thereby confirm my present observation. To see this, try to imagine that all such micro-expectations are disconfirmed: would anything then count as disconfirmation? But how do I distinguish, according to Kripke, the expectation I actually have from the one that perceptual confirmation requires me to have? Since this is a *reductio ad absurdum* question, no answer is required. The upshot of this critique of semantic scepticism is that this latter indeed combines the incoherent and the self-refuting.

2.4: A New Theory of Consciousness

Are there further insights to be gained from our refutation of semantic non-factualism? Indeed there are, all the more so if our findings are conjoined with the system-based theory of consciousness and intentionality about to be very briefly sketched, more having been said in the introduction, with a full account awaiting us in the penultimate chapter. Our theory, to begin with, will be metaphysical, hence the contrast made between the conscious and the non-conscious rather than the unconscious, which is too closely associated with Freudianism and perhaps, nowadays, with neuroscience. The crucial claim, for which

I argue in great detail, is that the system-based theory transcends the distinction between physical and mental and therefore between brain states and consciousness. With regard to this latter, we need to ask whether one's notion of consciousness has any need of that of the non-conscious; and it is easily shown that indeed it does.

The basic argument, as we saw in the introduction, albeit articulated differently, is that bare consciousness is not the stuff of memory or other forms of the intentional, this being shown in the case of language. Linguistically, a word in a spoken sentence derives its meaning from the semantic context, as with the last word of the present sentence being the one I am about to write down. If I hear the previous sentence from someone speaking it to me, the last word being "down", then I do indeed register it in the context of the sentence to which it belongs; but I hear only that single word at the time, the body of the sentence having fallen away into the void of the past. Since nothing counts as the meaning of that sentence having been passed on to the last word of it, there is a gap into which, or so I claim, only the non-conscious can fit, which in the nature of the case must be all-pervasive of language; hence the theory of the non-conscious.

In the present case, we may now depict my non-conscious memory and understanding as obtaining within the same realm as the non-conscious events or states underlying my conscious auditory experience of the whole of the spoken sentence. But also, we may now depict the non-conscious workings of my memory of the spoken sentences being manifested in my conscious memory, hence its particular experiential character. This is such that phenomenology, narrowly construed, cannot do any justice to it. Nor, for that matter, can any form of the psychophysical, the reason for which, at the level of metaphysics, will become apparent in the following chapters.

This theory of consciousness will form the backdrop or take centre stage in much of what follows; for if intentionality belongs within a system, the problem of avowals, which we are about to confront, should be amenable to a particular form of treatment. That is, one should be able to exhibit self-ascriptive authoritativeness as being governed by assertibility conditions and constrained by its connections within a system. This is the task we now set ourselves.

Chapter 3: The Problem of Avowals

The discussion thus far has focussed on intentionality according to Wittgenstein, its difficulties also exhibited in the problem of avowals, which is our present concern. In the first chapter I rejected the thesis that inner processes need outward criteria, the converse carrying more conviction, and I argued that mathematical calculations, as in the case of working out a formula, are self-contained. In terms of avowals a corollary is that even if my reasoning is unsound, my report of it is epistemically privileged. Again, if I wake up and wonder whether the front door is unlocked, I can be unsure about the door but not about whether I am thinking about the door. Thus it is that intentional avowals involve, among other things, propositional attitudes, as when we think, fear or hope that something is the case. It may or may not be, but either way it seems that we cannot doubt but that we think, fear or hope that it is, hence the claim that avowals are authoritative.

In some instances, the propositional content as well as the attitude may be intolerant of doubt, for example if recent and more distant memories are compared. I have a vivid childhood memory of being bitten by a dog, but I know that recollection is the plaything of the past, which is more playful the longer the playground in time, so I cannot be absolutely certain it was that way around. That said, it would be odd indeed if I started to doubt whether I typed a sentence to that effect a moment ago, as I now remember doing, and if I did not expect to see it when reading back. Taking this further, to say that one is reading is arguably to authoritatively attribute to oneself a process which typically is as much behavioural as mental, the one feeding into the other. Should it not count as an avowal for that reason? Even if it should not, the fact remains that it blurs the distinction between self-justifying avowal and externally corrigible self-description. When, in the first chapter, Wittgenstein asked, perhaps ironically, how one knows that one is reading, my response was that the question cannot arise and that we should take the reader to be in reading mode. And, too, I have argued that necessary conditions attach to the deliverances of memory, which can be questioned only in particular instances. Thus it is that the problem of avowals is continuous in many ways with problems already addressed, perhaps the same being true of solving it. That being the case, my present finding in relation to a solution is that we have already finished the footings, the concrete having set, and even that the first bricks have been laid.

Since, however, we do not know what the completed construction will be, we should perhaps examine the theoretical structures already in place, the initial focus being on the way in which the problem is framed. According to Dorit Bar-On and Douglas C. Long, 'A sincere, linguistically competent subject' (2001), when she self-ascribes mental states in the present tense, may be deemed to be authoritative in her self-knowledge, or even to be infallible. The examples the writers give include declaring that one has a headache and that one is thinking about philosophy, the one perhaps causing the other. Whether avowals of the phenomenal and the intentional should be lumped together is one of the questions we shall discuss, and partly in connection with Crispin Wright distinguishing between them in his critique of Colin McGinn's irreducibility thesis. The fact is, after all, that the problem of avowals is that of how they can be both authoritative and seemingly ungrounded; but the self-ascribing of sensations is taken to be grounded in the sensation itself.

Apart from an individual needing to be sincere and able to understand the avowal, one assumes that this latter must concern an occurrent mental state— or perhaps, given that stipulation, we should speak of an immediate mental event. Note, however, that if an earlier argument of ours is correct an assumption as to immediacy, strictly understood, would have no application; hence the reference very often being to occurrent process rather than, or as well as, momentary event.

The problem of avowals is, as is no doubt already apparent, a tangled skein, the point being that there are framing assumptions that are treated as background enabling conditions, so that the further assumption, or so it seems, is that they are not otherwise relevant to the problem or to finding a solution. Such an approach, given our track record and the remarks just made, is to be initially fostered rather than permanently adopted. And one consideration here, the significance of which would seem to have been overlooked, is that the understanding by which avowals are made possible, both one's own grasp of them and that of external observers, is itself something that implicitly implies an avowals-like self-ascription. One cannot state a belief, for instance, without implying that one understands the avowal; and it is arguable that the cognitive self-ascription is itself an avowal. Again, then, this harks back to the first chapter, in which the case for necessary cognitive conditions was made, and in terms of the notion of a system. Just as one can cogently doubt one's own understanding only in ways unthreatening to one's grasp of the doubt, so it is that one can epistemically doubt one's avowal only if subject to the same constraint. Clearly, the problem of avowals has pricked up its ears at this, but the dog was already at the door, its tail wagging for two other reasons. Firstly, the quoted reference was to a 'sincere, linguistically competent subject', to which it was tempting to respond by asking how, in her sincerity, a competent speaker might misavow her mental states. And secondly, I mentioned being unsure whether a door is unlocked but not whether I am thinking about the door. But again, what might this mean? It just is a fact that being unsure is itself a mental state, the self-ascription of it an avowal. Clearly there are doors of a different kind to be unlocked; but for the moment, having inserted the keys, we should leave them unturned, our concern being with the attempted solutions already exercised.

3.1: Observational Models

It is commonly held that avowals conform to an observational model, usually along Cartesian lines, so that introspection yields direct awareness of one's conscious mental states as they unfold. For Descartes, such inner observation is unmediated, avowed conscious objects being self-illuminating and indubitable. Any comparison with perception will depend on one's theory of it, but a salient difference, one might think, is that outward observation is at least in some cases inferential, as when we listen to a trilling sound and say that we can hear a skylark. As against this, one might argue that seeing the skylark, or even hearing it, is not in itself inferential, this latter attaching, rather, to observation in a wider sense. And we know from previous work that avowals, or what seem to be avowals, depend on inference insofar as memory and expectation are involved. If we deny for that reason that they count as avowals, then this is a stipulative definition for which a case needs to be made. Not that it would do any good, for memory—and expectation— enters into all avowals, however circumscribed.

It is possible to argue, then, that perception is mediated by sense-experience, whereas awareness of a conscious mental state seems intrinsic to the mental state itself. Let us grant, at least for now, that this is a clear distinction— but only in the context of asking whether a parallel that is conducive to a solution to the avowals problem may be drawn between introspection and perception, the bars being sturdy enough for the philosopher as gymnast. She is required, after all, to land on her feet after the triple somersault of accounting for the apparently authoritative status of avowals. But the point conceded militates against the possibility of that performance, concerning as it does a difference, not a similarity, between looking out and looking in. This use of "looking" is by design, my intention being to illustrate its naturalness and that of the lexicon as a whole by which we use observational equipment to exercise mental-state descriptive concepts. The question of the debt that the observational model owes to a pre-existing metaphorical conceptual scheme is not, however, one that we shall directly pursue. That said, those who speak of an inner sense—an implicit analogy if a certain construction is placed upon it—would seem to hover between like and unlike: perhaps misled by metaphor.

Such considerations help to explain why it is that the appeal to observational models has been much criticised, one of the main critics being Sydney Shoemaker (1994). In a series of lectures he analyses in detail the points of epistemic disanalogy between introspection and perception, his critique in its turn being challenged by other theorists, some of whom share his views as to the importance of comparative analysis if a solution is to be found. Since I do not count myself among them, despite the ease with which one becomes embroiled in disputes of this kind, I shall join the fray by focussing initially on what I take to be the central question: is it the case that the parallels between physical-world perception and mental-realm awareness are such that the former may serve as a model for the latter? Whether this question can be answered by compare and contrast will depend on the meaning of "model" in its present use. It is reasonable to take this to be such, given the centrality of the problem of authoritativeness, that perception qualifies as a model— one that preserves the epistemic status quo in the case of avowals— only if certain conditions are satisfied. First, that the deliverances of perception should be authoritative; second, that this elevated epistemic status should not itself be vulnerable, which is to say needing the support that avowals need from it; and third, that somehow or other that support, with avowals in receipt of it, equates with underpinning their epistemic authority, and in a way that has advantages over directly analysing them.

Note further, lest it be overlooked, that perceptual deliverances themselves involve avowals: seeing or hearing a skylark is a subjective experience which it should be possible to describe in that way, the description being an avowal on the same level as, and perhaps incorporating, a statement of perceptual belief, which clearly qualifies as an avowal of beliefs of that kind. Several hands are raised here, each of them vying for attention, but all that counts for the moment is that perceptual avowals cannot be ignored.

Keeping that in mind, we find that Shoemaker distinguishes between two classes of observational model, namely the object perception model and the broad perception model. On the object model one gains factual information from the perceived object as opposed to the facts themselves being perceived, this being the prerogative of the broad model. Shoemaker now focusses on the conditions associated with what he refers to as the perceptual stereotype on which the object perceptual model is based, the list of which runs as follows, the comments about each condition, and some of the examples, being mine.

(1) Perception involves a sense organ, over which the subject has more or less control. For instance, I open my eyes and see a book.

(2) It involves a distinction between sensory experience and its

object and associated belief. For instance, I am looking at a book, the looking being one thing and the book another. As for belief, I need not recognise the object as a book.

(3) Perception of an object reveals observational facts. This is in line with Shoemaker's distinction between object perception and broad perception model. It is by looking at a book that I know that it is one, or that it satisfies a particular description.

(4) Perceiving objects enables one to pick them out from others and to re-identify them.

(5) It involves awareness of their intrinsic, non-relational properties, without which we could not perceive their relational properties. To register that one book is to the left of another I must see them as they are in themselves, for instance as having a particular colour and shape.

(6) One can shift one's attention from one object to another and thereby learn more about them. Keep in mind here that Shoemaker's concern is to contrast perception and introspection.

(7) The relation between perception and its object involves causation. For instance, it is because a book is in view that I see it, the visual experience being causally connected to properties of the book, and in such a way that my seeing of the book is veridical. Shoemaker now comments on the links between this property and the first and second on the list.

(8) Physical objects exist unperceived and in general are independent of the existence of perceivers. For instance a book——unless, that is, one wrote it.

This is an interesting list, some of its distinctions and definitions being eminently debatable, as is to be expected given the issues involved and the polarisation of different points of view. Shoemaker's concern, however, is not to arrive at a definitive account of what it is to perceive a thing; rather, he wishes to undermine the notion of an observational model by showing that none of the listed conditions has its counterpart in the introspection of avowable mental states. That it may be possible to confound this aim is attested by the attempt by Cynthia McDonald to demonstrate that the conditions do indeed have counterparts if one digs deep enough.(1998) Common to all parties to this debate is the taking for granted of its relevance to the analysis of avowals and therefore, one must insist, to the issue of their epistemic authority. Not everyone finds it obvious that perception holds a mirror up to introspection, and in any case there is the linked but separate issue of why anyone would seek answers by reflecting a question when introspective features reveal themselves directly. This they must do if introspection is to be compared to perception; but then the comparison may be dispensed with. It is not as if the deliverances of perception are secure in their epistemic authority, or as if perceptual analysis meets with more consensus; on the contrary the opposite, if anything, is the case. But even if perceptual belief were epistemically secure, I fail to see how the authoritativeness of mental-state avowals might thereby gain support. Note, too, that since mental state avowals already include those in perceptual mode, this would oblige us to ask how these latter fitted in. Should we, all considered, look to introspectional models of perception, the mirror turned the other way?

That progress can be made via modelling is, then, an assumption that is open to challenge, the place to start being with Shoemaker's interpretation of the list. He takes (3) to (6) to be distinctive of the object perception model, which he thinks is the one that theorists have in mind when they consider whether introspection should be regarded as an inner sense. This, however, is to leave out (8): that physical objects exist unperceived— and independently, Shoemaker adds, of the existence of any perceivers. He discusses this condition in connection with the broad model, but in fact the property of unperceived existence is at the very core of our conception of the physical world; so much so, indeed, that it is difficult to conceive of the lack of it unless, that is, we imagine solipsistic multi-sensory patterns with, for instance, the visual field reduced to a kaleidoscope of changing images. Condition (2) would also seem to characterise perception, and what this double omission indicates is that the distinction between object- and broad-perception model has questions attached, the answers to which may undermine it. Again, we shall return to this.

In the meantime, consider condition (5) such that we perceive relations between objects only if we register the objects themselves as having intrinsic non-relational properties. Thus, we see one book as being positional relative to the other, perhaps to the left of it, only if we see the books as having intrinsic non-relational properties, for instance of colour and shape. Shoemaker now compares perception and introspection and points out that no such condition governs consciousness of mental states, this being another significant difference between the two modes of apprehending the world. There are several questions here, but he now goes on to say, with regard to the perceptual object model, that intentional mental states, not just sensations, are taken to be 'nonfactual objects of introspective perception'.(page 11) Thus it is that my belief that it is raining must now be conceived of as a mental word sequence, in which case it is, one might think, short lived, unlike the rain itself.

3.2: Externalism and Avowals

What goes around comes around and we are now in the same arena as in the earlier discussion of Wittgenstein and intentionality, from which we fought our way to the exit via the irreducible intentionality thesis. The terms of that discussion are not, however, the ones favoured by Shoemaker, who uses the coordinates by which the thesis of externalism is mapped onto the issue of introspectible intentional content. Citing Putnam, Burge and Boghassian, he suggests that an intentional state cannot be such that one's awareness of it, on the object perceptual model, is of its intrinsic non-relational content, the reason for which is that its content is in fact relational, which is to say accountable to external conditions. These consist in the subject's 'standing, or having stood, in perceptual relations to external objects of certain kinds, in his belonging to a linguistic community in which certain practices exist, and so on'. Shoemaker now briefly brings Putnam's Twin Earth problem into play, his response to which is to claim, in a footnote, that 'whatever fixes the content of the first-order belief I express by saying "there is water in the glass" also fixes in the same way the embedded content in the second-order belief I express by saying "I believe there is water in the glass"—assuming that "water" would be used by me univocally in those reports'. This would seem to be correct, as also his thesis that the relation between first- and second-order belief is not that of inner perception and its object. I remain attached, however, to the view

82

that the implied comparison enjoys no advantage over direct contemplation of mental-state avowals.

That being the case, I shall focus not on the difference between water and twater on the two Earths but on the less contentious general question of whether a full account of the intentional can be rendered in terms of phenomenal consciousness. So much less, indeed, that the answer, sanctioned by the earlier establishing of the irreducibility thesis but also by glaringly obvious fact, is quite simply no. And the reason, here below and of single planetary origin, is that such an account, in fact any indicative statement, is freighted with semantic content, the sentences being vehicles for the meaning thus conveyed. In its absence, they grind to a halt, and the stranded passengers are word-shapes or word-sounds, one's experience of which may be assimilated to exposure to a foreign language. I am not sure what Shoemaker would make of this, apart from shoes, but in any case he asks whether inner sense objects can be perceptually modelled by such items as 'drawings, maps and sentences'(page 12), all of which he says are perceived non-intentionally but also as having representational content. His point is that there are no non-intentional features of beliefs and so on, or none that might serve as inner sense objects. Is it really true, though, that sentences when spoken or written are perceived non-intentionally but also as having representational content? Well, a foreign sentence may be taken to express a statement, its content unknown, and to be non-intentional in the sense of not being understood. But the contrast here is with sentences that we do understand, whereas it is these that Shoemaker is referring to. This betrays a common confusion that it is worth trying to clear up, the place to start being with the sentence " I am looking at a glass of water", which I use to convey my belief to that effect, or to express it to myself, for instance in silent thought. What leads us astray is the assumption that we are capable of detaching the phenomenal part of that sentence from its intentional content, thereby suspending our grasp of its meaning, and this becomes clear when we consider an actual instance of a suspended sentence, in the present case "Je regarde ce verre d'eau" in the mind of a monolingual Anglophone. But qualitatively this is not the same at all as it would be if he learnt French or saved himself the trouble by actually being French; and this is to say that our mistake is to think that the statement that one is looking at a glass of water can be separated from its intentional content when expressing one's belief that one is looking at a glass of water.

This is not, I have to admit, a completely satisfactory account of the link between the phenomenal and the intentional, as becomes clear the moment we ask what the difference between "qualitative" and "phenomenal" is meant to be. A complete account will emerge from the theory of the non-conscious already dipped into but with full immersion in a later chapter. All that can be said at present is that if I issue the observation report that 'I am looking at a glass of water', then that is what I mean, where this is to imply that I am suitably disposed. But my dispositions, insofar as they are verbal, are themselves realised semantically, in line with intentionally being irreducible.

The crucial issue, as I see it, is indeed that of the analysis of intentionality, the externalist approach of Putnam and others being relevant here; though as before we need not follow them into outer space with its Twin Earth and its own chemically different water or twater, depending on one's point of view. The fact is, after all, that intentional avowals are accountable to externals in much more obvious and familiar ways, for instance if what seems to be water is really gin, or vice-versa if one is a surreptitious teetotaller. And what this indicates is that physical-world reference renders mental state avowals less than logically certain, which it might be thought we should already know, and that the distinction between proposition and attitude, to hark back to it, is not clearcut, which again is obvious. If I say "I have toothache", do I thereby imply that the cause of the pain is dental? If subsequently I say that the toothache has eased, how do I know that the proposition is true? If I now appeal to my memory of the pain being more intense, then what of the fact that memory is fallible? If I acknowledge uncertainty on that account, then I must accept that avowals cannot be authoritative, since they all depend on memory. But my uncertainty as to the epistemic status of avowals itself depends on memory, an incoherence thus exposed. So much, then, for the distinction being clearcut; but looking beyond it there is also the debt that meaning owes to cognitive fact, for to say that one has toothache is to imply that one understands the avowal, with all that this entails about being suitably disposed, and in ways that transcend any epistemic acquaintance with the sensation of toothache, assuming that the notion of knowledge of that kind has any application.

Since Shoemaker now moves on to sensations and sense experiences, we need to keep in mind the earlier insight into the fact of perceptual avowals and the uncertainty in pinning them down, depending on one's theory of perception. He is of the opinion that sensations, for instance localised pain sensations, as with a pain in one's elbow, seem suited to the modelling role if they are taken to conform to an act-object notion associated with perception, this being partially explicable in terms of taking at face value the surface grammar of, in the present case, "I have a pain in my elbow". I have a doubt about this, not in my elbow but in my mind, for what would count as my taking it at face value? That the doubt can exist independently of my having it? But I could just as easily have written that I am doubtful whether..., or that it is doubtful that. And similarly for "I have a pain in my elbow", which taken at face value means what exactly? That I regard it as an object analogous to a perceptual object? But that "object" is *pain*, as in "my elbow hurts" and "the pain has gone", but no-one asks where it has gone or where it was before moving to one's elbow. Perhaps it was in a scarecrow's knee, as befits the targeting of a straw man. It is true that one's elbow is a perceptual object, but all that this does is to highlight the conceptual opposition by which physical object and sensation increasingly seem fundamentally incomparable the more that we reflect on them. As Shoemaker himself points out, one can always find similarities, but this is not the same as there being 'a similarity between our access to those mental states and our access to the objects we perceive in cases of veridical sense-perception'(page 16). It seems to me, but apparently not to him, that similarities are established only if such access is detected in both parties to the comparison, in which case it need not be made.

3.3: Avowals and Sense Data

Much the same applies to what Shoemaker has to say about sensory experience, which he treats as if it were a species of sensation, at some points referring to it as such, for instance when assimilating localised pain references to saying that one sees a red, round after-image. This is more than a little tendentious, for it occurs in what is intended as a discussion of sensation and sensory experience, this latter being better served, one might think, by focusing on what it is to see red, round tomatoes rather than after-images. To show that there is a difficulty here, let us narrow the focus further, as Shoemaker does, and consider the notion of sense data. He makes the claim, as does A.D.Smith in *The Problem of Perception*, which we shall open in the next chapter, that if sense-datum theory enlists the notion of "being perceptually appeared to" then the appearances must be the same whether veridical or illusory. This, it seems to me, is of limited truth, if only because it is via perceptual experience that one is able to distinguish between reality and illusion; but in any case it may be shown that the notion of a sense-datum does not favour the modelling thesis.

For suppose, given the phenomenon of being appeared to, that sense data may be extracted from perceptual appearance. One's natural inclination here, given the connotations in the present context of the verb "to appear", is to single out the visual sense. This, however, should be resisted, for visual experience is transparent, and in a way that other forms of sensory experience are not, for instance in the case of hearing, as in hearing a skylark. It is mainly if one sees it at the same time that the reference is to direct perception, the contrast being with simply hearing it, which is taken to be both indirect and a manifest subjective experience. One difference this makes is that the concept of a visual sense datum has confusion built in, the case of colour proving the point, for normally-sighted people see the colour of an object as inhering in it, but philosophers' glasses reveal an otherwise hidden medium: that of subjective visual experience, in particular of colour, which seems to inhere both in the experience, on the present view, and in the coloured object.

Consider what it is to listen to a trilling sound, from which one infers the aerial presence of a skylark. Such inference is inimical to the notion of a sense datum, which must therefore make friends with the trilling sound itself, or rather with each note as it occurs if we take the data to be immediately given and directly known. This is in spite of the fact that it is of the very essence of a piece of music, where this includes a song, even the song of a presumably self-taught skylark, that it registers from one moment to the next as if transcending them, not as a note and then another and another. But now, the statement "I hear a trilling sound" is itself an avowal, in fact a perceptual avowal, and herein lies the difficulty just remarked upon; for sense data as presently characterised, far from lending themselves to a perceptual model, represent the extension of the problem of avowals into the sensory realm. Indeed, the present case illustrates the problem, and in terms of content as well as attitude, for how can I be sure that the source of the trilling is external, quite apart from all the other ways in which the avowal goes beyond the sound itself? Given this mostly negative critique of the modelling approach, one is tempted to ask whether observational models are capable, even, of doing the work required of them.

Resisting temptation, let us at least ask what Shoemaker and others expect to gain, or to show cannot be gained, from aligning perception and introspection? By way of answer, and referring to the object-perception model, he writes 'To the extent that this model incorporates the act-object conception of sensation and sensory states, it populates the realm of the mental with what many, myself included, regard as philosophically objectionable entities—sense-data, reified images, etc.' (p. 19) There are issues here that gain in complexity what they lose in clarity if the following is added to the mix. First, that the natural tendency of language is to gravitate to the nominative when verbs and other speech parts are in orbit, thereby adding linguistic substantiveness to them when they land. Since the solidity of nouns owes as much to grammar as to content, one should be circumspect in one's use of the verb "to reify". Lightning, for instance, is always, unless they order things differently in other skies, a fleeting event, but my use of the noun to begin the present sentence does not betoken a misplaced act-object notion populating my electrically charged mind with reified meteorological phenomena. One might as well be accused of reifying events in one's description of them as, well, events. Second, and again linguistically, one should be alert to the difference between the act-object notion and that of object and reference. If I say that I hear a trilling sound, the subject-predicate structure does not correspond to an act-object auditory experience structure; rather, I have a single auditory experience, at least if allowance is made for the complications of auditory intentionality. Third, and taking a stricter view of the second, is there really such a thing as an act-object auditory experience? Or even one that is visual?

But surely, it will be said, the act-object paradigm of perception has application, in which case we should take seriously its extension to sense data, sensations and sensory experience. Taking it seriously, then, one may speak of a perceptual act as being distinct from its object, as with seeing a skylark. This example, however, conflicts with the impression of "act" and "object" being a dynamic duo when juxtaposed, for all that happens is that one squints into the summer sky while out rambling, and if a motionless black dot is discerned, one may recognise it as a hovering skylark, an observation perhaps aided by unconscious triangulation based on change of position and birdsong—and, of course, by past observations. Clearly object and awareness are taken to be distinct because that is what they are, but what the skylark example also indicates is that nothing automatically follows as to the significance of their separation for the analysis of avowals. The fact is, after all, that they remain separate even when other senses are considered, for instance if the skylark is heard but not seen, the auditory experience being one thing and the skylark another. The common factor across all the senses is that they fly back to base with perceptual information on board, all such flights penetrating an independently exiting physical realm of, in line with the present avian conceit, skylarks and other birds that commute between earth and sky.

This, then, is the act-object notion in relation to perception, which is to say no more than that the perceiving of a physical object is distinct from the object perceived. There is nothing over and above this content by which the notion, if sense data are set aside for the moment, might extend to sensations and sensory experience, which have their own acts and objects, namely those that are suited to them. The essential differences, if we return to elbows, are as follows: perceiving one's elbow, perhaps by looking at it, the elbow being one thing and the seeing of it another; feeling a pain in one's elbow: in other words one's elbow hurts, the pain being one thing and the elbow another; believing that one's elbow hurts, the belief being one thing and the elbow another; avowing one's belief, the belief being one thing and the avowal another; avowing one's pain, the pain being one thing and the avowal another. In all these cases a philosophical game of compare and contrast may be played, and very interesting it would be, no doubt, if that is what it would be; but if the aim is to solve the problem of avowals, then much of the board should be cleared away, the remaining pieces coming under scrutiny, for instance if the avowal of pain and of the belief that one is in pain are kept, with a question arising as to pleonasm.

Finally, there is also the view that the perceptual act-object notion is intimately linked to acquaintance-based observational knowledge, this being the point at which sense data become prominent. On this account the certainty attaching to external-world perceptual belief, for instance that one sees a skylark, or at least a bird, or the sky itself if all else fails, is now located in sense data, usually defined as immediate perceptual objects, the skylark now a black dot in a blue expanse, its aerial singing reduced to a trilling sound, which oddly enough is what it always was. What this indicates, as already pointed out, is that the reference could just as easily be to avowed sense experience or qualia as to sense data, given that the object in both cases is a sequence of sounds.

All of this makes it easier to understand, though not to endorse, Shoemaker's bracketing of sense data, sensations and sense experience, the common thread being that of knowledge by acquaintance. Again, however, observational models play no part, the thread being obvious in all three cases, and quite independently of any comparison being made. But is it really true that the thesis of knowledge by acquaintance rises above the fray and cannot itself be assailed? It is, after all, a central pillar of the empiricist edifice, with only the weightiest arguments, one might think, being able to shift it from the vertical. In fact, it is easily shown to lack reinforcing bars in the case of sensations and sense experience, for there is nothing in the sensation itself, if one has a pain, that compels a pain avowal; and if one sees a red object there need be no colour-experience avowal that clicks into place. All that need happen is that the conscious event occurs, which in itself indicates not at all its capture by language or the ability to use it. Indeed, one's being non-lingual is very much the norm in the natural world, with linguistic ability confined to members of the human race, so that the question as to whether or not any particular member possesses it is empirical. By "non-lingual", by the way, I mean "lacking a language", for which in the case of human beings there does not seem to be a single descriptive term for those thus deprived, apart from "babies", which is not really germane to the point I wish to make. As for what that is, my aim will be to show that linguistic enabling conditions do not equate with extraneous scaffolding, or not if the notion of a system is brought to the fore and applied in the present context. "I am in pain" is a pain avowal only if certain connections are made and conditions met, all of which goes beyond the sensation itself. For instance, we grasp the concept of pain only if we are suitably disposed in our use of the word, where this includes not using it incorrectly, which itself implies the correct use of other words. The upshot of all this disputation, assuming that we won, is that avowals need to be analysed, not modelled.

3.4: Interim Recapitulation

What I now propose is to recapitulate the main points of the discussion thus far, no doubt with some elaboration thrown in, and at the same time to broaden our purview and make a smooth transition to the analysis itself. This will feature a guest appearance by Crispin Wright and Colin McGinn on the subject of irreducible intentionality in relation to avowals, my aim being to contribute a detailed system-based analysis of these latter in the particular form of avowals of belief. Zooming back out again, my conclusion will be that avowals thus treated form an epistemic continuum with empirical knowledge in general, the unifying factor being that of belonging to an interconnected system of necessary conditions of discourse. The emphasis will be on those by which the problem of avowals is articulated, it being taken to be an ontological truism that the problem exists only because language does. Since this is true of all philosophical problems, with epistemology centre stage, one begins to appreciate the potential for system-based solutions, the anthropic principle perhaps already humming along the rails of a complex system.

According to Shoemaker, it may be recalled, one may distinguish between a perception object model and a broad perceptual one, this distinction being at odds, I suggested, with the thesis that perception is intrinsically inferential. Looking at this pen, which is only partially on view at any particular moment, its appearance changing as I turn it in my hand, my idea of it as a three-dimensional object transcends these different perspectives, testimony to which is the essential role of memory and expectation, which link past and future views of the pen from one moment to the next. My perceptual experience is of seeing object-parts thus related, in line with the thesis that such inference is encompassed in perceptual intentionality. For what I see is a curved surface, not a coloured patch, and if to this it is objected, perhaps on behalf of sense-datum theorists, that I can see only a two-dimensional coloured shape, the rest being inferred, then this corresponds not at all to my experience and seems to be little more than numerical dimension prejudice.

The upshot is that my claim that I see, say, a curved object-part, which I recognise as the near side of the body of the pen, does not separate out into an avowal of what is perceptually given, namely a colour patch, and an inference to its being part of a three dimensional object. Nothing is perceptually given, or not in the way intended; and this is to say that there is no colour patch on which the avowal might infallibly gain purchase. Even if there were an actual colour patch, say a blue wall completely monopolising one's field of view, the visual perception being of a uniformly blue surface but nothing else, one's avowal of the subjective experience would still go beyond it, and in all the linguistic and cognitive ways we have recently outlined. Thus it is that not even the purely subjective, as in "I am having a visual experience as of a uniformly blue surface" is epistemically unaccountable to surrounding facts. There is no unbridgeable epistemic chasm, then, between that avowal and "I see a uniformly blue surface", which is to say that there is no need to hedge the self-ascription, perhaps by saying that one sees the surface or seems to, thereby allowing for illusion.

But would we not be epistemically less exposed behind that hedge, even if only marginally? If so, it would not upset any applecarts—indeed, they would not even lift off their wheels; for to allow for illusion we should have to grasp the concept, our cognitive burden being increased and the marginal gain thereby cancelled out. Besides, we could not coherently allow for illusion, or not on the basis of logic possibility, which would be all that we could appeal to, there being nothing of substance that we could evidentially adduce. All told, then, there is no significant difference between seeing a blue surface and seeing a curved object-part, notwithstanding the visual inference by which curvature is claimed. To appreciate at the micro-analytic level that such inference is involved, we note that if the pen's visible surface is indeed curved, then it will exhibit curvature from at least two, and in practice many, perspectives, only one of which can obtain at any particular moment, so that the claim as to curvature draws inferential credit from parts unseen. If some of these have already been on view, the pen turned between my fingers, then again this is not significant when it comes to analysing avowals; for it is assumed that these now unseen object-parts, or the present object-part seen from previous angles, would be similarly displayed if the pen was turned forward or back. Analysis of this kind, with its Kantian resonance, has general application to all physical objects and all configurations of shape and colour, other things being equal—though not needing to be quite so equal if only stable, relatively unchanging objects are considered.

Very well, one might think, but surely there are limits to be confronted. Not all self ascription is authoritative, and if our aim is to analyse avowals, central to which is their elevated epistemic status, then the analysis of this latter will not result in rejecting or diluting it. Rather, our intention, or mine, is to rehabilitate it within a system, about which enough has already been said, in particular about memory, expectation and understanding, to indicate that appeal will be made to necessary conditions of personal self-ascription of a certain kind, at which point a discussion of the limits to its extension will ensue. This returns us to the present case, for a curved object-part is one thing and a pen is another, its defining function not being a perceptual object at all, unless we pick it up and write with it, and yet it is recognised as a pen, just as a dot is recognised as a skylark. In the perception chapter, Smith favours typewriters over pens in addressing the issue raised, but he is obviously more dextrous than I am, for I have yet to succeed in twirling a typewriter between my fingers without dropping it. Fortunately, a simple writing instrument suffices, for we have already established that an avowal, as far as perception is concerned, cannot target only the perceptually given, presumably taken to be experiential, since nothing is given in the sense intended. We are dealing, then, not with a clear distinction but with differences, it being a matter of judgement as to what may be presupposed, at least when an avowal's epistemic authority is placed under strain. In the particular case: that of recognising a pen, as in "I am looking at this pen", this description differs from, say, "I am looking at a cylindrical object about five inches long and pointed at one end", which presupposes less but is inconsistently overcautious. For if that is the level of epistemic security required, then the reference should not be to a cylinder, since only a curved surface is actually visible, and it should not be to a curved surface, since..., and it should not be to a length, and so on. So much, then, for Shoemaker's distinguishing between object- and broad-perception.

3.5: Beyond Observational Models

I now propose to apply our findings to the views of others who reject the modelling approach, the place to start being with the attempted solution advanced by Barry C. Smith, one of the contributors to *Knowing Our Own Minds*.(1998) He rejects modelling accounts because very often there is no conscious item that would serve as an inner sense object, the example he gives being that of intending to go to Scotland. The problem as he sees it derives from the tension between first- and third-person accounts of mental states, such that other people infer to them from an individual's behaviour and actions, whereas she herself enjoys immediate epistemic acquaintance with them, and without having to consult anyone else. This, however, invites a question, for in what way should the inference from observed behaviour to mental state be understood? For Smith, the answer is that there is just the one mental state, whether inferred from behaviour or immediately known; and it is only on this interpretation that a problem of authoritativeness arises. For how can I claim to know my intentions simply by having them, which is to say without any evidential requirement, when those observing me may disagree as to my intended holiday destination and are expected to give reasons? Perhaps that I say every year that I am going but never actually go. But now, it seems to me that the presuppositions by which Smith's problem of self-knowledge, as he calls it, is framed are open to challenge, and at several points.

To begin with, it is generally untrue that one's avowable mental states are externally ascertainable, the exemplar of which is pain and pain behaviour. Even here, it is quite possible that the particulars of my pain or other sensation are conveyed to others only through description, as when I say that my fingers are tingling, a question immediately arising as to whether this counts as observable behaviour, with no clearcut answer as far as I can see. This in itself suffices against Smith, but it is possible to go deeper. At a greater depth, then, I now maintain that the analysis of avowals encompasses both first-and third-person standpoints, but with no opposition between them. Arguing from the particular case, suppose that I wake up in a hospital bed and complains that my feet hurt, a nurse now informing me that they, for whatever reason, perhaps that the bed was too short, have been amputated. Then the nurse does not find my localised self-ascription of pain authoritative, aware as he is of the anatomical impossibility. But he does credit me in that way when I now amend my statement and avow that I have a pain that feels as if it is in my feet, the point being that epistemic retrenching of this kind is always possible. We would both agree that I have a phantom pain, this being a ready-made adjective, but in any case, there is always the

94

language of appearance to fall back on. Having said that I am looking at a bent straw in a glass of water, only to be told that it is an illusion, I now correct myself and say that I am looking at a straight straw that looks bent. Or this also being possible, I insist that it is an actual bent straw, knowing as I do that it was bent when placed in the glass. In such cases it is clear that the avowal, or extended avowal, reaches beyond conscious experience into objective fact, this also being true, albeit less obviously, of even the most restrained subjective self-ascription.

Moreover, the point being made that the fact of one's behaviour belying one's mental-state avowals is not at all problematic, may be generalised to cover any external counter-indication in relation to what is avowed. Suppose, for instance, that leaning on a gate and looking into a field I announce to my companion that I can see a rabbit, her reply being that it looks more like a hare. Then I stand corrected, perhaps twice over if what I now take to be a hare is really, according to my companion, a manufactured item, placed in the field for real hares to mate with. The point is that this discontinuity between belief and fact signifies not at all a deeper fault line between introspection and observation. Told that the apparent rabbit looks more like a hare, I believe that it is a hare and believe that I was told it. Also, when corrected again, I believe that I was corrected again, that the object is really an artefact designed to look like a hare, that the object is in a field, that my companion is more knowledgeable and less myopic or more observant than I am, that I was mistaken in what I originally believed..., and so on. In short, the errors to which one is vulnerable in one's avowals, or extended avowals, about one's mental states are accommodated within the same system as the avowals, the problem being that of analysis in terms of conditions and connections, in particular insofar as it concerns the epistemic status of certain aspects of my knowledge of myself. Going deeper again, the possibility of observational or perceptual error is accommodated within the same system, such that mistaking a hare for a rabbit, or a teddy bear for either, threatens not at all the authoritative status of perception in the general case. And the reason, with both perception and introspection, is the same: that it is only within a general framework of correctness assumed by default that particular errors can be made, and only in ways that do not pose a general threat.

Since we are now directly solving the avowals problem, insofar as this is possible given the fact of intentional irreducibility, the next step is to consider in more detail the conditions that govern the application of the notion of elevated epistemic authority. Suppose again that I announce, on this occasion at time t, my intention to visit Scotland with my friends, and that, as before, they do not believe me, because I always cry off. Then the conclusion to be drawn is only that very likely it will be the same this year, not that I do not intend to take the trip. There is nothing in my avowal of intention at time t that commits me to its permanence, or even to its persistence from one minute to the next. It may be, for instance, that in response to my holiday announcement someone warns me about the plagues of Scottish midges in summer— or even that I simply change my mind about going, and for no apparent reason. This illustrates one of the ways in which avowal assertibility conditions operate within a system; but clearly there is more to be said, for knowledge of a person's intentions is possible, the associated behaviour predictable, which it would not be if the slightest fickle breeze might snap them. This connects induction and necessary conditions; but setting that aside, that only way to press further into such terrain would be to survey in detail its network of conditions and connections. Since analysis of that kind is already earmarked for avowals of belief, it is to this that we now turn.

3.6: Wright and McGinn on Avowals

My aim in this final part of the chapter is to bring analysis and intentionality together by discussing Wright's criticisms of McGinn's thesis that intentionality is irreducible, in the course of which I hope to be able to analyse in detail avowals of belief, and in such a way as to present a system-based solution to the problem of avowals of that kind. To begin with, it may be recalled that McGinn presented his irreducibility thesis as a rejoinder to Kripke on semantic non-factualism; but the thesis also ramifies into the problem of avowals. Suppose, for instance, that my partner complains that she is bored waiting for Christmas, and what

96

do I propose to do about it? My reply, as the clock strikes noon, is that there is always patience if all else fails, to which she retorts that she is very patient, having been waiting since midsummer, with another three months to go; to which my answer is that I meant the card game, not the mindset needed to play it. Then I know, or I am certain, that that is what I meant, and that I meant it at noon, the time now being a few minutes past, notwithstanding my also being certain that at noon I said 'There is always patience if all else fails.' which I might easily have said if I had meant that she should be patient. It is these and other such considerations that induced us to embrace the irreducibility thesis, a consequence of which is that Wright's objections to it impact upon our own standpoint, so we need to address them.

His main criticism is that McGinn makes no attempt to account for the paradoxical nature of avowals of meaning and understanding, the paradox arising from the fact that they combine authoritativeness with dispositionality, so that correct usage goes beyond the particular occasions of use on which avowals are made. According to Wright, 'How is it possible to be, for the most part, effortlessly and reliably authoritative about, say, one's intentions if the identity of an intention is fugitive when sought in occurrent consciousness, as McGinn grants that Kripke's Sceptic has shown, and the having of an intention is thought of as a disposition-like state?' (2002: p. 113)

His concern is with the distinction between self-ascription of experiential states on the one hand and of particular forms of intentionality on the other. Examples of such phenomena are given by 'pain, tickles, the experience of a red after-image, and ringing in the ears'. (p. 113) They are characterised by our being aware of them because we have them: 'The subject is authoritative about such states because, since they are events in his consciousness, he is in the nature of the case conscious of them.' (p. 113) If, on the other hand, we take intentionality to be irreducible, so that meaning addition by "plus" is not to be identified with its mental accompaniments or with any other experiential state, then how can we be authoritative with regard to it? To mean addition involves, after all, having certain dispositions, so that its content goes beyond the present experience. But this marks it out as being epistemically vulnerable in a way that the reporting of an experiential state is not.

What we have seen, however, is that there is indeed a difficulty here, in the sense that there is a question with no obvious answer, but that it cannot be used against the irreducibility thesis, to which it is not particularly relevant, and does not lend itself to scepticism about intentionality. Rather, it is a difficulty of analysis, and its resolution depends on the notion of a system in which both intentional and experiential concepts have application. Presently, I shall exhibit in great detail the conditions by which that application obtains in the case of belief avowals.

If, in the meantime, we ask whether it is really true that intentionality is not to be found in occurrent consciousness, as Wright maintains, then to this, too, we already know the answer: a conscious item, say a memory image, cannot be prised away from the recollective experience, for a mental image is not a memory image, the difference being that this latter belongs to the intentional experience of remembering. Such experiences are by definition conscious, the point being that the conscious and the non-conscious are bound tightly together—so much so, indeed, that the non-conscious informs the conscious. If we turn to a different example, the irreducibility thesis implies that descriptions of seeing lines and squiggles cannot do justice to what it is to read and understand a text, nor can the account one may give of one's dispositions in relation to such non-intentional shapes. This is the sense in which the reader's understanding may be said to be irreducible; but clearly it cannot be separated from the process of reading as an intentional flow, the cognitive experience of which is just as much a conscious state as is ringing in the ears or feeling pain. On the theory introduced in the last chapter, such conscious understanding taps into or derives from or is informed by cognitive non-conscious processes within a system. It hardly seems to matter which expression we use, provided it is vague enough, for nothing is known about the nature of the non-conscious in the realm of metaphysics.

This leads to my second point, which concerns the fact that in maintaining that descriptions of experiential states are categorical, unlike references to understanding, Wright implies that the difference this makes is epistemologically significant. If his reservations about McGinn's approach are to make sense, then it would seem that he takes us to enjoy privileged access to our own experiential states, on the basis of which we are authoritative in our claims to have them. Such claims, he would say, are more secure than the corresponding claims about belief, expectation, understanding and other intentional states, which obviously have a dispositional component. It seems to me, by virtue of previous argument, that there is no such difference, for to self-ascribe a conscious experience is to bring into play one's awareness, for example of ringing in one's ears, which for present purposes we may take to be verbally expressed, so that one is able to refer to or describe one's irritating aural sensations, with all that this implies about understanding. If I utter the words "I have tinnitus", they are taken to be authoritative if given their conventional meaning, which is to say that my understanding of them is correct. Since understanding is partly dispositional, the implication here is that authoritativeness is compatible with dispositionality. The fact is, after all, that logical or mathematical reasoning is also dispositional as well as occurrent. It follows that if the authoritativeness of self-ascriptions of belief, intention and so on is called into question, then it would be inconsistent for this to be by virtue of the fact that their truth conditions have a dispositional component. Although experiential states are not themselves dispositional, the self-ascription of them is, for it involves understanding. It is a mistake, I believe, to assume that knowledge can be more certain than the understanding – and memory and expectation – on which it depends and from which it derives its content.

This brings us to the third point, which is that the distinction is superficial not only with regard to dispositions but in another way. If, again, I have ringing in my ears, my awareness of which is verbally expressed, then strictly speaking the reference is to a past event, for there is always a time lapse before the end of the sentence in which I refer to the sensations I am having. In any case, I cannot be aware of it now occurring without having the concept of it as a past event, otherwise I could refer to it only in the present tense and only until the ringing stopped. Also, my reference is conditionally predictive, for I imply that I am able to use my words in a variety of contexts, other things being equal. But now, if I imply knowledge of the past and future in ascribing a present experiential state to myself, and also in ascribing forms of intentionality, so that both go beyond the present moment, then in that sense there is no difference in the authority with which I self-ascribe them.

If the foregoing is correct, so that epistemically intentional avowals do not compare unfavourably with direct experiential reports, then it is arguable that far from solving the problem this extends it, for we now have to justify not only such avowals but also the self-ascription of occurrent sensations. The rejoinder to this, it seems to me, is that it is not the problem that has been extended but the range of application of the notion of a system. This is in line with our treatment in later chapters of the problems of perception and induction, the concepts involved all turning out to be system-based. For instance, the thesis of intrinsic perceptual inference has already been introduced, and in the next chapter we shall renew our acquaintance with it. In the meantime we may continue to show that Wright's reservations about McGinn's irreducibility thesis, if that is his target, and his own sceptical thesis about avowals, are unfounded.

Note, too, that Wright seems to be taking a third-person stance when he refers to disposition-like connections to behaviour, rather than to the subject's conscious reasoning and understanding. Since this may conflict with our own first-person use of the notion of a system, we need to discuss it. First of all, it is undeniable that avowals are authoritative only if understood, and that there are public standards of correct usage and concept application by which criteria of understanding may be brought to bear. But it is also true that in any individual case it is possible to hold a belief that may turn out to have been incorrectly or misleadingly expressed. For instance, if I claim to believe that I can count up to 100, then it is possible that there is a disparity between what I mean and what others understand, as would be the case if what I meant was that I could count up to 100 in tens, not in units.

In discussing Wittgenstein, our thesis was, indeed, that public standards have to be subjectively understood by each individual, in which sense the first person is logically prior to the third. In practice one finds that philosophical discourse about the intentional borrows freely from both perspectives, as one would expect from their intimate embrace at every entry and exit of the edifices of psychology, philosophy and everyday interpersonal exchange. It is only when attempts are made to separate them, in philosophy and psychology, that the distinction becomes an issue, at which juncture it should be made clear, if our reasoning is correct, that the first-person perspective is privileged. What micro-analysis reveals, after all, are the conditions by which processes of belief, perception and other forms of the intentional subjectively unfold, with no reference needing to be made to other people. When I look at this table edge, my belief as to what I see is accountable to my visual experience if I move my head slightly to one side, the new appearance of the table being confirmatory of my belief about the old, but only if it marries up with it. But this owes nothing to any public standards, perhaps best described as being non-existent, to which perceptual verification must conform.

Taking this further, suppose that the house of a French person learning English is flooded, the waters rising, to which her verbal reaction is 'I fear for the future.' Her interlocutor, a fireman, has no reason to doubt her sincerity but is not sure whether she meant what she said, which was in reply to his asking why she was trying to drag an armchair up the stairs. He then realises that by "future" she meant "furniture", the point being that her mistake would seem to detract not at all from the authoritativeness of the avowal. It follows that evidentially the epistemic weight of the self-ascription falls on the utterance not in itself but as a linguistically intentional—or intensional— vehicle. This places the emphasis on what the woman meant rather than what she said.

3.7: Avowals Analysis

There are one or two points that need to be clarified before we turn to a detailed analysis of different kinds of avowals. They connect with our earlier gloss on a passage from Wittgenstein in which a teacher and a pupil are having communication problems. The pupil adds 2 up to 1000, 4 up to 2000 but then has to decide, when adding 6 takes him as far as 2996, whether to add another 6 or start adding 8. Many such decisions then have to be made if the pupil continues on that path as best he can. As part of that earlier discussion, I maintained that such examples make light of the fact, insofar as it obtains, that it is as if we traverse all the steps in advance. Perhaps all that it amounts to is that we may feel confident. We have seen, however, that for Wright, too, the authoritativeness of avowals does not sit comfortably with their dispositional properties, the example he gives being that of avowing an intention. Interestingly, intentions would seem to be less awkwardly seated than, say, the self-ascription of understanding, but I shall argue, in any case, that avowals have the posture that suits them and are quite relaxed.

Still, we shall focus on understanding, our concern being with criteria of application. One insight we gained from the Wittgenstein passage is that he fails to distinguish between individual and interpersonal understanding. The pupil, as an individual, believes that he can add 2 up to 1000, ..., 6 up to 3000, which in fact he cannot do. And now it might be thought that this reinforces a difficulty similar to Wright's: how can one be authoritative in one's claim to understand a rule if the path it may take is branched in all directions and in any case continues on the blind side of yonder hill? Note that if this presents an obstacle, then it could not be removed by traversing the steps in advance—in other words by reconnoitring the route, for the information would have to be retained, with all that this implies about memory; and also it would have to be applied at each step and each crossing of paths, with all that this implies about knowing how to go on, which takes us back to the original or associated difficulty.

I shall now maintain that what is taken to be a sceptical problem about the grasp of a rule is really a difficulty of analysis, the problem being spurious in that it arises from a misconception about the epistemic conditions of authoritative avowals. These are conceived of as committing the avower to a set of determinate steps by which the route of understanding is constituted, irrespective of the unfolding of events elsewhere along the way, as if any response to them, if it leads one away from the route, will automatically disqualify the avowal. But this is not at all the way it works: if it were, then being suitably disposed would itself be strictly determinate, whereas in fact it involves ceteris paribus clauses by which the epistemic status of the avowal is preserved. An obvious example, corresponding to permitted deviation from the straight and narrow, would be that of a public performance of reciting one's 83-times table as far as 83000, halfway through which the hall has emptied, with only the cleaners blocking their ears. There is no point in the performer continuing but the avowal of his grasp of the table still stands. If this use of "avowal" raises eyebrows, given its propositional content, then the same point can be made about the avowal of one's belief that one has that skill. This brings us to the promised detailed analysis of the concept of an avowal.

The first step is to confront a particular difficulty which a comparison between belief and understanding may bring out. If I speak in a particular case of believing that I understand what it is to count to 100, say, then the meaning is clear and unambiguous; but if I speak of believing that I believe that I can make the count, then either this locutionary device is pleonastic, nothing being added to the simple statement of my belief, or it qualifies that statement as being less than certain, more clearly conveyed by my saying that I think, but am not sure, that I can count to 100. Such uncertainty and vagueness, however, sit awkwardly and are in any case of no interest to us, for our concern is with simple, unqualified statements of belief. With regard to these, the expression of belief as an object of belief still has a use, but only, this being our working assumption for the moment, in the past or future tense, in which mode it may still be somewhat circumlocutory, as when I state that I believe that yesterday I believed that I could count to 100. Still, this may unequivocally be referred to as a belief claim, since I claim that yesterday I had a particular belief, where the claim and the belief utterance are distinct entities. Nothing but confusion could arise from merging them by referring, without the present clarificatory remarks, to the form of words, "I believe that..." as itself a belief claim when it refers to itself, for this is to imply that one either has or pretends to have the belief, whereas it is also possible that one does not understand the belief sentence. There is a pitfall here, and clearly we do not wish the question of authoritativeness to fall into it, for the authority with which we self-ascribe belief would then turn out to be spurious. A similar risk would be incurred if, harking back to the beginning of this chapter, we spoke of my sincerely claiming to believe that I can count to 100. If this is to imply that I am sincere in making the claim at the time that I utter the words, then what immediately follows is that the claim is true, since I sincerely, which is to say genuinely, believe that I believe that I can count to 100, which reduces to my believing that I can count to 100.

In order to negotiate this terrain we need to start with "I believe that..." regarded as an utterance or a sentence, so that we may trace out the epistemic and semantic conditions of its use as a statement of belief, thereby allowing for the possibility that they are not satisfied. A belief claim implies that they are, for it is the proposition that the sentence expresses the particular belief, and it has truth conditions attached to it, such that oneself and sometimes others are able to judge whether it is correct. We shall take the interval between belief statement and belief claim to be as short as possible, one reason for which is that it enables us to bring micro-analysis into play; but since we need to ascertain what happens at the limit, we shall initially extend the interval. Suppose that I utter the words "I can count to 100", and for reasons of simplicity let us always hear "I believe that I can count to 100", but without implying hesitation or uncertainty or change of belief if the past tense is used. Next, let us agree to call it sentence A. Then if sentence A was uttered yesterday, my belief claim today is that yesterday it expressed my belief about my counting skills. Now shorten the interval until almost at the limit, as with sentence B: "I believe that a moment ago I believed that I could count to 100". We now need to work harder to not read the usual subtext of uncertainty into this, not to mention the strong implication that I still believe that I can count to 100. The fact of such difficulty is itself significant, or it will be when we now reach the limit and allow belief and belief claim to merge into sentence A: "I believe that I can count to 100". This is risky, but keep in mind that we can always utter sentence A and then reaffirm our belief a moment later with sentence B. That will serve as a reminder of the difference between belief and belief claim.

At the limit, then, sentence B is incorporated into sentence A; but also it merges with it, the fact being, after all, that we would never say "I believe that I believe that I can count to 100". Concomitantly, the account just given contains intimations of the persistence of intentional states, in the present case belief, and previously intention, as with intending to visit Scotland. The connection is with necessary conditions of discourse and, indeed, of reasoning and empirical knowledge; and the problem of induction, as also of perception, is waiting in the dressing room.

Given our present concern, suppose that I utter sentence A and thereby appear to avow my belief. Then a concomitant of my having this belief is that a moment after the utterance I should be ready to oblige if asked for the immediate successor to any natural number between 1 and 99 inclusive. Now imagine that I do oblige but with the wrong answer; then it could be that I have made a slip, easily rectified, or perhaps the conclusion to be drawn after further testing is that I do not know how to count to 100. So my belief turns out to be mistaken, and therefore lapses, but I am still taken to have held that belief, albeit erroneously, for I was ready to oblige with answers and I understood the questions. Clearly the belief claim, taken to be sentence B, would also hold good, and would not lapse, if the answers I gave turned out to be correct. Note that all these processes at every point themselves involve beliefs.

Now suppose that when it comes to it, I am not ready to oblige with an answer or to start counting if asked, though perhaps I originally was. This is unlikely but at least conceivable, depending on the length, in any case short of the interval between the belief ascription and the question; and if it does happen then it could be that I understand what is required of me despite being unable to comply. Realising this, I now say that I did believe that I could count to 100 but no longer do. In this case, as before, my belief claim is correct; and in both cases there are possible circumstances in which originally my belief was true, my ability to count to 100 having lapsed in the meantime. If, however, the belief claim is not correct and never was, despite my having uttered the appropriate words, and if I was not feigning the belief, then we are free to imagine all manner of inconsistencies. It could be, for instance, that I am asked for the next number after 81 and admit that I do not know it, yet continue to utter the words "I believe that I can count to 100". In that case it may be suspected that I do not understand my own statement, so that the question of authoritativeness for an external observer lapses, since a necessary condition will not have been fulfilled. What, though, of the way it would seem to me? I, the author of these words, am trying and failing to imagine such a situation; and to this I have nothing to add.

So far, we have investigated a variety of situations in which a particular belief claim has been put to the test, the results of which have been instructive in what they reveal about the difficulty of undermining avowals of belief. Increasing the pressure, suppose this time that I utter sentence A at time t and make the belief claim a moment later, adding that I continue to have the belief. Try to imagine circumstances in which a moment later again I withdraw that claim, my disavowal being expressed as follows: 'I believe that I can count to 100, but I no longer believe that I had that belief at time t.' Is this possible at all? No doubt one could embrace this exciting challenge to one's creativity, but the point is that the circumstances thereby imagined would have to be exceptional. In fact, the actual challenge is even more formidable; for it involves entertaining the idea, unencumbered by any evidence in its favour, that in a perfectly ordinary setting, perhaps at a counting symposium, one wrongly believes that one believed a moment ago that one could count to 100, the context being that in which one does now believe that one can make the count. Here there are two elephants in the conference room, the first of which is the gross implausibility of that kind of belief revision claim from one moment to the next; and the second is the targeting of some beliefs but not those involved in so doing, which we have already remarked upon and are familiar with.

What does this rather overcrowded account tell us about whether self-ascription of belief is authoritative in the sense of commanding acceptance by others? That the question, rather, is that of how it could fail to be, given that we seem unable to conceive of such a failure in anything other than special circumstances. If this is correct, then perhaps we can take it further; for

106

if a condition upon a belief claim being authoritative is that it should be understood, then the question of whether it is entitled to that status has already been implicitly settled. For understanding is itself intentional and involves belief and being suitably disposed; but the interlocutor in sceptical mode can be consistent only by challenging belief claims in general, except that these include his own avowals of belief and understanding, thereby obliging him to acknowledge that he refutes himself.

Continuing in this vein, recall that Wright demands to know how we can be so confident about our intentional state if we may never have envisaged some of the dispositions involved. This is weak, for why should it matter about our limited powers of envisaging? But mainly, it is incoherent if read as radical scepticism; for being confident about an item is itself a form of the intentional, in which case Wright should rhetorically ask how we know that we are, and similarly he should ask himself to justify his own implicit claim to know that he is asking it, and that question too, and so on. Thus it is that the sceptical problem of avowals cannot coherently be stated.

Time, now, to focus on the avower rather than to include both internal and external judgement in the mix. Suppose, as before, that I ask myself how I know, having just uttered sentence A, that I thereby expressed the particular belief. I believe that I did express it, this being my belief claim, which in everyday terms I have no reason to doubt. But I cannot interrogate that claim without implying present beliefs on my part, including my belief that a moment ago I had a belief about being able to count to 100; and if these are to avoid being incriminated, then my reason for targeting the original apparent belief must be such as to exclude them from suspicion. Since no such reason has been given, we are left with Wright's contention that the problem is that avowals require one to be suitably disposed, which we cannot know that we are. If we now look into this, the first point is that all avowals, indeed all beliefs, have a dispositional component, hence their belonging within a system. This alters everything, entailing as it does that the beliefs involved in checking one's dispositions would themselves entrain further dispositions to be checked, and these in their turn, the tracks endlessly branching. Worse again, the train could never depart the station, for in the first carriage would be the belief that one's dispositions need to be checked, its own dispositions being subject to the same exponentially proliferating demands.

3.8: Time Passing and the Analysis of Avowals

Now that our concern is with analysis rather than radical scepticism, it may be of interest if we tease out the deeper implications of our treatment of avowals, the emphasis this time being on their temporal properties. I have argued that it seems insuperably difficult to doubt one's own belief claim in a philosophically interesting way, and certainly not on the basis of belief being dispositional; but not on any other general basis either, for the expression of doubt would itself be an avowal. What follows is that avowals of belief and other intentional states are fundamental within a system, which is to say that they are the pathways along which intentionality travels; and each path branches into many others, occasionally in such a way as to sever a connection, where this corresponds to, for instance, a deliberately false belief claim, the remaining connections enabling this to obtain. In order to dissemble in this way, one must have the same grasp of the relevant concepts as those who speak truthfully. The reference to travel along pathways is a reminder, in the unlikely event of its being needed, that the application of concepts is inseparable from temporal process, a fact which in its implications veers towards the metaphysical, the path going deeper rather than broadening out.

Teasing out those implications, consider not sentence A or B, overfamiliarity being something with which we are all too familiar, but the freshly minted sentence C: "There is a swan in that box." Let it be uttered by myself and followed immediately by my belief claim in the past tense: 'I believed a moment ago that there was a swan in the box.' Now suppose that this implies, as indeed it more or less does, depending on context, that I no longer have that belief, perhaps because I now notice that the box has been opened. There is nothing untoward in this, and only a hungry crocodile would shed any tears over it; but now try to imagine that all one's beliefs changed from one moment to the next, in which case there would indeed be much distress, and with the sheer frustration of not being able to avow anything at all. That belief in general has duration, the measure of which is given by language use as temporal process, is indicated by the unusualness of the earlier retrospective belief claim. Normally, I would say not that I believed a moment ago that there was a swan in the box, which strictly speaking is true, but that I believe that there is a swan in the box. This is the present tense, but what that word hides in plain sight is that it is always the continuous present, in other words the past, present and future functionally overlapping over short intervals of time, this being a necessary condition of intentional avowals, indeed of discourse itself. It takes a moment to say "I believed it a moment ago", or to think it, at which point it is now two moments ago; but the same is true of "I believe it". We are well below the waves here, and our fundamental insight ramifies into the problem of induction — but that can wait.

3.9: Return to Avowals of Sensation

Is it really correct, as Wright maintains, that avowals of sensation are a special case? Not in the way that he had in mind, or so I argued, but might it be in some other way? An obvious distinguishing character is that of direct acquaintance, a pain, for instance, being exclusively phenomenal, whereas a memory image is charged with intentionality. Perhaps, then, we should now extend our sweep to see if sensations can also be caught in the net of the present method of analysis. Let us ask, in other words, whether knowledge of one's beliefs can be assimilated to other forms of authoritative awareness, for instance to knowing that one is in pain, which again is something we would lay claim to, just as we are certain as to our beliefs. Again, we could go into detail about assertibility conditions, pointing out that, for instance, one could utter the words "I am in pain" and know that one is in pain without thereby giving voice to it. For instance, such awareness would not be verbally expressed by a suffering monolingual Frenchman uttering the words "I am in pain" when learning English phonetics. To forge the semantic and cognitive link between pain and utterance, we need to take account of dispositions as well as the conscious qualitative character of the utterance, and in much the same way as with belief claims.

It is true, of course, that a belief is different from a sensation, which we know directly if it is the immediate experiential object of self-ascription in the present tense, as with "I am in pain." This belongs to the class of what A.J.Ayer calls basic propositions, characterised by their truth conditions being identifiable with the immediately given. These contrast with wider-ranging descriptions associated with physical-object concepts, such as that of a rabbit, which one may understand while frequently confusing rabbits and hares. Although it points to an epistemic difference, the distinction thus illustrated does not, or so I have maintained, have the epistemological significance which some philosophers attach to it, claiming as they do that basic propositions are infallible or incorrigible, thereby lending themselves to foundationalism. What is true is that if I believe that I am in pain, as expressed by "I am in pain", then I understand what I say, otherwise no sense could attach to my believing it; and then it follows that I am in pain, for I do not understand if, without pretending, I say that I am in pain when I am not. Such is the difference between " I am in pain" and "I am in Wales". But now the question shifts from how I know that I am in pain to how I know that I understand. Here we should keep in mind the claim, which Wright advanced in the quoted passage, that my knowing that I am in pain is directly grounded in the sensation itself, an example, perhaps, of what Ayer refers to as an 'act of knowing' (1959: p.111), a form of words which he thinks is highly misleading. Indeed it is if it is taken to exclude dispositions, for on any particular occasion of use one has to be not only in pain but also suitably disposed with regard to one's use of "pain". Note that awareness of one's dispositions is itself both occurrent and dispositional, so that the difference between these two modes of awareness or understanding is not fundamental.

If the foregoing is correct, and if my use of "I am in pain" is considered, then I may not understand it even if I think that I do, for that understanding depends on my being suitably disposed with regard to the use not only of "pain" but also of the other words in the sentence, all against a background of general competence in English. It is not possible to specify exactly how far my command of the language must extend, partly because understanding admits of degrees, which is why I have concentrated on essential cognitive and semantic conditions. One of these is that I must be able to repeat or paraphrase the sentence, other things being equal, and what this indicates, as so much else does, is that the required dispositions are utterly dependent on my memories being correct, which again invites a question as to how I know that I understand.

Does this mean that we cannot know that we are in pain? Not at all: in starting from "I am in pain" regarded as an utterance, all that we have done is to reject a particular view of what it is to know that one is in pain, that which presents awareness of pain as grounded in the sensation itself, no account being taken of disposition, memory and expectation; and a corrective to this, as we have seen, is to analyse that awareness in terms of a system. But that analysis enables us to reinstate authoritativeness on a different plinth, very much in the same way as with self-ascription of belief. If we consider, as before, the epistemology of memory, then it is true that self-ascription of pain is conditional upon one's memories being correct, which in particular cases they may not be; but what must also be said, by way of balance, is that it is in the nature of the system to impose constraints on any doubts we may have as to the legitimacy of memory claims. These are such as to rule out general philosophical scepticism about memory, given that the sceptic argues from within a system in which no statement can be made that does not presuppose that the memories it calls upon are correct. Reliance on memory is part of the structure of the system; and this is to imply that if on occasion I doubt whether I remember correctly with regard to my understanding of "am in pain", then my reasons must be appropriate to the particular case, not general reasons such as to render incoherent the doubt itself. It could be, for instance, that owing to cognitive deterioration I am no longer certain as to the meaning of "pain", having lost confidence in particular linguistic memories — though not, let it be noted, in all of them, otherwise I should not be able to verbally express my misgivings about some of them. The point, anyway, is that my loss of confidence would debar me from stating that I was in pain, or that I knew that I was. It is conceivable that I confidently utter the words "I am in pain", as if self-ascribing pain, when in fact I am not in pain; but then, pretence apart, I do not understand what I say, so that I am not mistakenly self-ascribing pain.

Furthermore, if scepticism about the understanding of "I am in pain" is based on the argument that it is logically possible that one utter that sentence without understanding it, the necessary dispositions being absent, then the same is true of any sentence, including that by which the argument is conveyed. It follows that if I state that I am in pain, and then it occurs to me as a philosopher to ask how I know that I am, then this immediately rules out any sceptical answer based on logical possibility. But further, and as already explained, if I can ask how I know that I am in pain, thereby exhibiting my grasp of the concept of pain, then it must be that I am in pain when I say, without feigning it, that I am, so that the question answers itself.

This should all be enough to establish the qualified authoritativeness of pain avowals, depending as they do on dispositions in a system partly defined by necessary conditions of discourse, especially if it is noted that a condition of one's grasp of the concept of pain is only that one should be suitably disposed at the time, not that one's dispositions should permanently obtain. Thus, it is possible that I know on a particular occasion that I am in pain, but that my understanding then lapses, so that I am no longer able to refer to my pain on other occasions, perhaps because I have forgotten the meaning of "pain". It is a significant fact that one has to make an effort to imagine such a thing, for it indicates how well entrenched is our grasp of basic psychological concepts, such as that of pain. There are inductive connections here, which await investigation; but for the moment, and by way of gaining insight into the entrenching of such concepts, we may note that the grasp of them is taken to extend over the continuous present as a necessary condition, the same as with belief. That is, one can imagine that my claim to know the meaning of "pain", to know it now at time t, is tested by my being stimulated in various ways and asked to describe my sensations, and, less painfully for me, by my being asked what I infer from the screams of other subjects. It may be, as in practice it almost certainly would be, that I am deemed to have passed the test. But this all takes time, so in a sense the verdict is retrospective; or, rather, it is taken to cover the period between time *t* and the continuing present. Now, it might be thought that this reveals only that one's abilities tend to persist; but I would argue, as with belief and as in the next chapter, that persistence of this kind, with its predictive implications, is a fundamental semantic and cognitive condition and is part of the structure of the system of language use.

To sum up: conscious experience ranges over a world of differences, with pain in the west, pleasure in the east, but with intentionality both north and south, its myriad longitudes mapping sensation at all points, but overlooked if the focus is on latitude instead. All such points belong within the same coordinate system, its origin at the centre, and with no fundamental difference between avowals of pain and of belief. The fact is, after all, that reference to one's pain requires that sensation to be simultaneous with it only if self-ascribed in the present tense, this being complemented by its not being felt at all if the reference is negative

3.10: Recapitulation and Conclusion

Finally, it should now be possible to exhibit more clearly our findings across these chapters as providing solutions, in particular to the problem of avowals. If we start with avowable sensations, an empiricist preconception is that they are self-luminous, their luminosity being that of, as Bertrand Russell put it, knowledge by acquaintance. Thus, it is that for Wright, as already quoted, 'The subject is authoritative about such states because, since they are events in his consciousness, he is in the nature of the case conscious of them.' Note the elision from consciousness to awareness via being conscious of; but wordplay apart there need be no connection, at least if we try not to connect them when reflecting on whether they are connected. Think not of present pain but of a momentary twinge two moments ago. In what way is it in the nature of a twinge that we authoritatively avow it when, apart from a fleeting sensation, we do not feel it? Is it possible to avow it in and for that instant? Let it be granted that we can conceive of such a thing; but why bother? For in the next instant we would cease to avow it; and how can epistemic authority be so strictly a function of its object? Very well, it will be said, but we remember it. This, however, is to increase the interest on the epistemic debt, for now we take the question of authoritativeness to extend to avowals of memory, which in any case is where it also belongs. What matters is that our criticism of Wright's thesis is thereby conceded.

What, though, if pain if prolonged? There is a metaphysical answer to this, but it will have to await the later theory of consciousness. Meanwhile, we can say that on one interpretation a sensation is either a momentary event or a sequence of such; but in this latter case each moment of pain would the same as in the case of a momentary pain, so that we are no further forward. On a different interpretation, the psychological experience of time is of a continuous present, the same for momentary as for prolonged sensations. Since the concept of time is by definition intentional, courtesy of being a concept, and since the self-ascription of memory is an intentional avowal, as also of expectation, and since intentionality is irreducible, we begin to wonder again about the limitations of epistemology. Does a fog of mystery surround the planet and impede our vision of what lies beyond? Clearly, it is not as if the notion of psychological time has penetrative power or, indeed, explains anything at all.

If the foregoing is correct, then it makes no difference if we take Wright to have in mind co-occurrent awareness of sensations, the notion of which we have subjected to analysis. More generally we have shown that avowals of sensation belong within a system in which language gains purchase by going beyond its objects and attaching them to conditions and connections by which one thing predicated of another is both exposed and protected. If pain is the self-ascribed object, let us grant that the ascription has an epistemic advantage, its truth-conditions coinciding with the sensation itself, albeit only if we ignore the way in which memory goes out on a limb. But it is, as we have seen, in other ways exposed, this often overlooked if the reference is to cognitive conditions. One cannot self-ascribe anything, whether sensation or intentional state, without an implicit cognitive avowal making itself accountable.

Set against this, I argued, is the countervailing fact of the system being governed by necessary conditions, these in their turn overlooked, perhaps partly because one tends to assume that the individual case is always extrapolatable. If it is, then one should credit with perfect sense this damning indictment from a judge to a car thief about to be sentenced: 'If everyone behaved like you, the owners of cars would live in constant fear of theft.' Error is possible only within a system of assumptions as to true belief; and avowals of sensation form a continuum with increasingly empirical propositional content. There is no sharp epistemic distinction between "I am in pain", "My feet are hurting" and "I have a phantom pain in my amputated limbs". None of this is to deny everyday difference in degree of belief, but it does indicate that one's room for manoeuvre within a system is less than we think, partly because if there are beliefs that we would not countenance and others we would not deny, then we may not be aware of not having or not denying them. Looking at a teddy bear with its unsettling vacant gaze, one's visual experience cannot be that of looking at the person who holds it, and one's visual impression of him cannot be that of looking at a teddy bear. Perceptual experience must be such as to conform to the necessary conditions of perception by which misperception is made possible; and what this means in terms of a system is that the veridicality of particular perceptions is judged against surrounding perceptions, themselves not in question in the same way. But also, the notion of a continuum still uppermost, there are more abstract facts, no doubt feeding off the physical, about which we are very certain indeed. Earlier I mentioned my belief that I live in Wales, whereby I would be extremely mortified if it were to transpire that I live in Scotland.

If we now broaden our retrospection to encompass avowals of both sensations and intentional states, it may be recalled that one of our key findings turned the lock on a particular aspect of the passing of time. If at time t I boast at a very boring party that I can count to 100, then my implicit belief-claim, that I believe that I can count to 100, requires me to be suitably disposed, and in ways that depend on whether the time is now $t + 5$, $t + 10$, $t + 15...$, and on whether the increments are in seconds, minutes, hours..., all of which is best kept vague, if only for the reason that it also depends on other relevant changes or the absence thereof. If, for instance, the time is now 5 seconds after t, and if I have not collapsed with a stroke in the interim, and if I am asked to make the count, and if I am confident when attempting to comply, then others will accept that I believe that I can make the count, irrespective of whether I succeed. If I fail, the expectation will be that at that point my belief no longer holds, provided there is no suspicion that I am dissembling the opposed belief: that I cannot count to 100, in which case I never believed that I could.

Turning now to my own perspective on these events, one epistemic advantage I have is that I cannot deliberately mislead myself, or not unless the notion of the subconscious is brought into play, the possibility of which would muddy the waters too much were we to wade into it. I can become uncertain as to whether I had the belief at time t, this being more likely the longer the intervening time; but my avowal of that uncertainty is itself authoritative, as would be any admission of error on my part. For instance, it may occur to me, perhaps the day after time t, that it was unlikely that I had the belief in question, given that I am semi-numerate and in fact cannot count to 100. The point is that this revision would itself involve avowable beliefs and other intentional states, in recognition of which I now maintain, as the last word on this matter, at least in the chapter about to close, that one way in which avowals are authoritative is that they are *inescapable*.

Finally, we are about to move on from direct grappling with Wittgenstein, having earned the right to critically pronounce upon his world view, and without being accused, or justly accused, of ad hominem strictures against him. Wittgenstein wishes to convert us to the belief that we are misguided in our notion of what it is to mean or to understand. He maintains that there are misconceptions in the usual philosophical notion of correct use being determined by what is meant. After illustrating various senses of "determine" in this connection, he suggests that we mistakenly think that it has another sense, or that there is another sense in which the steps are determined by what we mean; and he also implies that our being misguided in this way is linked to the picture we have of the steps being traversed in advance. He then indicates that such a picture makes no sense, and thereby suggests that we are wrong in the notion we have of the steps being determined. The impression given, as elsewhere in the *Investigations*, is of peering into the depths of truths too profound to be stated clearly, and this owes a great deal to his style of writing. His sentences are on the one hand oracular and opaque, and on the other they announce their importance by the profligate use of italics. Sometimes, that said, a particular passage may register with the reader straightforwardly—or would do if Wittgenstein permitted it, as with the section about the order to "add 2". Instead of construing it as an example of individual understanding but interpersonal misunderstanding, perhaps checking first that its author is not looking, one freezes mentally or, for all I know, suffers a cognitive seizure, or perhaps feels a headache coming on. At the very least one is left with a feeling of intellectual unease, a prisoner in Wittgenstein's camp, as it were, who is being made receptive to the new ideology of equating meaning with use. We, however, are non-political and have work to do, this being the last sentence of the present chapter.

Chapter 4: The Pure-Applied Problem

My plan for this chapter is to continue to chart the deeper currents of the human intellect, by which I imply that carpet mites, at least of the aquatic variety, will be left to their own devices in the shallows of instinct and conditioned response. More particularly, I first introduce the pure-applied problem, to give it a name, via the device of a dialogue in which various aspects of the problem are debated, the object being to survey them as they are traditionally understood. I then develop the thesis that everyday factual inference is essentially similar to applied logic or mathematics. In so doing, I hope to be able to emphasise the fact, as I see it, that if reasoning of a particular kind belongs within a system, then the system is to some degree closed with respect to standards of correctness. Probability, for instance, is a case in point, and I shall try to show that the application of the notion of equiprobability, a lynchpin of the probability calculus, can be scrutinised in particular cases only if taken for granted elsewhere. First, however, we need to introduce the pure-applied problem.

Let us consider the geometry of plane figures drawn on paper. If I construct a right triangle and measure the length of the sides, then it seems that I may predict with certainty the length of the hypotenuse, unless Pythagoras made a dreadful mistake all those years ago. Discounting that possibility, a question arises as to whether geometrical prediction has logical force, my present aim being not so much to answer it as to exhibit its difficulties. Consider the following dialogue between persons F and D, father and young daughter, who are hunched over a school exercise book showing a right triangle.

D: You don't mind helping me with my homework, do you, Dad?

F: No, love, not at all.

D: Would you agree that the two sides of this triangle are three and four inches long and are perpendicular?

F (using a ruler and protractor): Yes, I agree.

D: Then if we apply Pythagoras to get $3^2 + 4^2 = 5^2$, it follows that the hypotenuse is five inches long, this being a conclusion deducible from true premisses.

F: In geometry it's easy to confuse mathematics with physical facts. If a conclusion follows deductively, then it and the premisses are mathematical. The hypotenuse being five inches long is a contingent fact about lines on paper.

D: But Dad, if the sides are three and four inches, we *must* believe that the hypotenuse is five inches.

F: You seem to take the physical embodiment of the theorem to be synthetic *a priori*, as if its logical force somehow leaps the gap between pure and applied; but I would say, following Ayer, that the theorem is analytic and logically separate from empirical fact.

D: Well, Dad, serious doubt has been cast on the notion of analytic truth, notably by Quine, who argues that we have no clear and distinct idea, as Descartes would put it, of the synonymy on which the notion of the analytic depends, partly because of the way in which the synonymous and the analytic feed into each other. Besides, what makes you think that the theorem is logically separate from empirical fact? That, surely, is just what we are debating. Can you show that it is analytic in that way?

F: No, and you are right to challenge me, though perhaps I would have more success in simpler cases, and in a way that, *pace* Quine, would be unproblematic. Don't forget, too, that he would question the notion of synthetic *a priori* truth on which you seem to rely. What I can still say, in any case, is that it is an empirical question whether this hypotenuse is five inches long, irrespective of whether the theorem is analytic or whether it is logical, assuming any difference; and also, again following Ayer, that nothing is allowed to count against the truth of the theorem. If the hypotenuse turned out to be other than five inches, I would seek an explanation, but not at the expense of the theorem, which would always be sacrosanct, the problem lying with its physical depiction and not with its mathematical validity. I would check the measurements again, confident that they would turn out to be incorrect.

D: But it is precisely because our belief about the length of the hypotenuse relative to the sides has logical force that we check our measurements when there seems to be a discrepancy. Why else would there be any reason to doubt whether we have correctly measured lines and angles?

F: Well, I suppose our reasons must be inductive. If all the right triangles we have ever encountered have been Pythagorean, then there is no reason to think that this triangle is an exception; but it isn't logically impossible. Before drawing and measuring the hypotenuse, I can easily imagine that it is 6 or 7 inches long, even when I know the lengths of the other two sides. Put another way, I am in the same state of nescience when I look at the end points of the lines and the gap between them where the hypotenuse will go, irrespective, that is, of knowing the lengths of the sides.

D: You've crammed a lot into that, but here goes. Perhaps you can imagine different lengths for the hypotenuse, but what of it? Before multiplying two or more large numbers, I can easily imagine different values for their product; but the correct value is uniquely determined arithmetically. As for the other way of putting it, what do you mean by 'state of nescience'? Would you expect to have a *sensation* of logical force? Then good luck in trying to identify it. Another thing: I promise not to tell Mum, but which star system did you say you were from? How many millions of these triangles would you have to be acquainted with in order to be absolutely certain that the hypotenuse squared is *always* the sum of the squares of the other two sides? How, in any case, would you account for this universality? How many different sizes and proportions of such triangles would you have to measure in order for it to count as a fair sample from an infinite population?

F: OK, you won those points; but reflect on this: if I took a ruler or tape measure to numerous right triangles of sides a and b, their sizes limited only by practicality, and if I found that the length of the hypotenuse, c, was given by $c^2 = (1.01a)^2 + (1.01b)^2$, then I would say not that Pythagoras was no longer valid but that it had ceased to have physical application, at least to triangles drawn on paper. What say you?

D: 'What say you?' Not the coolest of locutions, Dad, but, tit for tat, I would say that you know not of what you speak. That which you invite me to suppose to be the case is impossible, or so I claim, therefore your invitation begs the question against me. If the sides are at right angles, then this determines, by Pythagoras, the length of the hypotenuse.

F: The notion of begging the question has its own problems. Surely, in any case, you can imagine a world in which this deviant formula, as it would be in our world, was taught in schools and had physical application in the way that the Pythagoras theorem presently now has. This latter would still be valid as an abstract theorem but not as applying to actual triangles.

D: But it wouldn't be — it's a geometric theorem about lines and angles on paper or screen, so it *would* be invalid. We are back with your deviant theorem being impossible, so we seem to be going around in circles.

F: Circles, triangles, it makes no difference, but let's focus on triangles again. This hypotenuse you've drawn: it *looks* about five inches, even before being measured; but just imagine that the sides were much longer, say thirty and forty miles – would you then insist that the hypotenuse must be fifty miles?

D (failing to sense a trap and trying to imagine a ruler that long): Yes. It would be difficult to measure, but it would have to be 50 miles, given sides of 30 and 40 miles and an included right angle.

F (springing the trap): But then you would be mistaken. Because of the curvature of the earth the triangle would be curved, not planar, and the hypotenuse would be longer than 50 miles.

D (recovering quickly): But that just means that a different but related formula would apply; and in spherical geometry it would be the counterpart to Pythagoras and would dictate, in the same way as the Pythagoras theorem in planar geometry, the length of one side of the triangle if the other two sides and the included angle were given.

F: But you said that only Pythagoras makes a geometric fit, and now you have to qualify that statement; so how far can the cloth be trimmed before the suit is ruined? what it comes down to is that Pythagoras, as with any theorem, is derived from axioms, the ones pertaining to figures in a plane being different from those in spherical geometry. Side and angle on a sphere have to be *defined*. If you try to draw a triangle on a football, you'll see what I mean. If a right triangle constructed on a flat surface satisfies the appropriate axioms, then *of course* the length of the hypotenuse is logically determined.

D: Are you sure that came out right? And why are you speaking italic? Practice makes perfect, and your "*of course*" is wrongly placed. *Of course* a right triangle in a plane satisfies the axioms; but the whole issue is that of whether the length of the hypotenuse is thereby logically determined — and you've acknowledged that it is. The issue is not whether we can be certain that a triangle is really a right triangle of sides three and four inches. The theorem states that *if* it is, then the hypotenuse is 5 inches. Also, you said just now that this hypotenuse looks about 5 inches, possibly 6 or 7 — but could it be a foot long? No, absolutely not; but doesn't that sound like logical certainty to you?

F: You've lost me — how did you get from logical truth to visual appearance?

D: On foot.

F (laughing): it must have been a very small foot.

D: I was following in the footsteps of Kant.

F: Now you've really lost me. He never mentioned feet.

D: That's because he was German and used the metric not the imperial system.

F: I thought imperialism was widespread in 18th century Europe.

D: OK, Dad, that's enough.

F: Very well; shall we just agree that the world is such that mathematics always has application, though not necessarily the one it happens to have in any particular case?

D: If you like, but I've got question marks ringing in my ears. Shall we just agree that on this flat piece of paper on this flat table any side of any triangle is logically determined, given the other two sides and included angle? It's called the cosine rule. Also, that this triangle in front of us has perpendicular sides 3 and 4 inches; and this means that the hypotenuse *must* be 5 inches long.

F: Very well, but what about probability and the theory of arrangements? I suppose you would endorse the claim that a relation of partial entailment binds population to sample, and perhaps sample to population. But what does it even mean?

D: I suppose you would endorse the claim that I am totally predictable in my views; and I would endorse the claim that you need to get out more. In fact, I have no idea what partial entailment looks like when out of the box; but I do think that a logical imperative presides over arrangements. A black ball and two white balls may be pairwise combined in precisely two ways: white with black or white with white; or arranged in three ways if sequence order counts: bw, wb and ww; or six ways if in addition the balls are treated as individuals, perhaps b, w_1, w_2, so that we have $bw_1, w_1b, bw_2, w_2b, w_1w_2, w_2w_1$. Try as you might you will not find more than six, or three if a restriction is imposed, or two if it is tightened.

F: What a clever little girl you are, and very special, even in the matter of your punctuation- mark tinnitus.

D: Dad, are you patronising me?

F: No, love, I wouldn't dare.[4]

And so on. Looking back over this dialogue, we can see that it plays over difficult issues, the father and daughter dug into opposing trenches. But Kant was mentioned, as also the force of apparently empirical certainty in relation to perceived length. And Quine, to whom we are indebted for the seminal idea of challenging any strict distinction between fact and logic, albeit given that this needs to be clarified. Perhaps, then, we should venture into the seaways, all the better to close the gap between pure and applied, the middle lane, pending further enquiries, being that of the synthetic *a priori*.

4.1: Tea Behaving Badly

Note first that the whole of our waking experience is conveyed from one moment to the next by certainties of detail, which fa-

---

[4] The references in this dialogue are to the views of W.V.O.Quine and A.J.Ayer, in particular Quine's *From a Logical Point of View* and Ayer's *Language, Truth, and Logic*

miliarity both channels and obscures. Consider, for instance, my reaching for this cup without looking, whereupon I bring it to my lips and sip the tea, every step of which is automatic. There is always, of course, the possibility of surprise, as when I lift the cup only to find that it is lighter than it should be. But suppose that I glance inside, expecting it to be empty, only to find that it is full of what seems to be tea, which, bewildered and not being house-proud, I try to expel from the cup by turning it upside down, except that nothing comes out. Now imagine the shock of it and the associated cognitive cluelessness, an exercise which may suggest that if we focus on logical force then we underestimate the power of apparently contingent fact.

But surely, one might object, there are crucial differences here, at least between geometrical prediction and the expectation that a cup of tea will not be proof against gravity. The rules of geometry admit of no exceptions and in the father-daughter dialogue one argued that it is on the basis of the Pythagoras theorem, not inductively, that we appreciate that all right triangles *must* be such that the length of the hypotenuse is determined by that of the sides. If this imperative is denied, it is because we misconstrue the fact, entailed by it, that all encountered right triangles have satisfied the theorem, whereupon we reach for the induction label. My argument, or one of them, was that inductive evidence could never rise above its own inadequacy, given that the theorem is infinite in range. Be that as it may, we must now face up to an entirely different approach by which empiricism answers its enemies, the method being that of radicalising the theory rather than moving to the centre ground.

According to radical empiricism, fact and logic are not only opposed but strictly separated, the bridge between them unsuitable for traffic, so that not even applied logic or mathematics is able to span opposing views. On the contrary, it splits into factual statements on the one side and analytic propositions on the other—hence my earlier comment about clarifying what is meant by a strict distinction. In discussing these issues, we shall cover geometry, probability, arrangement theory and everyday reasoning. We may start with A.J.Ayer, who in *Probability and Evidence* has little to say about geometry, concentrating instead on probability. He maintains that very often there is a failure to distinguish between *a priori* probability, which concerns the calculus of chances, and statistical theory. This latter, he says, involves probability in the form of the relative frequency of the features of interest, as with the probability of heads if a fair coin or one with a known bias is tossed. The problem, he thinks, is that these two approaches are illicitly conflated, even by theorists, whereas in fact they are quite distinct. Since the calculus of chances is purely mathematical in character, he says, the probability values derived from it do not determine what it is rational to believe about actual events but refer only to relations of ratio and proportion among abstract possibilities. It is therefore quite separate from facts about relative frequency with regard to dice, coins and games of chance in general, about which he says:

> If we are going to apply the calculus of chances to actual games, we have to make the assumption that all the logically equal possibilities are equal in fact, and this of course is not a mathematical truth. It is an assumption to which one has to give an empirical meaning.
> Unfortunately, this is often overlooked. It is a common mistake for those who are writing on this subject to start with a well-defined notion of *a priori* probability, namely that of the incidence of certain features in the total of all possible mathematical combinations of a given sort, and then go on to talk of its being or not being equally probable that this or that possibility will be realised in nature, thereby using the word 'probable' in a way that their definition no longer covers. (p.30)

In this passage Ayer focusses on the features exhibited by abstract possibility sets derived from the theory of arrangements, and he speaks of the incidence of such features, which he associates with *a priori* probability theory. Take, for example, the probability of independent events h and t and of the possible sequences of three such events. Given that h and t are equally likely, then so are the eight alternatives, in which case the mistake to which Ayer alludes, if heads and tails are substituted for h and t, would be that of taking them to be equally likely in the case of a particular coin being tossed. There are several areas of enquiry here, one of which concerns the association just mentioned; but a prior question is that of whether combinatorics can be purely mathematical, as Ayer implies that it can. Consider the fact that two letters may be combined from four letters a,b,c,d in six ways: ab, ac, ad, bc, bd, cd, the ratio of each to the total being 1:6. More generally when r objects are combined from n objects, the number of combinations is given by $\dfrac{n!}{r!(n-r)!}$. Now let the objects be the letters of the alphabet, with $r = 2$ as before. Then the number arrived at is $\dfrac{26!}{2!(24)!} = 325$ and there is no reason why this should not count as applied logic or mathematics. For the fact is, after all, that one may check that there are 325 possibilities by, tedium notwithstanding, systematically listing them. That being the case, let us now ask whether the letters qualify as being abstract as opposed to concrete. They are not actually made of concrete, this monitor being too flimsy, but even if it were more robust the concrete shapes would have to register as letters, and registered letters have to be read and understood and signed for as having symbolic content, and the same with cardboard letters or those made of ink or digital display pixels. Thus it is that even the distinction between abstract and concrete is not clearcut, this therefore being true of that between pure and applied in relation to the theory of arrangements. This enables us to maintain, without the concepts involved coming under too much tension, that the present cases are indeed examples of applied mathematics.

Keeping that in mind, let us ask again whether Ayer's distinction has the significance that he attaches to it. He refers to the 'incidence of certain features in the total of all possible mathematical combinations of a given sort', one example of which, if he is correct in what he seems to imply, would be that of the proportion of the 325 letter pairs that include the letter "a", namely $\dfrac{1}{13}$.

We have seen, however, that there is no valid reason why this should not come under the heading of applied arrangement theory, contrary to what Ayer seems to think. But also, he associates that theory, in what he deems to be its purely mathematical form, with *a priori* probability, the notion of which he links to proportions among mathematical combinations. We have just shown that this is mistaken in one way, but it is, too, in another; for in what sense are combinatorial proportions *a priori* probabilities? Of the letters a,b,c,d there are six ways of combining them in pairs, any one of which, this being a surprise to no-one, represents one sixth of the total number of selections. But this is proportion, not probability, as would continue to be the case even if the letters were physical shapes, perhaps pilfered from a baby's toy box. Similarly, we have quoted Ayer as claiming that if we 'apply the calculus of chances to actual games, we have to make the assumption that all the logically equal possibilities are equal in fact'. But in what sense are our six possible letter pair selections logically equal? What Ayer has in mind, I suspect, is the notion of equipossibility, in which case the selections, if he is correct, are not equipossible, for this connotes equiprobability, and Ayer's thesis is that pure and applied are distinct.

4.2: Frequency

Why, it may be asked, should this issue loom large? Because in making the distinction, Ayer implies that the propositions of *a priori* probability theory belong to logic only in the sense of being truistic, by which he seems to mean analytic, whereas empirical propositions are synthetic. But if by this latter he has in mind probabilistic applications, the focus being on frequency, then the distinction is not a happy one and may, indeed, be suicidal. What drives it to the edge is the fact, as I shall now show, that relative frequency is itself a probability construct.

Suppose that we conduct a coin-tossing experiment in order to ascertain whether a particular coin is biased, the resulting sequence being subjected to statistical analysis according to our preferred method. If the estimate arrived at is that $P(h) = \dfrac{1}{3}$, where "h" = "heads" then this is a formal interpretation of the sequence, which is to say that the distribution of heads and tails is taken to conform to the requirements of independence and randomness and yields the proposition $P(h) = \dfrac{1}{3}$, all of which involves the probability calculus. Otherwise, and with regard to numerical values, the probability of heads would be taken to be a third only if this was exactly their proportion, in which case it would not be a probability estimate at all but simply a precise measure of such proportion in a finite sequence, one that would change at the next toss of the coin. Finite, that is, because its expression as an infinite sequence limit would be mathematically technical. Its predictive utility, if it had one, would derive not from abstract probability theory but from inductive extrapolation. Hume, as we know, would compare them and see no difference. Again, consider randomness in particular as a condition, the lack of which would mean that the probability of heads would be taken to be a third even if all the heads in the sequence came first, followed by twice as many tails. If we are correct about these conditions, then to say that $P(h) = \frac{1}{3}$ in a formal probability context is to imply that the sequence of heads and tails exhibits appropriate probabilistic frequency characteristics and that this will continue if the coin is tossed again.

Less formally, which is to say in everyday life, one's understanding of the sequence may be more pragmatic. It may be obvious, for instance to a bookie who examines the sequence and wishes to offer odds on heads or tails, that the incidence of heads is about a third; also, that the arrangement of heads and tails is random in the practical sense that it offers no clue, apart from that proportion, as to the outcome of the next toss of the coin. Quite possibly, then, she will offer odds of two to one or skew them to her own advantage.

Having countered the empiricist approach to relative frequency, let us now enquire into its connection with proportion, and more generally with the notion of numerical probability. If a bag contains three black balls and two white, then $P(black) = 0.6$ if it is assumed that each ball is as likely to be drawn as any other. And now suppose a series of trials in each of which a ball is drawn and its colour noted, the colour sequence at the close of the experiment being subjected to statistical analysis, as already explained. If, other things being equal, the resulting relative frequency value deviates beyond acceptable limits from the expected three-fifths, perhaps when maximum likelihoods are ascertained, or if it does not seem to converge to that limit when continued indefinitely, then the original assumption may be placed under scrutiny. This indicates that a truth-conditional connection obtains between proportion and frequency, at least in those cases in which a clear sense may be attached to repetition of instances treated as trials in a statistical experiment.

Continuing in this vein, I suggest that we discuss more generally the standard arguments by which the dispute between empiricist and rationalist has become polarised, not in order to take sides but to show that the problem lies with the very distinctions which permit a partisan approach. Let us begin with the claim that a distinguishing property of logical or mathematical knowledge is its *a priori* status. Such knowledge, in contrast with that which is empirical, is regarded as being independent of the state of the physical world, or what we know of it. Since pure maths operating over abstractions is by definition independent in this way, enabling conditions apart, the reference must be to applied maths, or, given the fluidity of the distinction, it must be to the purely theoretical aspects of applied mathematics.

Note that Ayer makes little attempt to explain how it is that we mistakenly take pure maths to exert logical force, and concomitantly how it is that applied mathematics impresses upon us an imperative which, if he is correct, is all symbol and no logical substance. He would say that with two coins nothing is allowed to count against the number of couples of heads and tails being four, and 2^r with r coins. But now, what does he mean by "nothing is allowed to count against..."? Presumably that if the number seemed not to be four, we would check again, or we would explain away the discrepancy in some other way; but that is because we know that the formula cannot admit of exceptions, so there would in fact be a valid explanation, such as that we had miscounted. What Ayer needs to show is that something *could* conceivably count against, but he makes no attempt, and for the simple reason, one suspects, that he is aware of its futility. Suppose again that we take two coins, the formula giving four ordered couplets *hh, ht, th, tt*, and that we wish to set out all four arrangements on a table at the same time. Amassing more coins, we place the eight and then we take two more. Standing one of them on edge, its partner tails uppermost, we announce that it is *et*. But this is either a joke about aliens or an extension of usual practice. If the latter, then this gives, or so we may suppose, *et, te, eh, he* and *ee*. But there still are precisely four ordered arrangements of heads and tails among the nine pairs displayed.

Turning now to the mistake we make, according to Ayer, in crediting pure maths with logical force, it is presumably because we fail to notice that its deliverances are propositionally analytic. Perhaps we can, by way of atonement, be more attentive when considering the following example of mathematical magic, so that the trick of analyticity will be exposed. Consider the binomial coefficients in the expansion of $(a+b)^n$ for n=0,1,2,....This gives an array known as Pascal's triangle:

$$
\begin{array}{ccccccc}
& & & 1 & & & \\
& & 1 & & 1 & & \\
& 1 & & 2 & & 1 & \\
1 & & 3 & & 3 & & 1
\end{array}
$$

One could spend many a happy hour investigating its properties, but for present purposes the one that stands out is that the terms of each row sum to 2^n. This is indeed magical, and if it relies on a conjuring trick, then it should be possible to explain, in terms of the notion of analyticity, how it works. But one does not need to be Quine to expect a long wait for such an explanation, and for the simple reason that it would itself involve mathematics. By what trickery of analytic prestidigitation, with different expressions meaning the same thing, do the terms in each row sum to a power of 2? Well, one might exclaim, the trick is obvious! Take the binomial expression $(a+b)^n$ and substitute a =b =1: $(1+1)^n = 2^n$. But in what way is this a reductive explanation in terms of the analytic when what it indicates is that mathematics is characterised by interconnection?

Renewing the attack, let us now consider a physical-world probability application, illustrated as follows. Suppose that a bag, A, contains two black balls and six white balls, and a bag, B, a black and a white ball, giving $A(b_2 w_6)$ and $B(b_1 w_1)$. In an experiment a bag is picked at random, and a ball from the bag. The assumption here, for the sake of simplicity and because in practice one assumes it by default, is that the bags are equally likely to be drawn, as are the balls. Let the drawn ball be black, the subject being asked to guess the probability of its coming from bag A. If she is unfamiliar with the probability calculus, she may indeed resort to guesswork — or perhaps her impression is that bag A is the more likely because it contains more black balls than B. Using the conditional probability formula, on the other hand, and with the usual notation, one finds that:

$$P(A|b) = \frac{P(A \cap b)}{P(b)} = \left(\frac{1}{2} \times \frac{1}{4}\right) \div \frac{1}{2}\left(\frac{1}{4} + \frac{1}{2}\right) = \frac{1}{3},$$

so that $P(B|b) = \frac{2}{3}$, which is to say that B is twice as likely as A.

This epistemic inequality may be truth-conditionally interpreted in terms of relative frequency, and as follows if the technicalities are set aside: in a series of trials in which a bag and a ball are picked at random, about a third of the bags from which a black ball is chosen will be A, and about two-thirds B.

But now, the equiprobability of the balls and that of the bags partakes of both fact and logic; the process by which numerical substitution into the formula yields the result $P(B|b) = \frac{2}{3}$ is mathematical, and the results are such as to determine rational choice. That is, one should choose B over A, where this corresponds to relative frequency as a statistical truth condition. How, in that case, could it be denied that this is an example of mathematically derived prediction within a system? If this is not what is meant by mathematical force being exerted in application, then I do not know what is.

I argued earlier, with regard to the number of possible triples of heads and tails given three coins, that it *must* be eight, and that in general the number of arrangements must be 2^r given r coins, this being an instance of synthetic *a priori* truth. There is always, however, a ceteris paribus clause by means of which, or so I shall now maintain, fact and logic may be further assimilated.

Consider the possibility that a geometrical theorem may fail in a particular case. If I draw what I think is a right triangle of sides 3 and 4 inches, except that the hypotenuse when measured turns out to be 5.5 inches, then *either* I have mis-measured, the hypotenuse being 5 inches as required, *or* the triangle is not a right triangle of sides 3 and 4 inches: they could, for instance, both be 4 inches. Moving away from geometrical figures, consider the following inequality argument: if $a > b$ and $b > c$, then $a > c$. Here a, b and c are abstract symbols and " $>$ " means "greater than" and marks the transitive inequality relation between them. Now let a, b and c be planks of wood such that $a > b$ and $b > c$. Then *either $a > c$ or* the failure of the inequality argument requires explanation: perhaps a has shrunk or b has expanded. The possibilities would seem to be endless, but note that they are limited as to type; for they are required to be explanatory, and it is only in a stable world that this requirement can be met. If there were no physical constancy, in particular of length, then the enabling conditions of the inequality would not be satisfied. For instance, the planks would not be such and nothing would count as their shrinking.

This is interesting, even more so if I now maintain that exceptions to a purely contingent rule, to use the old way of speaking, also admit of a limited range of possible explanations. Why, for instance, would a plane crash? Because of pilot health issues, error or sinister intent; because of mechanical or software failure, perhaps linked to poor maintenance; because of a design flaw; because there was a bomb on board or the plane was hit by a rocket or another plane; because of a bird strike or space debris or accidental projectiles from some other source; because of a volcanic eruption; or bad weather, or...aliens; and already we are struggling.

4.3: Are Fact and Logic Now Married?

I believe that they are, this being one of the conclusions in which the work of this chapter will now culminate. The children that issue are a blend of their parents, except perhaps at their extremities, as micro-analysis of their genomes will reveal if the focus is on geometry and then on probability, each subjected to less formal scrutiny than before. Taking geometry first, we shall initially use the term in a very general sense as applying to the constraints imposed on particular shapes and their continuations; for it is obvious enough that a visual appearance from one perspective is accountable to change of appearance from adjacent points of view. Looking at the speaker next to this monitor, I see it as an oblong object, thereby expecting it to present itself accordingly if I turn it slightly, and then again, or if I look behind it. This, however, needs to be properly balanced, for what is also the case is that from any particular perspective the constraints on appearance are limited, beyond which the possible configurations are spoilt for choice, the only way to zoom in on them being to look and see.

For instance, the back of the speaker, which I can see not at all, enjoys a great deal of freedom of shape within certain constraints imposed by the way in which it appears to me. Since the back is less than two inches away from the wall, as far as I can tell when seated here, there cannot be a design feature that juts out more than that distance—or not unless, quite oddly, it goes into the wall. But then I would very likely have noticed and would now remember not being able to lift or move the speaker. None of this is being denied or overlooked when I now propose a thesis about applied geometry and necessary conditions of perception.

Perhaps we may start with examples of such conditions. An object of uniform thickness will have a shape on one side that is the obverse of its shape on the other unless it is flat, which is a limiting case. If an object is curved from one perspective it must be curved from others. If an object appears to have a particular three-dimensional shape from one perspective, and then from others, the different appearances must dovetail together, which is to say in conformity with geometry. If an object seen from a particular perspective has partially occluded features— which is always the case— then very likely the hidden lines and surfaces will be continuations of what can be seen; otherwise it would be by coincidence that the discontinuity occurs at the very point where one feature is hidden by another.

But let us now go deeper, nothing having been said so far about the link between geometrical projection and the sense of sight. When I look at an object, I see it from a particular perspective by which the apparent shape of the object accords with projective geometry as it enters into the science of optics in connection with vision. It is through the sense of sight that the science of optics has been developed and applied to that sense, the point being that projective geometry enters into the science and informs our visual perceptions. When a draughtsman draws a box on paper the drawing is two-dimensional but we see the box as three-dimensional, as if the drawing is a projection of the box onto a plane surface. That we should take the theorems of this form of geometry to be correct, assuming that we have at least a basic grasp of optics, is a necessary condition of our trust in the deliverances of the visual sense.

As regards probability, consider the attacks on the World Trade Centre in September 2001. When the first plane struck the North Tower, no-one seemed to know what to think; but that uncertainty lasted only until, about twenty minutes later, the second plane hit the South Tower. It immediately became a coordinated terrorist attack; and yet, the first plane also had a probability link, not to a recent event but to the bombing of the World Trade Centre in February 1993. One could enquire into similarity and difference here, perhaps under the rubric of the psychology of probability reasoning; or one could attempt to bring the calculus of chances into play, with selections from equiprobable alternatives yielding a probability ratio. That attempt would perhaps be very difficult or very easy, this latter reminiscent of previous remarks about its always being possible to rationalise prediction in terms of induction, something thereby being missed. The overlooked object is perhaps the same here, for even if applying the calculus presents difficulties, one can always fall back on what is known as the no-miracles argument, as in "If we assume that the first crash was accidental, then a second such event, whether accidental or not, would be too improbable even to contemplate". But if we are to be dismissive, albeit only up to a point, of the giving of reasons, hence the reference to rationalisation in the sense used by psychologists, then in what way do we propose to fill the gap? What, in other words, is the missing object?

The missing object is the fact that we just *have* the mental states by which reasoning unfolds, for instance in the case of the sudden certainty, when the second plane struck, that the two events were connected by design. We just *have* a memory, expectation or belief, all of which have experiential correlates in some cases, as with sudden certainty or a memory appearing out of nowhere, or with perceptual expectation that simply is there, at least before we seek the source of it. Even in this latter case, however, the epistemic link is via memory, for instance if I expect a label to appear when I turn this wine bottle in my hands, having seen the label when I picked the bottle up. And the memory is just there, even if we do not experience it in that way, so that it still is the case that we just *have* the memory.

What follows is that if we just *have* a belief, which we may or may not associate with probability, and if in the former case we appeal to the no-miracles argument, or if we do not but are simply aware that probability is in play, perhaps in the form of our belief that an event is probable, then the focus is on whether probability theory can be appealed to, irrespective of whether we are aware of it at the time. This greater scope manifests itself in an extended probability space in which much of what we believe gains epistemic licence. One example would be that of the destruction of the Twin Towers; another, more generally, would be that of the mutual support enjoyed by memory and expectation, the former giving rise to the latter, the fulfilment of which confirms the memory, sometimes very strongly indeed, as when they both enter into perception. In that case the no-miracles argument may be adduced, or one may simply declare that the juxtaposition of the relevant events cannot be coincidental.

Again consider any everyday state of affairs, say that of being seated, and now try to list the very strong probabilities in attendance. Very likely you cannot think of even one, either because of over-familiarity or because there simply do not seem to be any, and certainly none that you are aware of by virtue of being seated. We have, however, gone beyond awareness, our concern being with possible, not actual, probability support. To begin with, it is virtually certain—in fact certain— that at some point in the last twelve hours you sat in that chair, this being the only possible explanation of why you are now seated in it if you do not remember differently. Also, that the monitor in front of you was there when you sat down if you have no memory of its being disconnected and removed and then re-installed. You would, after all, have noticed, particularly as you are sitting directly in front of it. Also, that a myriad other items in your study have certainties or strong probabilities attached, such that there is no evidence pointing the other way. This, as we know, is all that is required, the allusion being to necessary evidential conditions in relation to underdetermination.

What is true of probability is, as we have seen, true of induction; but now let us take it further, for we are left with memory and expectation, each amenable to the same treatment given their interdependence, and also with the concept of the past. What is it that recollective memory consists in? Well, it is via memory that one becomes aware of past events—but if we ask about the nature of past events, they are just events that have occurred; but what is it for them to have occurred? It is, surely, for them to be past events. Very well, then perhaps we may exit the loop via memory; but without it we should know nothing of the past, and then a question arises as to whether the concept of the past would still be available, bound up as it seems to be with that of memory. This implies not synonymy but the feeding of one concept off others, which is to say within a system. What, though, of the intentionality of the concepts thereby circulating? But the intentional is irreducible, a thesis arising from, among other things, the experience of remembering a thing. We know that the phenomenal cannot be dissected out from the intentional in the case of memory, for then there would not, for instance, be memory images but only mental images. There is nothing in the concept of memory by which it appropriates to itself a separate identity from that of belief that reaches into the past, and by the same token we know that the concepts of memory and expectation are interdependent, so that this latter, too, belongs within a system. That memory and the past are conceptually interdependent is proved,

136

if proof is needed, by a *reductio ad absurdum* argument, the same as in establishing the interdependence of memory and expectation.

The startling difference, however, is that these latter are clearly distinct, whereas the memory of an event and the belief that it occurred are not, or not in such a way that the appeal to memory vindicates the belief. On the contrary, the appeal to recollective memory goes further out on a limb, implying as it does a causal connection between the event and its recall. It only seems to be justificatory, an impression that lapses if one speaks not of memory but of the belief that the event occurred and caused the belief—or simply that it occurred.

It is clear by now, I trust, that the foregoing prefigures our theory of consciousness in which the non-conscious is paramount, this being in line with the fact of just *having* a memory, the surface features of which lend themselves to experiential suddenness, as when a memory knocks out of nowhere at the door. But it may be said of any memory, whether cold-calling or not, that we just *have* it, and very often that nothing is lost, at least at the surface, if we speak not of memory but of our belief that an event has occurred. Witness the ways in which the notion of memory is used non-recollectively, as when we say that we can recite a poem by heart, despite having no memory of learning it by rote. Similarly, I speak English because I remember it, but since I have no recollection of learning all those words, the appeal to memory is presumably a theory of language acquisition. Thus, it is that we just *have* our beliefs, a fact concealed under cover of the notions of memory, expectation and the past, aided and abetted by intellectual rationalisation in the form of giving reasons that seem to fit. The metaphysical implications of these findings will be teased out when the theory of consciousness is fully discussed.

But still, and in conclusion, the universe has much explaining to do, and new theories or insights only seem to intensify the need for explanation. We can emphasise the similarities between our epistemic approach to maths and to matters of fact; we can point to the existence of necessary perceptual conditions in relation to applied geometry and specify them insofar as it is possible— but the expression on the face of reality does not change. That said, can we at least account for the impassivity—or, better, the Sphinx-like physiognomy? Well, it is partly that mathematics, whether pure or applied, is a mystery unto itself, and entirely unperturbed by any attempt on my part to mediate between fact and logic and promote harmony between them. A brick building, after all, retains its opacity no matter how bright the stars that shine upon it. Speaking of which, a brick being a perceptual object, the chapter on perception is next, about which we have already mentioned necessary conditions; but also, we have hinted at the interdependence of different perspectives on the same object. Time, then, to move on.

Chapter 5: The Problem of Perception

The problem I shall try to resolve concerns itself with what is given in perception, or really given, and with the relation it bears to sensory experience on the one hand and physical reality on the other. Our primary senses, either singly or in concert, open a window onto the external world; and when other senses also play a part, including those pertaining to bodily awareness, they are the means by which we engage with the landscape thus revealed, perception and movement combining into action. Corresponding to the contours of this landscape there is, however, a conceptual terrain whose fault lines may seem to threaten continuity of thought. Surveying it, one may be struck by the subjectivity of perceptual awareness, as with vision, so that one focuses on the phenomenal character of seeing, thereby reducing it to visual sensation. But this conception of what it is to see is now confronted by the certainty one has that visual experience reveals an objectively real physical world capable of existing unperceived. The resulting conflict may then seem irresolvable, with opposing sides separated by a chasm of apparent paradox.

Such a conflict, inherent in the relation between the physical and the mental, may be represented at the level of theory by the opposition between phenomenalism and direct realism, the middle ground being occupied by various forms of indirect realism. In what follows I shall defend the view that phenomenalism and indirect realism are untenable, thereby paving the way for the reestablishment of direct realism in its native habitat, located within a system, of common sense about perception. The reasoning by which its competitors are eliminated will, I hope, be such as to remove the difficulties they were intended to resolve.

That said, it seems to me that the fault lines really exist and are permanent, their origins too deep, and that the apparently anomalous nature of the discontinuous conceptual strata of perception will always pose a philosophical threat. When we struggle across fractured ridges of thought, our preconceptions dragging us down, it is the sudden falling away of familiarity as a form of understanding, the horizontal become vertical and then vertiginous, and the impression of incompatible elevations, which engenders a sense of paradoxical unease; and to overcome it we need to gain the higher peaks from which the fault lines are less pronounced, merging as they do into a panoramic view of the system as a whole. From that vantage point, and employing this very notion of a system, we may come to see that the apparent shearing away of one concept from another derives from too narrow a view, the opening out of which reveals the slips and separations of the land to be surface features. What is also made manifest, however, is that such features have an impenetrable subterranean origin, so that the paradox, together with a resolution of the perception problem, merge into a profound mystery, one which reverberates from the centre of the world.

Let us begin with a survey of the irregularities of terrain just contemplated, starting with the observation that the content of perceptual experience depends on a multiplicity of factors which combine to vary the appearance of even the most solid and stable of objects, such as pebbles, tables and telephone boxes. Thus, this table in front of me presents itself as being subject to the play of light and shadow, as also to apparent change of shape according to perspective, or when objects are placed on it, or when I close one eye or when I close both, this latter causing the table to disappear altogether. What is also deemed relevant is the possibility of perceptual illusion, as with a straight stick, or even a telephone box, looking bent in water, or of perceptual error, as when we entertain hallucinations under the influence of, for example, recreational drugs. And, too, it is taken to be of sceptical significance that perceptual content is causally dependent on sense organs and nervous system. Finally, there is the fact that physical objects look different, oddly enough, at the microscopic level, the other senses losing all purchase on them, and that they fall away from the sense of sight, too, when the world of the sub-atomic exerts its pull and vanish into the black hole of quantum physics.

5.1: The Argument from Illusion

Clearly, these facts about perception are diverse, but their unifying feature is that they may suggest that physical objects are not directly perceived, or not in a way that accords with common sense. This is the conclusion of what is known as the argument from illusion, which initially we shall consider in relation to its treatment in A.D.Smith's *The Problem of Perception*. Smith is of the view that the argument should be taken seriously, and although he does not subscribe to it, he presents it in great detail and breaks it down into several steps. He begins by targeting what he refers to as basic perceptible features, about which he claims that if an object appears to a perceiver to exhibit such a feature but in reality does not, then that feature or apparent feature is nevertheless instantiated in his perceptual experience of the object. Using Smith's example, if a white wall looks yellow to me, where yellow is a basic feature, then, as he would put it, *something* is yellow, the reference being to a sense datum. We now have the sense datum inference thesis, for instance with regard to colour, according to which the immediate objects of one's colour awareness in cases of perceptual illusion are not, or not straightforwardly, the physical surfaces in which the colours apparently inhere; rather, one is directly aware of non-physical sense data which exist or occur only when perceived. Taking a further step, Smith now presents the sense-datum infection thesis, which again applies to all the senses. It states that if some features of an object are illusory, so that one's direct awareness is of sense data, then this is true of all features of the object in that sense field. Using vision as an example, he points out that the shape of an object is defined by the pattern of colour it presents; therefore, if its colour is illusory then so is its shape. Thus, if the yellow appearance of a white wall is a sense datum, then so is the shape-appearance of the wall, one's visual experience of the wall being of sense data and nothing else. The final step in the argument from illusion is that in which the sense-datum inference is generalised to cover veridical as well as illusory perception. What lends itself to this extension is the claim that illusory perception may be phenomenally indistinguishable from perceptual experience of real as opposed to illusory features of the physical world. Smith indicates that he takes the argument from illusion and the direct realism to which it is opposed, as being rooted in the everyday perceptual concepts that in some sense they systematise. What is quite striking about the theory just outlined is that it takes no account of

141

perceptual intentionality — a concomitant, one might think, of its emphasis on basic perceptible features.

That said, Smith now takes issue with the defence of direct realism mounted by those he refers to as new realists, whose contention is that in many cases of illusion the illusory feature attaches to the object in the same was as its other features, so that it has ontological parity with them. Thus, a straight stick looking bent in water is a publicly observable phenomenon, as is a white wall looking yellow if suitably illuminated. These visual appearances are explicable in terms of the behaviour of light and the properties of the bodies it acts upon, and they are just as genuine as those that we certify as real. Smith would seem to concede this point, his rejoinder being that in any case there are forms of illusion that are rooted in psychology or physiology, so that they are subjective in character. By way of example, he adduces the fact that the apparent colour of an object may change if it is juxtaposed with contrasting colours. And, too, when a colour-blind person sees a red object as green, this is not because of any change in the object itself or its illumination, the same being true if an individual becomes myopic. Subjective illusions also occur, or conceivably could occur, in the case of the other senses, he thinks, and it is mainly by appeal to subjective illusion that he rejects the new realists' proposed solution to the problem of perception.

5.2: Parting of the Ways

Perhaps it is time to intervene, the place to start being with Smith's contention that the difference between objective and subjective illusion is a sceptically significant one. Since it seems to me to be no such thing, I shall advance arguments to that effect, the first of which exploits the fact that all perception depends on the physiology of the perceiver; and, too, that the distinction in question is not dichotomous. For much of what one perceives is mediated by events interposed between oneself and object without impinging on the object itself. Looking at this black monitor stand on the table at which I am seated, I see it as blurred because my glasses are smudged. Is this an illusion, even on Smith's easy-going construal of the term? If so, then perhaps we should

142

say that it is an objective illusion, for it cannot be subjective in the sense of being purely physiological. Very well, but what if I clean and replace my glasses, the stand now more sharply in focus? Is this the way the stand really looks or does it count as an objective illusion? We need not worry, for in either case a sudden switch must take place, if Smith is correct, when I now remove my glasses again, given that myopia is purely physiological and that I now have a blurred image of the stand. But the blurriness is partly a temporary effect of my having just removed my glasses, so it is anyone's guess as to how we should categorise it. The point I wish to make, in any case, is that there is no sceptically significant difference between looking at an object with smudged glasses, with clean ones and with the naked eye. The difference, in fact, is explanatory, for in the first case I would say that the stand looks blurred because my glasses need cleaning. in the second that it looks clearer because I am wearing corrective lenses, and in the third that it looks blurred again partly because I am short-sighted and have just taken my glasses off.

Let us now reinforce this point at the same time as we also challenge the sceptical reading of the distinction between appearance and reality. Suppose this time that I watch a red tractor being driven into an alfalfa field and that it thereby acquires a purplish hue; then I will say that the tractor is red but looks purple, and perhaps I will give an explanation. But if the tractor continues to look purple after exiting the field, then perhaps it is because I replaced my glasses with purple-tinted ones, in which case everything looks purple, not just the tractor, the question of generality always being a prime consideration with regard to observational explanation. There again, perhaps I believe, on the basis of a recent shower of purple rain, that everything really has turned purple. If the tractor appears purple out of the field, but not everything else, there will be possible circumstances in which the explanation would be that I have become colour blind for red, which I see as purple, depending on what I now see when I look at objects I know to be that colour. Clearly, one could expatiate on the assertibility conditions that govern the everyday distinction between apparent and genuine red objects, as also purple ones, as also the colours by which I perceive other people and bring testimony into play. What I shall now suggest is that the sceptical view of the nature of perceptual illusion is thereby undermined.

To see this, note first that it is not as if the red tractor's looking purple in the field is a rare event, decidedly out of the ordinary, such that red objects and purple ones almost always look red and purple respectively. On the contrary, an object that always looked uniformly red would violate not only colour-ascription conditions but also the established laws of optics and perhaps others in physics more generally. Imagine seeing it the same whether short- or long-sighted, in the dark the same as in the light, this latter on a cloudy day the same as in full sunshine, with no contrast between the sunlit and the shaded sides of the object, or between the object close-up and at a distance. If this is correct, then colour variation according to circumstance, whether objective, subjective, both or neither, is a necessary condition of colour ascription, whether in relation to objects that vary in colour or to those that are constant in this respect. What is true of colour is also true of shape or size and therefore of visual properties in general, a concomitant of which is that it must also be true of all the senses. This conclusion is borne out by even the most cursory glance at what it is to touch, hear, taste, smell, or otherwise perceive if one is a bat, an object in the physical world. Such necessary conditions of perceptual variability provide the framework in which apparent and real observational features may be distinguished, that distinction therefore being unconducive to the argument from illusion.

5.3: Perceptual Variability and Illusion

But is this really true? A.J.Ayer would say that it is perceptual variability itself that is problematic, irrespective of the argument from illusion. If an object which persists over time, the usual example being one which in itself changes very slowly, such as a pebble, is known to us only by its appearances, which vary according to conditions, then in what sense, he asks, does it preserve its physical identity? How, in other words, are we to distinguish between the object and the range of appearances by which it manifests itself to the perceiver? In *The Concept of a Person*

(1973: p.78) Ayer follows Russell in detecting a difficulty here, and it is one which obliges him, he thinks, to treat appearances as entities in their own right. This is a pivotal point, but we have pivoted on it already, in view of which it suffices, by way of addressing Ayer's concerns, to repeat that perceptual variability is indeed fundamental and thereby immune to scepticism. Remember that since this cannot be radical scepticism, in the sense of entailing solipsism, it would have to be moderate scepticism which is to say that Ayer must be understood as insisting only that there is a case to answer, the existence of the physical world not being in question. But then, the answer is all around us, for we do not live in a mirror-world, as it were, in which only reflections or appearances are encountered. We live in a world of physical objects, and it is these that I see, and what I see is not an appearance but an object, object-part or event as it appears in the particular perceptual or observational conditions. Similarly, what I hear is a skylark or the sound of one, the singer thereby announcing its physical presence.

But surely, it might be said, the particular fact of perceptual illusion does pose a sceptical problem, even if the general fact of perceptual variability, at least in some cases, does not. Suppose that a normally sighted and a colour-blind person are looking at the same time at a red post box. The one sees it as red, the other as green, say, but it cannot be both red and green at the same time; therefore, and arguably as a synthetic *a priori* truth, it must be at most the one, the other then being illusory. But now, this is to ignore the point I made, which concerns not the bare fact of what the sceptic takes to be illusion but its analysis and sceptical import. I argued that the sceptical distinction between genuine and illusory perception necessarily involves perceptual variability, which includes apparent perceptual conflict of the kind in question, instances of which are ubiquitous across the senses. If the two observers of the post box are at different distances from it, then they see it as different in size; and now it might as well be said that it cannot be different sizes at the same time. But then there would be no post box, with all that this implies about numerical identity, for the argument from illusion to gain purchase on.

145

The fact just is that perceptual illusion, as conceived of by the sceptic, most likely the sense-datum theorist, equates with perceptual variability, not with the misperception conscripted into the imperialist forces of the argument from illusion. That is, the sceptic commandeers the ordinary distinction between illusory and veridical perception, gives it ontological muscle and invades the South Seas of perceptual variability. Ordinarily we speak of a straight stick looking bent in water or a bent stick looking straight or more bent, thereby distinguishing between veridical and illusory perception, not sceptically but in recognition of the possibility of being observationally misled; for instance, if one feels about in the water and expects to find the stick where visually it appears to be. The implication here, however, is that expectation enters into perception, so that immediately we break free of sceptical constraints and embrace the theory of intrinsic perceptual variability and intentionality mentioned in previous chapters and developed in this one.

5.4: Can Sense Data be Located in Perceptual Experience?

The sceptical thesis with which we have grappled is that the fact of perceptual illusion entails the existence of sense data. We have, I believe, shredded the sails of that thesis, with radical perceptual scepticism now listing to starboard, but we still have work to do, our concern being with the terminology and concepts of sense-datum theory. Far from their being elucidatory of perceptual experience, it seems to me that they derive from everyday physical-world or perceptual concepts being press-ganged into a servitude all at sea, the sceptic on the bridge having to cope with an unruly crew. To prove myself wrong, perhaps I should indulge the sense-datum theorist by trying to reconcile sense data and actual visual experience. If we consider a particular object such as a bird in a cage, which in the present circumstances can only be a parrot, then our aim is to see it in a way that would vindicate sense-datum theory.

To that end, one could narrow one's focus until a two-dimensional coloured shape is all that can be seen. A pocket lens might be useful here or one could pick up the parrot and hold it very close to one's eyes, thereby reducing it to a patch of blue and yellow. These are not, except in the case of a very short-sighted tropical-bird keeper, standard observational conditions; and one wonders how the visually impaired aviarist, even if he is a philosophically motivated genius at jigsaws, proposes to construct the physical world, visually perceived, out of colour patches. Better, one might think, to zoom out a little, to hold the parrot a little further away, the coloured patches thereby acquiring spatial depth. If this also fails, the reason is not that there are always going to be pieces left over and others that don't fit, or that the finished product will turn out to be deceased. The reason is that the flat or curved colour patches have conflicting demands made on them, for they have to be both non-physical and, when zoomed out or held further away, apparently part of the physical surface of the parrot. But then we see them as object-parts, and even when viewed as flat colour patches they appear to occupy physical space.

In view of the foregoing, the sense-datum theorist mistakenly believes that the existence of sense data follows from that of perceptual illusion; and, too, that sense data are exhibited in actual perceptual experience. How, in particular, are visual sense data to be aligned with seeing physical objects as exhibiting spatial depth in three-dimensional surroundings? So far, we have traded on their being misaligned; hence the quixotic attempt to identify the sense data of the parrot with blurred-parrot images in visual-distortion space. But how could it possibly succeed? The result, irrespective of the distortion, would still be a physical feature; but sense data are required to be perception-dependent, which would suggest that they are items of perceptual consciousness. The problem here, given the sense-datum theorist's aversion to perceptual intentionality, is that the collapse of perception into its conscious interface with the physical world would be solipsistic, which is contrary to common sense and, indeed, to basic sanity. Since the putative middle ground between the mental and the physical has now turned into a quagmire, it would seem that there is no point in the sceptic continuing to tilt at that particular windmill, for the anti-sceptic will always be able to unhorse her.

5.5: Sense Data Abstractly Posited

But is it not possible, one might ask, that sense data should be regarded as neither physical nor mental nor intermediate between them? They fall, rather, into the category of mysterious theoretical entity, imposed on us by the argument from illusion and other forms of scepticism about perception. The fact is, however, that we have to be able to connect the notion of a sense datum with established perceptual concepts, as indeed is implied in the argument from illusion. We are told that when we see a red post box as purple, perhaps in the middle of an alfalfa field, then something is purple, namely a sense datum, and that it is the bearer of the phenomenal quality of purple, the sense datum being what we actually see or "see". And now, a multitude of questions and comments immediately raise their hands, where these include a query as to whether it means anything to speak of a sense datum as being a bearer in this way. Suppose that the sceptic's rejoinder is that it is no use claiming that only a physical object, given its numerical identity, can be a bearer in the required sense, for a sense datum is a special theoretical entity, completely alien to one's acquaintance with the physical and the mental, such that it is perfectly capable of being inhered in by, say, the phenomenal quality of purple. Suppose further that a rejoinder of this kind confronts any anti-sceptical argument premised on requiring the sceptic to assimilate sense data to the physical or the mental. Then the sceptic wins a Pyrrhic victory by bringing all discussion of her views to a deeply unsatisfactory end.

Time, I think, to lighten up a little, now that the sunrise of the second part of this chapter, with all its dispelling of the opacities of sense-datum theory and perceptual scepticism more generally, is on the horizon. Heading west, let us consider the difficulties that, if I could make sense-datum theory come true, this being the right time of year, I would encounter in posting a Christmas card. When I look at a post box I recognise it as such by its mouth always being open and by its red surface, except that this could easily be some other colour, provided that *some* colour gives it shape – otherwise it becomes an invisible box, one which I would have to locate by touch, sound or smell, or possibly taste. Let it be red, then, my encounter being with a standard post box, one which is out in all weathers waiting to be fed. But how is this to be accomplished? How am I to post a Christmas card, or the sense datum of it, into the sense datum of a post box? The positing of some kind of primary analogue of the physical, a parallel post box itself beyond the reach of vision but known by its visual sense data, is not going to be of any practical help; and to speak of an unperceivable "physical" realm in this way is, to say the least of it, to invite scepticism as to semantic content. We are left with sense data in their own right, except that they exist only when perceived; and what this means in practice is that my card is unlikely to be delivered on time, despite being posted first class, for I cease to experience it as a sense datum as soon as I drop it into the sense datum of the box. Even if the postman happens to drive up at that very moment I cannot rely on her to keep looking at the card in order to maintain its existence, for she, too, is a sense datum, one which ceases to exist when back in the sense datum of the Royal Mail van. We have said enough, I believe, to establish that the theory of sense data is no longer in contention.

5.6: Primary and Secondary Qualities

The distinction between primary and secondary qualities belongs to John Locke's theory of perception, the essence of which is that the primary qualities of shape, size and motion belong to the structure of the physical world, whereas secondary qualities of colour, taste, smell and so on are subjective in their effects. This is to say that the primary physical properties of an object determine the qualitative or phenomenal character of our perceptual experience of it, this being a reference to sensory qualities. Thus a standard post box, though not itself coloured, has objective properties such as to cause, or to be disposed to cause, one's visual experience of the colour red when looking at the box.

But now, an obvious difficulty presents itself, for shape, according to Locke (1997), is a primary quality and colour is a secondary quality. What this indicates, in my view, is that Locke's theory is untenable, this being a conclusion deducible from the fact that colour defines shape, as also from the implausibility of the Lockean thesis about secondary qualities. Taking this latter first, we are invited to believe that to see the coloured surface of a physical object, as common sense would phrase it, is to have a visual experience such as is produced in us by a property or disposition of the physical object. This, as it stands, is truistic, for we already know that perceptual experience, at least of the objective kind, is externally caused by its objects. What is needed, if the secondary quality thesis is to be of interest, is that it should imply that the everyday belief that colour inheres in physical objects, foisted upon us by the phenomenology of seeing, is erroneous or in need of re-formulation. If we consider the possibility of error, this would mean that our seeing colours as inhering in physical surfaces is misconceived and incorrect. Since that is what we are convinced, even upon reflection, that we see and that others also see, other things being equal, this is a counter-intuitive implication of the secondary quality colour thesis, the evidence for which would have to be convincing, especially in view of its targeting colour but not shape.

Not only that but it would also have to be such as to impart sense to the secondary quality thesis — for what exactly does it mean? By way of answer, one cannot appeal to the everyday distinction between real and illusory colour, and the reason is that the thesis is meant to apply to veridical colour perception. Very well, then perhaps what is meant is that a wall, for example, is out there in all its three-dimensional solidity, whereas its colour is just a chromatic conscious item inside my colourless head. But we are back to this not being my experience at all, which is that of seeing the coloured exterior surfaces of the wall; so the question of meaning still awaits an answer. I know what it is to hallucinate an object, say this tiny kangaroo on my keyboard, and if it were real I would know what it was to misperceive its colour; but I do not know what it is to see it as being coloured when it is not. What we return to, then, is the fact that colour defines shape, in which case Locke's distinction is unsound.

With Locke's theory it is just about possible, I suppose, to read a semblance of sense into it, for instance if we look at a football and try to imagine it as an empty circle, one which we fill with colour by utilizing our palette of subjective colour paint.

The result would be a disc, not a ball, but practice makes perfect and in any case it hardly matters, the point being that we at least think — wrongly because a circle is not colourless — that this helps us to grasp the concepts involved in the claim that some of what we take to be objective features of the world are in fact subjective. That said, we should not be deterred from distinguishing in some other way between subjective and objective aspects of perception, since clearly they both obtain, as is immediately apparent if we consider the non-visual senses. It is arguable, indeed, that a philosophy of perception in which the visual sense was out of bounds would be more clear-sighted than is the case with the terminological impairment of vision that results from focussing on the sense of sight. Suppose, for instance, that I am listening to the song of a skylark on a bright summer's day; and now ask how exactly my auditory perception should be analysed into components in the form of sense data and phenomenal qualities. 'With great difficulty', one might reply, the reason for which is that the notion of perceptual intentionality is anathema to the sense-datum theorist. That being the case, his analysis would be in terms of auditory sensation, but the hearing of a trilling sound is perceptual, which is to say that it conveys physical-world information, as do all the other senses. Time, then, to bring perceptual intentionality down to the ground.

Chapter 6: Intentionality and Perceptual Scepticism

What is it about sense-datum theory and its phenomenological approach to perceptual analysis that renders the whole enterprise unseaworthy? This is rather like asking what it is about a tattered old millionaire that an attractive young blonde finds irresistible, one answer being that there are aspects of her wealth which take his breath away. What the sense-datum theorist's account of perception entirely neglects is the notion of intentionality and inference, which are taken to be extraneous to the essential nature of perception. This, as indicated in the last chapter, is the source of much that is unbelievable in sense-datum theory, so that it is time, perhaps, to prepare the ground for an entirely different treatment: one which takes intentionality and inference to be intrinsic to perception, the analysis of which will involve the notion of a system. What can already be said, in very general terms, is that this is a system of connections and necessary conditions within and between the senses, such that their deliverances presuppose the existence of the physical world. What I suggest is that initially we should target perceptual inference and intentionality as they enter not only into sight but also into hearing — in fact into all the senses.

6.1: Intrinsic Visual Inference and Necessity

Reprising the argument in the first chapter by which the intrinsic perceptual inference thesis was introduced, suppose that I report that I am looking at this keyboard, the palm rest of which I see as curved, my seeing of it being an occurrent perceptual event. Yet what I see at one moment or from one perspective is evidentially accountable to further perceptual experience. If I move my head a little to the side, I expect the palm rest to continue to look curved and any newly visible part of it to dovetail with the old. Such micro-expectations, as I call them, are necessary to perception, as is perceptual expectation at further remove. If I hold the keyboard at eye level, turning it until it is end-on, then I expect to see the palm rest in curved profile, confirmatory of its previous appearance and of the corresponding perceptual beliefs. A condition here is that I remember that appearance and, since the keyboard is a solid, stable object, that I expect it to persist from one moment to the next, other things being equal, and to be able to re-identify it. Note, crucially, that necessary conditions are involved at all points. For instance, the distinction between correct and incorrect memory or expectation as it enters into perception is applicable in any particular case, but only within a framework in which the other memories and expectations on which applied criteria of correctness depend are themselves taken for granted along with memory and expectation in general. This has already been explained in more detail in previous chapters.

Audition belongs to what is known as distance perception, the reason for which will become apparent if we now subject it to analysis, both for its own sake and in order to locate within it the required intrinsic properties. Since, to begin with, we speak of hearing a sound, it might be thought that the auditory object is the sound itself. But although there is much that is of interest in the way in which we speak of sounds as if they were substantive perceptual objects, it is difficult to separate a sound from the hearing of it, even given that the sound is public in the sense that other people in the vicinity would also, other things being equal, be expected to hear it. A sound is intentional and imparts information, which even at its most scanty will signpost, however vaguely, the source direction. If the sound is recognised, its physical source identified, then one may associate it with the object heard, as when one says of a trilling sound that one can hear a skylark. This demonstrates very clearly the inferential character of audition. At this point, by the way, one may be tempted to try to analyse the co-dependency of the senses, for instance as it concerns audition and vision. This would be interesting, no doubt, and to some extent one would rely on the notion of conceivability, for instance in finding it difficult to conceive of audition without vision; but it just is a fact that congenitally blind people hear perfectly well, and that they gather information about the physical world via the intentionality of the senses. Thus it is that the temptation, in my view, should be resisted, the existence of epistemic limitations thereby being recognised as a first step towards acceptance of irreducibility and mystery.

That being the case, perhaps we should ask what it is that perceptual intentionality consists in, given its intimacy with inference. My answer, or first answer, is that intentionality as it enters into perception is irreducible, though not in such a way as to preclude analysis in terms of a system across and within the sense modalities. That said, it is possible to argue against this answer as follows, the focus being on audition. To hear a skylark singing is to register a sound sequence, which itself, phenomenologically, is to have an auditory sensation. The picture thus painted is of the intentionality of perception reduced to perceptual sensations and the memories, expectations, inferences and connections by which in occurent and dispositional form the mind operates on such sensations and turns them into perceptual processes. This picture is flawed in two ways, the first of which is that if the physical world reduces to a realm of sensation, which is to say of pure sensory experience then its only occupant, no matter how it is organised, is the solipsist, about which no more need be said. The point is not that perception does not belong within a system but that it is a system in which perceptual intentionality is irreducible. Secondly, the picture in question is in any case inclusive of intentionality, as manifested in memory, expectation and inference.

If we focus on memory, the problem of its intentionality revolves around conceptual conflict and is ultimately irresolvable, for it cannot be forced into a lower orbit, perhaps in the hope that it will burn itself out in the atmosphere of bafflement that surrounds the main body of one's understanding. How can these conscious phenomena, these mental images, mental sentences and nostalgic feelings constitute my memory of that afternoon with my sweet love long ago! The answer, of course, is that thus characterised they cannot, for my description is phenomenological. What it entirely bales out with the seawater is that I remember those events, something I know to be both irreducibly intentional and to involve a conscious recollective process. I cannot reconcile inert mental image with memory image, this latter differentiated in virtue of its intentionality, which is both irreducible and perplexing. This is a reminder of comprehension deepening into

154

the appreciation of mystery; for it is at this point that we have to disembark and wade through the evening surf into a different darkness from that of resolvable philosophical problems. This does not preclude our shining a light into the undergrowth and onto a theory we are already acquainted with: that experience is constituted by the conscious and the non-conscious, this latter being the operations room of intentionality.

6.2: Perceptual Intentionality

Our present concern is with what it is to perceive an object in one way rather than another, or in each way at a different time, and I suggest that we focus again on audition. I hear a trilling sound, for instance, as being external to my body, unlike tinnitus, the difference between them, with regard to the auditory experience itself, being traceable to its intentional character. Suppose, then, that two people hear the sound, one of them an ornithologist and the other newly emerged from a subterranean cave. If this is the first time for her to see the sky, let alone locate a sound in it, then clearly her experience of the sound might be different from the ornithologist's, the troglodyte not hearing it as external to her body, and not, in any case, as birdsong. The point is that such intentionality is perceptually significant only within a system, one in which it manifests itself in the interplay between those experiences that exhibit it or occur within a framework in which it is exhibited. It also manifests itself in the form of actual or dispositional relations within perceptual experiences. Thus the ornithologist, as compared with the troglodyte, may have a different auditory experience, and in any case is differently disposed in any of a multitude of ways, each of them, if realised, involving further occurrent and dispositional differences. If we focus on perception as a process, then the differences between the two observers quickly become apparent as events unfold. It is likely, for instance, that the ornithologist's experience of the trilling sound will be epistemically richer, especially if he cocks his head, a habit he picked up from birds, all the better to attune himself to distance and direction, whereupon he shields his eyes from the sun and scans a particular region of the sky. He would say, no doubt, that in listening to the trilling sound, he hears it as the song of a skylark. The troglodyte, meanwhile, listens to the trilling sound for itself and appreciates its insistent cheerfulness. If the ornithologist is able to spot the skylark, he perhaps descries it as a black speck in blue space or as an amorphous blur which nevertheless is the still centre of such clarity of song. It is a distant object, too tiny to exhibit spatial depth but embedded in a voluminous sky.

Let us begin to go deeper, the need for which arises as follows: firstly, the ornithologist claims to hear a trilling sound as the song of a skylark; secondly, he claims to see a black dot in a blue sky as the bird itself. If these claims are correct, or if we can make sense of them, then the intentionality involved goes far beyond seeing an object, say the skylark, as three-dimensional or as a skylark on closer examination, when that is the way it looks. As for hearing it as the song of a skylark, we already know that one hears it as external to one's body, this being intrinsic to one's registering of the sound, which to that extent is intentional. But once this is recognised, as against the sound being purely phenomenal, the difference between the external source experience and hearing the sound as the song of a skylark is only one of degree. What I suggest is that we compare different interpretations of the same sound. Suppose that on a previous day in the summer I was, vertically speaking, in the vicinity of birds, butterflies also being needed so let us include them, when all at once I heard a trilling sound, which I interpreted, in the usual way, as being made by a skylark. Judging by the sound, I expected the source to be high up and almost overhead, which indeed is where I saw it when I craned my neck and looked into the sky. Clearly, the inferential step from sound to source is contingent at this level of detail, such that it might have been a butterfly that I expected to see, given that they, too, are known to behave irrationally at altitude, albeit not in the form of breaking into song. Suppose, though, that that is what I did indeed see, hence my conversion to the view that the trilling sound is made not by skylarks but by butterflies. Now take it that re-visiting the scene I find myself listening to a trilling sound again, which this time I hear as the song of a butterfly, much to the astonishment of my companion, a lepidopterist, with whom I have shared my discovery. Then I ex-

156

pect to see a butterfly if I look up; and if it fluttered down and perched on a finger of my outstretched hand, I would presumably expect to see its mouth, if I could locate it, opening and closing as the little insect sang. If, on the other hand, the butterfly was at skylark elevation, I would see it as a black dot or not at all.

What I am suggesting is that intentionality in perception goes beyond the experience of "perceiving as" and is all of a piece, in fact, with intentionality in observation, or even more generally again. Intentionality in the present case has many forms, being manifested in, for instance, my listening to a trilling sound that I hear as the song of a butterfly; my expecting to see one if I look into the sky; my seeing it as a black dot; my memory as it enters into all perceptual and observational processes; my worry that my lepidopterist friend will not believe me; my use of language now and when trying to convince him, and so on. In all these different cases I take for granted, in a perfectly obstacle-free way, all the multifarious manifestations of the intentional, not just those that are narrowly perceptual. Note that this is not to imply that perception, or narrow perception, is distinct from its interpretation, this latter imbuing it with intentionality. Clearly, that said, there are cases that may be thus understood, as with seeing a black dot in the sky as a skylark or vice-versa, the point being that this is perceptual intentionality at work, given that all perception is inferential. Since the point now being made is a pivotal one, we need to examine those views that are opposed to it.

Turning again to *The Problem of Perception*, we find that Smith, having rejected the dual component theory, according to which perception comprises sensation and the exercise of concepts, these being separate functions, now considers what he refers to as the monistic counterpart to the theory. This is the view that perceptual sensation is intrinsically conceptual, it being distinct in this way from bodily sensations. If I close my eyes and feel with my fingers an object which I thereby recognise as a wire tensioner on a fence post, then this is an example of tactile perception; but if I jump back in pain, realising too late that this is an electric fence, the object being an insulator, my fingers having touched the wire running next to it, then this is an example of bodily, not perceptual, sensation, despite all the information it conveyed to me in that particular observational context. The theory I outlined earlier, that perception is intrinsically inferential, invites comparison with – or to – the conceptualism which Smith rejects, claiming as he does that concepts are irrelevant to *what it is that makes any sensory state a perception at all*' (95.) At the same time, however, he acknowledges the 'enormously important role' of concepts, even going so far as to say that they suffuse the perceptual. This indicates that he is hedging his bets or that the point he is making must be a subtle one.

Pursuing it, he asks whether one can perceive a typewriter without having the concept of it as a device for performing certain functions. The gist of his argument, If I may take the liberty of updating his example, is that both a modern computer user and a former typist see the same physical object, despite the computer user, if she has led a sheltered life, having no idea what it is for. They would, Smith would no doubt acknowledge, have different reactions, intentions and so forth, in relation to the object, and different uses for it, this being an example of the agreed close link between perception and concepts; but they would see the same object in more or less the same way. I put it like that in order to allow for the possibility, as Smith does, of slight perceptual difference, his point being that this would not be the difference between having perceptually meaningless sensations and perceiving a physical object.

But now, this example is questionable, leaving open as it does the possibility that the two subjects see the typewriter in the same way because their basic visual concepts are the same; and, too, because the non-basic concept of a typewriter, which only one of them possesses, is not such as to interfere with their mutual seeing of it as a physical object of a certain size, shape and configuration. They would have different expectations in very limited ways, for instance if the carriage return was activated. Of more import is that their micro-expectations and memories would be the same from one moment to the next if they examined the object. What counts, really, if Smith's tacit comparison is with sensations, is the thesis that perception is inferential and that it reveals a three-dimensional world.It is inferential in that it depends on memory, expectation, confirmation and extrapolation. Turning this pen between my fingers, I see the clasp disappear around the pen's dark side, whereupon I wait for it to emerge into view again, thereby confirming the veracity both of my memory and of my seeing the clasp a moment ago, from which I inferred to my seeing it again. Clearly, my seeing the pen as three-dimensional is also thereby illustrated, as is the intrinsic perceptual inference thesis.

It just is the case, it seems to me, that the notion of a perceptual concept, as in the claim that 'concepts are irrelevant to what it is that makes any sensory state a perception at all', is far too vague for the claim to co-exist with its being admitted that the conceptual suffuses the perceptual. If it does, then where, exactly, is the irrelevance? Be that as it may, Smith now distinguishes between what he refers to as high and low conceptualism, the former being the view that perception necessarily involves high-level thinking and conceptualising, naturally associated, one might suppose, with the use of language at the level of human communication. Smith rejects this version of the theory, partly on the grounds that non-human animals are able to perceive, as also that human perception does not necessarily involve sophisticated thought. A non-typist, as it were, can perceive a typewriter as an object having certain physical features, just as a non-electrician may give a detailed description of an electrical insulator, ignorant of the fact that it has that function. There is nothing here I would wish to reject in itself, the point being that the difference between high and low in this context is one of degree, both of them involving the occurrent and the dispositional, rather than that high concepts involve conscious thinking, thereby distancing themselves from those at a lower level. Thus it is that the distinction is not such as to save Smith's argument or to close the gap between his approach and mine.

He would not agree, however, contending as he does that concepts are irrelevant to perception even at this lower level. In presenting his argument, he targets recognition as a necessary component of perception, to which end he distinguishes between recognising an object and being able to discriminate between it and others. This latter ability, he says, is necessary to perceiving anything at all, but the same is not true of recognition. He maintains that we can perceive a familiar object and have no idea what it is, as in the case of agnosia sufferers, who fail to recognise such objects as keys and combs in terms of their function, though at the same time they are able to perceive them and to describe their physical features. But in that case, this is not a counter-example to the claim, for it just is a fact that with visual agnosia some forms of recognitional ability are impaired but not others. This is obvious from the example, for if the sufferer describes a key, let us say, his seeing of it being normal, then he must be able to recognise it as the same object from one moment to the next, not just by virtue of phenomenal resemblance but also through changes of perspective and, correspondingly, of appearance, including apparent shape, colour and size. A difficulty here is that recognition and discrimination are closely connected, as with Smith's own example of our being able to distinguish between two colours, or shades of colour, on a particular occasion and yet not be sure, when shown one of them shortly afterwards, which of the two we are seeing again. This is meant to indicate that we can discriminate without recognition, but it seems to me that the point is lost in the overlap between these abilities, whence it cannot be retrieved. If I place two red balls of different shades in separate bags, and if I am presented with a third ball identical with one of them, except that I do not know which bag to place it in, then in what sense am I able to discriminate between the two shades of colour? Well, might it not be that I have forgotten them? Indeed it might, but this would indicate, unless it is just a momentary lapse, that I cannot make the discrimination, essential to which is the ability to remember what I perceive, this also being essential to perception itself. But now, a manifestation of that ability is *recognitional*, as when I place the third ball in the right box, and perhaps the fourth, if there is one, and so on.

Now that we have countered Smith's arguments, it needs to be emphasised that conceptualism, as he calls it, is also untenable, for what is meant by it, according to Smith, is that every perception involves concepts and that 'it is only in virtue of this that perception is anything more than mere sensation'. (p. 94) What is wrong here is the use of the word "sensation", which is misleading, hence the fact that normally, and more accurately, one would

160

speak of perceptual experience, as in the experience of listening to a skylark. Or perhaps a bird if one does not recognise the species; or a creature with wings; or an aerial object, the point being that one will never arrive at a sensation, to which one then adds a concept.

6.3: Perceptual Belief and the Perceptually Given

None of this is to deny that one may speak of what is given in perception, as with referring to the contents of one's visual or other sense field, one's experience of which is bound up with perceptual belief. In order to investigate further, let it be supposed that I am looking at an object about which I have no prior knowledge and that it is, in fact, a coin fixed on a stand in such a way as to be rotatable, like meat on a spit. Suppose further that I am not alone, my companion being in exile from a steeply inclined land where round coins have been replaced, on safety grounds, by oval ones, owing to the high incidence of injuries caused by coins rolling out of control. If the object is at present edge-on to us, so that its projected outline would be a narrow rectangle, then what is perceptually given is the curved edge of the object, this being what we believe it to be, our justification for which is that most apparently curved object-parts really are curved. To this it might be added that it is a necessary condition of perception that in general it should be veridical, for instance in the case of an object having the shape it appears to have.

This, however, is too simplistic, for "seeing as", and in general "perceiving as", need not be attended by the belief that the appearance in question corresponds to reality. When I watch a film, if it is an action thriller, I see, for instance, two climbers quarrelling on the face of a cliff, of all places, the context being such that my disbelief, as well as the climbers, is or are suspended. It is not just that I realise that the characters are actors, who are not really clinging to a cliff, or not unless they have fallen out with the director and over the edge of it, but also that I know that I am looking at changing patterns of shape and colour on a screen. Such instances are multifarious, each of them different in some respects from the others; and what this indicates is that perceptual belief is conditional within a system, the resultant of a range of factors which combine to determine the link between belief and perceptual content in any particular case. Thus, I may believe that an airborne balloon which presents itself as decreasing in size really is deflating, rather than, or even in addition to, moving away from me.

If we continue to ask what it is that perception informed by belief consists in, and if we return to the coin example, then we may suppose, as before, that my companion and I are looking at the object edge-on, and that we suspect that it is a coin. For my companion, however, coins are oval, whereas for me they are round, a question arising as to the difference this makes if more of the coin is revealed. Suppose, then, that the coin starts to turn from edge-on, so that its face comes increasingly into view; then my seeing it as round is now a continuous process of visual expectations confirmed, and others following on, these also confirmed and remembered, the flow of expectation, memory and confirmation merging smoothly into the observational experience by which the face of the coin reveals itself. What my companion initially finds, however, is that perceptual obstacles confound his expectations, the result being disconfirmation as the flow of consciousness breaks against the immovable reality of the coin being round, not oval. It may then re-form and run smoothly, expectation and "perceiving as" merging together as gradually the now-expected circularity of the coin takes shape.

6.4: Direct Realism and Moderate Scepticism

Consider the claim that if perception is intrinsically inferential, and intentional in general, then this in itself is incompatible with direct realism. If we now ask on what basis the incompatibility thesis is founded, the answer will depend on our interpretation of direct realism, the meaning of which is clear enough if the theory is opposed to that of indirect realism and phenomenalism, or to the underlying sense-datum account of perception. If we construe it as being antithetical to these, then what it states is that the relations between perception and the world are such that physical reality is objective and independent of being perceived, in line, as I have taken pains to show to be the case, with system-based per-

162

ceptual analysis. It is, in other words, perfectly compatible with the thesis that perception is intrinsically inferential.

If one hesitates to accept this, it is perhaps because perception being inferential is taken to imply that it is indirect. But what does this mean? With regard to the skylark example, I infer its presence from the sound that it makes if there are no counter-indications, such as my padding across Antarctica at the time, or listening to a recorded bird song, perhaps out of loneliness if I am a bird on its own. If the inference is made, then there is a sense in which my perception of the skylark is indirect, the implied contrast being with my seeing it. But this distinction is easily accommodated by direct realism, for I hear the trilling as external to myself, this being what I believe it to be, just as I believe that the song is that of a skylark, the belief itself being inferential. In different circumstances I might believe, given strong evidence, that it was butterfly song. When, to change the example, I look at this keyboard, my seeing of it may be continuous throughout its changes of appearance or from one moment to the next. Looking at what I take for granted to be a book on the shelf in front of me, I reach for it and suffer an observational shock, as it were, for the object turns out to be a dummy book with no pages, perhaps borrowed from a library in deep financial straits. But I saw it in the first instance, even if I misperceived it, and I see it now and saw it at all points in-between. But also, this was — and is — all within a visual framework in which the physical reality of my surroundings is inescapably taken for granted, this being a defining feature, as I said earlier, of perception within a system.

There is, too, another way in which perceptual inference is overlooked, so that we are misled into opposing it to direct perception, and it connects with processes of perception necessarily bringing the notion of objects existing unperceived constantly into play. Looking at this keyboard, only part of it presently visible, I know that the rest of it continues to exist, and correspondingly I experience it as if I can see the whole of it at once, this being an extension of seeing the visible parts of it as being three-dimensional. I experience it as if in a continuous present, or specious present as used to be said, the previous moment informing by way of memory the present one which it overlaps, the present one relating in the same way to the next, which loops back to the present by way of expectation. This explains, or helps to explain, one's impression of the physical immanence of surrounding objects and of the world beyond them. Perception is, in other words, transtemporal. To sum up: the thesis that perception is intrinsically inferential and intentional belongs to the analysis, not the rejection, of direct realism, this being the sense in which this latter obtains within a system.

6.5: The Shock of the Hallucinatory

Finally, I suggest that we apply our findings to the argument from hallucination, which is more powerful, some would say, than that from illusion. When I look at this non-existent kangaroo on my keyboard, the sense-datum theorist will say, there must be a perceptual object: if not a physical object, then a non-physical one, this being the point at which the theorist acquaints us with marsupial sense data. Since, however, we have already encountered and rejected them, along with phenomenalism and indirect realism, our concern should be not with scepticism but with analysis. That said, it would be useful if we could show that the argument from hallucination fares no better than that from illusion, and if this could be done by way of the analysis itself.

Note first, then, that when I look at this tiny kangaroo I judge that it is unreal by applying criteria that presuppose, as with all perceptual experience, the existence of the physical world. Thus it is that I reach out to touch it and thereby confirm that there is nothing to feel, where this depends on my hand and the keyboard being taken to be real, this being the default position if nothing countervails it. Since this is very similar to any attempt of mine to grasp the apparently bent part of a stick in water, it would seem that there is nothing especially significant, sceptically, about hallucination. In that case why do we have the impression that there is? The reason, I suggest, is that hallucinations can be epistemically and observationally startling; this kangaroo in front of me, for instance, looks much more convincing than the apparently bent part of a stick in water, this latter being familiar and explicable in a way that the kangaroo is not. Remember, too, that the stick is public, the kangaroo private.

Further to this, consider my looking out of the open window onto the street that stretches into the distance, whereupon I notice a very indistinct blur in the middle of the road and approaching at speed. Then in what sceptically relevant way is this blur in motion different from a hallucination? There is no actual blur, the blurriness being a distance effect, and I cannot reach out and touch it. Yes, you will say, but no doubt the blur will resolve itself into an adult kangaroo with an empty pouch and every intention of hopping through the window in order to rescue her joey, at which point I can expect more than enough physical contact with a mad Australian mother. But the fact remains that the initial blur did not exist and that, in blurred form, it could not be touched. Keep in mind, too, that the incoherence of the notion of sense data has already been established beyond reasonable doubt, in recognition of which the argument from hallucination would have to be very powerful indeed in order to succeed at a court of appeal. Since I submit that it carries no conviction at all, this being a plea that I have just entered, I shall have to leave it for the reader to decide, assuming that there is only one.

Perhaps it will be a fitting end to the present chapter if I now revisit the theory of consciousness mentioned earlier as already being familiar to us. If we take the brain to be the seat of consciousness then Colin McGinn and others will insist that the unidirectional, as they see it, causal connection between brain and consciousness, or body and mind, is wholly mysterious, the brain being a lump of matter and the mind not a lump of matter. My rejoinder is that the brain-consciousness connection belongs to science, the associated mystery to metaphysics, where it transcends the mind-body distinction. The mystery itself concerns intentionality, crucial to which is the distinction between conscious and non-conscious. By way of illustration, suppose that I now recall a summer's day long ago when I sat on a stile by Ewenny Priory with my first love and we kissed, the stile and the priory still there, though she and I, as we were then, are both dead and soon will be gone and forgotten. Then that feeling with which we are all familiar, of memory transporting us back through time, as if re-lived, yet here I am alone on that stile decades later, is one that manifests and is buoyed up by the non-conscious. This latter belongs to the same sea of intentionality as the non-consciousness by which I experienced so intensely the heat of that summer tryst now gone as if it had never been. But the nature of the currents involved in the non-conscious intentionality of memory is wholly mysterious, and the ocean in its profundity is inaccessible to human thought. This will all be fully worked out in the penultimate two chapters, if that can be said, our present task being to prepare for the next problem, that of induction and empirical inference in general.

Finally, and in anticipation, let us ask how this account of intentionality impinges on epistemology, in particular the problem of inductive reasoning. Since philosophy is necessarily mediated by language, scepticism about empirical knowledge is perforce constrained, and in ways that seem to me to have been overlooked by those who plot the sceptic's downfall. To begin with, I have argued against Kripke that memory is basic to stringing words and sentences together; hence the impossibility of radical scepticism about knowledge of the past. Note, too, that expectation is also basic. This is good, but it gets better; for my argument has also been that nothing counts epistemically as being immediately given, either perceptually or experientially. That leaves deductive inference, but I shall try to show that this, too, is epistemically vulnerable. It follows that all knowledge is intrinsically inferential, the notion of the infallible or incorrigible being replaced by that of necessary condition. This may seem to extend the potential for scepticism, but my claim will be that it removes the requisite epistemological benchmark, inference being fundamental to what we know of the world. Enough has already been said, I believe, to give shape to a resolution of the problem of knowledge and in particular of induction. All that remains to be done is to completely unveil the solution, the outlines of which are clearly visible in the folds of the discussion thus far; and to this we now turn.

Chapter 7: The Problem of Induction

Perhaps I may begin with an account of the problem from the point of view of David Hume, the philosopher widely regarded as its progenitor, at least in its modern form. He starts from the empiricist premiss that our concepts of the physical world are derived from experience, or in his own words that impressions give rise to ideas. Thus the notion of cause and effect originates in our experience of the constant conjunction of events, which we associate through relations of resemblance. He would say that what we know of events in the world, or the world beyond our immediate perceptual horizon, derives from our past and present experience of similar events and must be justified in terms of them.

This immediately raises a question as to what is to count as a particular event, given that it may be divided into sub-events under different headings; and a related question as to what is to count as being relevantly similar, given that one can always find similarities between events; and, too, a query as to whether one is misled by the habit of epistemically objectifying past experience of the physical world. We say that we know that the sun will rise because it always has; but this is potentially misleading, for we believe that the sun will rise because we believe that it always has, this latter belief being of prior epistemic status. What, then, of its justification? How do I know, for instance, that the sun rose today? Whatever the answer, it will involve unverified predictions the legitimacy of which is the very point at issue — especially if it can be shown, with predictions in general, that the verifying of them involves others that remain unverified. Clearly, memory is also involved, but how do we verify *that*? Is it even true that we are always able to find a causal antecedent for our predictions, as opposed, a la Wittgenstein, to just making them? Their aetiology need not, in any case, involve inductive inference, for it might be, for example, that we predict an event on the basis of a single glance, or on what we have been told. Of course, one can always find inductive reasons, in this latter case by appeal to the credentials of one's informant — but again how is this to be justified? Finally, and crucially, what does Hume the seemingly radical inductive sceptic actually mean — or what should he mean if we are to credit him with being self-consistent? Not literally what he writes, for he would then refute it in the very act of writing it. That is, micro-analysis reveals that expectation necessarily enters into the articulating of belief, and to expect is, as it were, to predict at close quarters. I dig deep at the outset, albeit by posing questions without answering them, only in order to point the way to a more penetrating analysis of inductive scepticism, without which, in my view, the problem of induction cannot be solved.

This digging down to a solution will be done in stages, our present concern, by way of clearing the ground, being with Hume's insistence that prediction can be justified, if at all, only by appeal to present or past experience of that which is relevantly similar in the particular case. Issuing a challenge as to what such justification could amount to, he now argues that inductive inference is non-demonstrative. If by way of example we again take my belief that the sun will rise tomorrow, and if in support of it I adduce the fact that the sun has risen daily since time immemorial, or at least since I was a boy, then it is clear that in this case evidence does not entail conclusion; for the failure of the sun to rise is at least conceivable, and no contradiction is involved in stating both that the sun has always risen in the past and that tomorrow will not be another day.

Is it not possible, however, that the appeal to past regularities could take some other form? Addressing this question, Hume first argues that there is no relation of natural necessity in which factual inference from observational premises may be grounded. Such a relation does not readily spring to mind when predicting a sunrise on the basis of previous ones, but if we think of mechanical effects, for instance the deflection of colliding snooker balls, then perhaps the impression we have is one of power or force, which we might then intellectualise as natural causal necessity. Hume's point is that this is an empty notion which contributes nothing to the bare facts of constant conjunction and regularity, there being no significant difference in this respect between indirect causation, as with the regular appearance of the sun, and the direct effect of one object impacting another, as with boxers, or when a teddy bear loses its temper, perhaps in a boxing ring. It follows that the question about justifying inductive inference still awaits an answer.

One possibility is that we may appeal to a general inductive principle: that of the uniformity of nature; but Hume's objection is that the principle must itself be inductively grounded, so that to appeal to it is to beg the question. That leaves the prospect of enlisting logic or mathematics to the anti-sceptical cause, in particular with regard to probability theory applications. But Hume is dismissive of any appeal to applied logical reasoning.

7.1: Aims and Methods

That, in barest outline, is Hume's anti-inductive sceptical thesis, a key feature of which is that it falls short of blanket rejection of all that we empirically know, depending as it does on our knowledge of past and present observable events. I shall refer to this limited but radical form of scepticism as Hume's problem, defined as the thesis that prediction is impossible to justify, given that such justification would have to be inductive in character. With regard to these limitations, my plan is not to work within them as other commentators do, or think that they do, but to expose the inconsistencies inherent in that approach. It is in this way that I hope to be able to show that the inductive sceptic is obliged to target present and past observation as well as prediction, the resulting global scepticism being easily refuted. In the same vein, I shall also maintain the thesis that the adherent of radical inductive scepticism is in any case, even without the global extension, self-refuting, and in two ways, one of them concerning the epistemic status of the basic statement of his position, the other his intellectual ambivalence.

What we are left with is the question of *how* not *whether* prediction or empirical knowledge more generally may be justified, given that the fact of its justification cannot coherently be denied. This is moderate as opposed to radical scepticism, but I shall argue that the moderate sceptic is mistaken if he continues to adhere to a strict dichotomy between logic and contingent fact. This becomes apparent if epistemological analysis is brought to bear on the given question: that of how it is that prediction may be justified. The answer will involve the notion of necessary conditions of discourse, these being such as to transcend the distinction between fact and logic, which is to say that they are metaphysical in character. This treatment is not exegetically derived and nor does it need to be; for my claim will be that it is only if Hume is treated as a moderate sceptic that his anti-inductive arguments give any impression of presenting a united front.

My present aim, which will involve capitalizing on the arguments advanced in the last chapter, is to show that perception is intrinsically predictive and retrodictive, this latter in the sense that it necessarily involves memory. Consider, then, this wine bottle in front of me, my identification of which goes beyond my necessarily partial view of it, for I cannot simultaneously see all parts of it or the varying appearances of any particular one. This is truistic, but let us now focus, in more than one sense, on my partial view, say of the body of the bottle on its label side. Then I see it as a curved surface and I believe what I see, so that I expect it to look curved from one moment to the next. This expectation also obtains if, for instance, I turn the bottle a little while keeping the label in sight, my altered perceptual experience jigsawing with the previous one. Such expectations, inseparable from perceptual belief, are intrinsic to my seeing of the bottle, as is the re-identification involved; but this needs to be clarified as follows. My visual experience of the bottle is not informed by a conscious process of interpreting that experience moment by moment, with perceptual belief, memory and expectation inhering in that process. Rather, they inhere in the perceptual experience itself, which is that of seeing the bottle or the part of it in view, this latter being in that sense directly seen. What this indicates is that perceptual belief, expectation and memory are both occurrent and dispositional; and this is also true, one might add, of what it is in general to believe, expect or remember that something is the case. The point about perceptual dispositions is that the conditional statements by which we describe them are predictions at one remove. Observing this bottle, I need not have in mind it's looking suitably different from a slightly different angle; but if prompted I will state, or should state, that I expect it to look different if my viewpoint changes. But a conditional statement of the form "if A occurs I expect B to occur" or "if A occurred I would expect B to occur" implies the possibility of predicting B on the basis of A. Thus it is that perception is intrinsically predictive.

If we now consider not expectation but memory, then it is readily shown that memory is intrinsic to perception, for remembering is the obverse of expecting. If I expect a thing, so that my expectation involves future events, then the way in which they unfold as expected necessarily depends on memory. Try to imagine walking around a table, one's visual expectations and the appearances of the table changing systematically but with no accompanying memory of any part of one's circumambulatory observations. What this shows is that memory is indeed intrinsic to perception. That leaves perceptual belief, but again the point to be made is obvious, for we are concerned not with insects or carpet mites, who are indifferent to philosophy, but with human beings, all of whom would agree that seeing is believing. That is, perceptual belief is intrinsic to the very notion of human perception.

If these findings are correct, then it follows that the radical inductive sceptic cannot stop short of rejecting perceptual expectation and prediction and therefore perception itself. What remains is to show that he must also target the deliverances of memory, this being another reason to reject perception, one that extends beyond it to include knowledge of the past in general. If he argues that predictions about the physical world are non-demonstrative, then the same is true of direct memory or of the reasoning, whatever the form it takes, by which one establishes that a past event has occurred. Also, it is taken to be a solid ground for trusting one's memories that they are strongly confirmed when predictions or expectations prove to be correct. For instance, I seem to remember that I placed black balls and white balls in a bag: if, for whatever reason, I wish to confirm the veracity of this memory, and if I do so by looking in the bag, then this is very strong confirmation, for how else is it to be explained that I was correct in what I expected to find? In different circumstances there would, of course, be other possibilities, for instance that it was by way of testimony, not direct inspection, that I knew what the contents of the bag would be. But then my looking in the bag would confirm my memory of having been told what they were, and again this would be strong confirmation. Suppose, to give a final example, that I seem to remember that I looked different from the front than from the back when I admired myself in two suitably aligned mirrors. If I look in the mirrors again tomorrow and find that I am indeed reverse asymmetrical, then this will confirm my memory of, so to speak, my present attempt at humour.

7.2: Interdependence of Memory and Expectation

I shall now argue that memory and expectation, already shown to be closely connected, as in the above examples of confirmation, are in fact necessarily interdependent. In that case it should not be possible for the sceptic to treat them separately, this being revealed if we allow him to make the attempt. Taking expectation first, we are asking whether it is conceivable that one should be sceptical about the future but not the past, this time from the point of view of a sceptic who simply chooses, and without making a case, to disregard all reference to future events. Perhaps this could be taken both at face value and as a device by which to spotlight the mutual dependence of the concepts in question.

Suppose, then, that the sceptic wakes in the night, opens his eyes, sees a yellow disc shining in the dark and, understandably, closes them again. He says, 'I saw a yellow disc', but as a sceptic about the future he also says, 'I have no reason to believe that I shall see or remember it again.' Now he opens his eyes, finds it still there, and says, 'I see a yellow disc, the same as before.' Then the first point is that he has no reason to believe that he remembers anything. In the normal world I see a disc, close my eyes, expect to see a disc, open my eyes and see one. This confirms my memory, and in the strongest possible terms, for how else is it to be explained that I correctly expected to see a disc?

In the world of the selective sceptic, however, nothing could count as confirming his memory or, indeed, any of his beliefs. Well, could it not be argued that even if he did not expect to see a yellow disc, or anything else, but did see one, then this confirms his memory of the previous observation? If we take the disc to be

172

a solid object, after all, then such objects have identity through time, other things being equal. But now, the sceptic cannot avail himself of such facts, for he has no conception of a physical object, since this would involve his expecting its appearance to remain the same or to change, depending on the circumstances; and, therefore, he cannot conceive of a physical world which exhibits any form of continuity. It is arguable, even, that he is not able to identify perceptual objects, for instance what he now sees glowing in the dark, as coming under a particular description, even in terms of colour and shape, or as being similar to a previous object, in this case one that he has just seen; and the reason, familiar to us from an earlier discussion, is that to identify or reidentify particular items is to imply constraints on future possibilities. If this is correct, then in what sense, given these epistemic and semantic limitations, his words not having their conventional meaning, does he remember having seen a similar object to this one? With regard to confirming his memory of the disc, he might as well have opened his eyes and gazed upon a starry sky — as we, but not he, would be able to call it, just as we are able to recognise the disc as the moon.

We may argue in the same vein if we now shift from scepticism about the future to that about the past. Suppose that once again the sceptic, this time a sceptic about memory, sees a yellow disc, at which point he closes his eyes and predicts that he will see it when he opens them. Then it is immediately apparent that the situation we are trying to imagine lacks all intelligibility. If the sceptic opens his eyes and sees a disc, then this confirms nothing, for he cannot confirm a prediction that, for the purpose of this discussion, he does not allow himself to remember making, just as he does not remember the beginning of what he says by the time he gets to the end. Thus, it is that the concepts of memory and expectation are intelligible only when linked together, a fact which indicates that a relation of interdependency may hold between intentional concepts in general, a consequence of their interconnectedness.

Taking this further, consider my claim at time t to understand the finite even number sequence composed of the first fifty terms, and suppose that I substantiate it, or so it would seem, by reciting them consecutively, at which point I meet not with applause but with its being denied that I have made good my claim, and for a reason which has nothing to do with strength of evidence. The point, rather, is that it was after t that I manifested my understanding, which it is therefore possible that I acquired at this later time. If that is what we suppose a sceptic to say, then his thesis is that criteria of understanding have application only to what it is that one now understands, at the time that evidence in the form of cognitive behaviour is forthcoming. But in that case, he does not go far enough, for by the same token he would have to add that it is possible, after reciting any term of the sequence, that I thereby lost the ability to repeat it. But it is the thesis itself which lacks all support, and for the simple reason that cognitive behaviour has duration, so that nothing could count, if the sceptic were correct, as one's present grasp of the sequence or, indeed, of anything at all. If I start to recite the initial terms at a particular moment, then immediately I am swept beyond it to the next, so that I call out the second term, strange to say, after I have called out the first. What this shows, apart from the incoherence of the problem of induction, already covered, is that intentional concept applications in the present tense are transtemporal, which in our case is to say that if at time t I claimed to understand the sequence, the initial terms of which I "now" call out, then I am judged to have understood it at time t, other things being equal, and to continue to understand it.

7.3: Objections to This Approach

What follows if these arguments are correct is that radical inductive scepticism entails the rejection of all inferential knowledge, whether of the physical world or of one's own and other people's mental states, thereby equating itself with epistemological solipsism. Since this conclusion occupies the main stage in refuting the radical inductive sceptic, I should perhaps consider those views that are opposed to it. A.J.Ayer (1972) takes Hume to subscribe to the theory of intrinsic description, whereby the description of the state of a subject at one moment is intrinsic to the subject if nothing is implied as to the state of the subject at a different moment or different subjects at the same moment. If we follow Ayer in calling the subject of such a description a distinct event, then Hume's thesis is now taken to be the ontological one that there are indeed events that are distinct in the given sense, such that, to quote from Ayer, 'they are sufficient to describe everything that happens'.(p. 6) He thinks, too, that such events should be equated with sense-qualia, which he takes to be the evidential basis by which perceptual knowledge becomes theoretical in character. The details of this analysis need not concern us, for what is already very clear, just as it would be if Ayer took Hume to be a simple phenomenalist, is that a foundationalist approach to perceptual analysis cannot save the radical inductive sceptic from the charge of being inconsistent by not targeting present observations. On that approach, after all, one posits direct perceptual objects from which physical-object concepts, or physical objects themselves, may theoretically be constructed. An account of this kind must incorporate into the construction project predictive and retrodictive relations between basic perceptual materials, whatever they might be. If all this is correct, then the thesis that perception is intrinsically inferential holds good under phenomenalism and other forms of perceptual foundationalism. This gives us what we need, but a direct challenge to Ayer's analysis of perception is now in order, for I would like the intrinsic perceptual inference theory to have no loose ends that a sceptical unraveller might seize upon.

What, then, does Ayer's notion of a distinct event consist in? The basic idea is perspicuous enough, for one may be more or less venturesome in one's descriptions, as with, respectively, "I see a round wine bottle" and "I see a curved object-part". This is interesting, but is it fundamental, given that an object-part exists in physical space, the same as a wine bottle? According to perceptual-appearance theorists it is, for they believe that bringing words and things into closer orbit can reach a point at which description spirals down to its object and makes a perfect fit — as opposed, that is, to all semantic content being flung off into space. This picture of perfection is one the lineaments of which I have already sketched in, thereby permitting myself to be more imaginative when I now add colour to it. Suppose, then, that a dense, turquoise mist envelops me while I sleep and that I open my eyes to a magical realm of pure colour. Suppose further, reality obtruding, that I immediately close my eyes again, too much turquoise being known to cause luscious dreams of a tropical atoll. Then the colour-flash I experience is a momentary event, but not my uttering of the sentence, "I see a flash of turquoise", which is the work of several moments. It follows that I must remember the flash, so that my belief that it is occurring — has occurred — is fallible, the same being true of any momentary perception and therefore of any perception. Further to this, I have to understand my own description, thereby being suitably disposed, with all that this implies about, as we have seen, conditional prediction. Not only that, but it is not strictly true, even in this extreme case, that I experience pure colour; for I am aware of looking at it, with all that this implies, and of being able to move around in it. I see it, in other words, as existing independently and objectively in the physical world.

Since the actual world is in any case composed of physical objects having shape-definition, we should now imagine that the mist starts to resolve itself into one such object bi-laterally symmetric about a mid-line, which metamorphosises into the body of a dragonfly, perhaps a lagoon dragonfly, its turquoise wings condensing from the mist on each side. Clearly, I cannot behold these wonders without the aid of recognition, memory, expectation and so on. On the contrary, they permeate the perceptual processes by which I register the unfolding of these events, without which the concept of a physical object could never emerge into consciousness and launch itself into three-dimensional space.

Perhaps it is time to take depth soundings. If perceptual processes are intrinsically predictive and retrodictive, this latter in the sense that memory inheres in perception, then it is a legitimate and obligatory target for radical inductive scepticism, my contention being that this equates with epistemological solipsism. The solipsist has no reason to believe in an external world, and he is debarred from remembering or predicting his own mental states. The rejection of the theory, this being the crucial point of logic, also sweeps overboard the arguments that entail it.

Let us now confront this theory broadside on, the place to start being with the solipsist's claim that all that can be known to exist is his consciousness from one moment to the next. If I cleave to that somewhat surreal proposition, then the solipsist must be myself, the only consolation being that my fear of death is misplaced, the concept of mortality no longer being applicable. Despite being hugely, and inconsistently, in favour of my own eternal existence — inconsistently because I would have no reason to believe in it — I cannot pretend to take solipsism seriously, for the waters would then part between word and action, my claim to be a solipsist capsizing over the cliff of the sea. It would have to be, for instance, that I am quite prepared to exit this loft by stepping through the dormer window, as Hume would say, even without opening it first — except, of course, that if the present moment is all that exists then there are no windows, the concept of a shortcut, of defenestration or of a window cleaner thereby lacking the slightest utility. Summing up: the theory of epistemological solipsism is *insane*.

What I shall now try to show is that Hume's problem, even if we stop short of invoking epistemological solipsism, cannot be sincerely entertained, even by its advocates, and that it leads, in any case, to self-refutation. With regard to the first point, is it really possible to articulate the problem without belying one's claim to take it seriously? One would, in trying to keep a straight face, have to think, thereby expecting to finish the thought, perhaps while sitting at a desk and reaching for a quill, which one expects to be able to lift from its inkhorn. One could, following Hume and updating him, try to bridge the gap between word and action by appeal to the induction instinct or the survival of the most expectant. But now, this is disingenuous, for the conflict is between what one says, or feels that one should say, and what one believes, not straightforwardly between one's beliefs. When Hume reaches for his quill, all the while repeating to himself the mantra that he has no reason to expect to lift it, he in fact expects to lift it, his protestations to himself thereby being insincere if ordinarily understood. To be sincere he would have to be consistently a radical sceptic, but he seems to be at best intellectually ambivalent, at worst an armchair epistemological nihilist. We are, however, too kind, for it is pretty plain that the latter obtains, the armchair at its most comfortable in study or seminar room, not out in a world that has weather.

If we now turn to the inductive sceptic refuting himself, our method will be to appeal to necessary conditions of discourse, to which end we need to be able to encapsulate inductive scepticism in a single sentence: "There cannot be prior knowledge of an event." Let us call it sentence C; then it is either understood or it is not. If it is not, there is no sceptical challenge and we can all dismount. If it is, then the sceptic implies that he knows the meaning of the constituent words or phrases, for he would be inconsistent if he said, 'I have no reason to believe that I know what "believe" means.' The implication, then, is that he is able to use the sentence parts in a variety of contexts or different parts in a similar context; that, for instance, he knows the difference in meaning between "there cannot be..." and "there can be...." The key point is that his use of the sentence involves restrictions on a possible future state of affairs in which he again encounters or uses it, or parts of it, the restrictions arising from his conditionally expecting, as it were, to behave in ways appropriate to his present understanding. But also, memory and expectation are involved; for in uttering the first part of sentence C, he anticipates his next words, so that he knows what he is going to say, at least when this is opposed to his having no idea, for then it would not matter what the first part of the sentence was, or whether he remembered it. But it does matter, as does the way in which the sentence continues, as would be obvious if the sceptic said, "There cannot be" – breaking off to announce that he has no idea what comes next, the announcement itself being truncated in the same way. Note, too, that the sceptic cannot argue that he need not be aware of his dispositions, not only because the argument would cancel itself out but also because we could in any case enlighten him as to the ways in which he is disposed. Very well, but what of the ceteris paribus clause by which all dispositional statements are qualified? The sceptic is entitled to point out, after all, that if his use of "believe", for instance, in sentence C is meaningful only if he is suitably disposed, then the implicit proviso is that other things must be equal when he next encounters that word, where these include his not having succumbed to dementia in the meantime, this being just one out of a whole range of exclusion clauses. The rejoinder here is that there has to be a limit to what is excluded, otherwise to say that I can correctly use a word again, other things being equal, is just to say that I can in all cases except those in which I can't. Thus, it is that even at the level of articulating his anti-inductive thesis the sceptic necessarily refutes himself.

All things considered, I now claim to have solved Hume's problem when taken at face value, both in itself if Hume is consistant enough to include memory when he places induction on the index, and when taken to its logical extreme in the form of epistemological solipsism. Moreover, I have shown that Hume's problem, in itself or when taken to extremes, is not the genuine problem that it professes to be. Since it is necessarily the case that one cannot sincerely bring one's actions, as also one's thoughts, into conformity with radical inductive scepticism, it follows that this latter must be rejected, thereby creating a vacancy for the moderate sceptic to fill.

What we shall find, however, is that changing course for moderate scepticism is not all plain sailing, for one is able to cut through the water, as before, only by churning it up; and the reason is that the moderate sceptic, hence the name, may still feel that there is much to be moderately sceptical about, despite the forcible undecking of his former radical self. He knows, or takes himself to, that on system-based anti-sceptical theory empirical inference retains its non-demonstrative logical status if particular cases are considered. By focussing on these, he perhaps indicates that he was not paying attention when the thesis about necessary conditions in the general case was introduced. Hence my now suggesting that he concern himself with how, not whether, we have knowledge of the world, rather than that he may be interpreted, already, as consistently taking that approach. But also, he may have misgivings about the notion of a system in itself if, as it were, he spent his formative years on a building site and looks to foundationalism to provide a benchmark. That said, we can ease him to some extent into being consistent if we continue to analyse empirical inference in terms of a system, thereby allaying his concerns – or re-directing them if our aim is for the notion of mystery to gain purchase at this juncture.

What I now propose is to tease out some of the threads by which memory, expectation and perceptual inference enter into empirical observation analysed as belonging within a system of conditions and connections. My aim is to show that there is nothing here for the notion of moderate inductive scepticism to grapple onto, the sceptic having to look elsewhere if he wishes to climb back on board. Accordingly, let us return to the wine bottle: I see it as curved and the default position, as one may call it, is that I believe what I see. That is, it is not a contingent fact that seeing is believing and that in general I take my perceptual expectations to be veridical. It is, on the contrary, a necessary condition of perception and misperception. With regard to this latter, if I see the label area as curved and believe that it is, then I expect this to continue if I change perspective and look again. But if the same area now appears to be flat, a necessary condition of which is that I re-identify it, then I may have expectations which would, if met, be confirmatory of flatness, just as I may have others which confirm the previous misperception and perhaps account for it; though we need to keep in mind how newsworthy it is for one to be perceptually misled in this way. Note, too, that necessary perceptual conditions are multifarious in their manifestations. If an object is curved along its length, then its base must also be curved, thereby instantiating the general rule that a curved body must always exhibit curvature in at least some cross-sections. This is arguably an instance of synthetic *a priori* truth within a system, probability concepts also having application in the present case. If the bottle is curved all the way to the straight line horizon, as it were, by which my view of it is delimited, then it is very unlikely, in view of the coincidence that would otherwise be the case, that the straight line delimits both my view and the curved area of the bottle.[5] In this, too, there may be implicit necessary conditions, hence my referring to the theory now being developed as perceptual conditionality theory. Now suppose that I hold the bottle steady and turn it a little, thereby

---

[5] For similar observations about probability see Sir Roy Harrod's *Foundations of Inductive Logic*. Note, too, A.J.Ayer's discussion of it in the chapter "Has Harrod Answered Hume" in *Probability and Evidence*.

expecting a slight change in visual appearance: one that again dovetails with the old. It is necessarily the case that one such change occasions another, all else being equal; and what this implies is that exceptions to the rule are limited, so that we are back again with the synthetic *a priori*. It might be, for example, that I am holding the bottle directly in front of me, the label not showing, and that I turn it in such a way that its appearance remains the same, the absence of change itself being informative, but only in the context of change of appearance elsewhere. As pointed out previously, change of perspective in tandem with change of appearance is required by the laws of physics. Clearly, we could go on in the same vein, with new conditions announcing themselves if we considered the complex relations between the different senses, both in this particular case and in general. We know already that their deliverances combine to reveal the physical world, together with our selves at the centre of it all.

7.4: Moderate Sceptic Seeks Role Definition

How is this connected with the former radical sceptic's attempt to re-position himself as a moderate subverter of everyday reasoning? I have suggested, by way of career advice, that he occupy himself with analysis; but first we need to go deeper into his discontent, and the place to start, appropriately enough, is with foundationalism versus our system-based theory. Drilling straight down, what is it about empirical knowledge that points to the need for a foundation, the emphasis being on basic items of direct perceptual acquaintance? It is puzzling when one reflects on it, and not only because the certainty attaching to such items breaks loose under scrutiny, as I think that we have established. The fact is, after all, that the epistemic strength of the base does not in any case transfer to the empiricist edifice built upon it, given that the bonding agent is inference in one form or another. All that happens is that the sceptic now aims higher in order to target the inference from premise to conclusion, for instance the passage from sense-data to physical object in the case of phenomenalism; or, in the case of everyday realism, from direct perceptual acquaintance with object-parts to more structured observations. In fact, the appeal to foundations is itself, but in a different sense, without foundation, for in the sense that concerns us the analogy of a base on which a structure is built leaves out of account the passage of time. We should speak, rather, of a perceptual flow, with temporal change being intrinsic to it, the notion of a system arising quite naturally from the concepts involved. With system-based direct realism, inference is bound up with perception, as is the intentionality that merges with it, the dynamics of the system deriving its force from these and from necessary conditions of operation. Since we know, too, that in terms of a system radical scepticism is either incoherent or self-refuting, it is not yet clear whether the erstwhile radical sceptic may be reinstated in some other role.

Part of the problem is that the sceptic is in thrall, as we all are, to the everyday certainties by which the notion of acquaintance gains spatio-temporal flexibility. We stretch it to cover physical-world dimensions the existence of which we necessarily take for granted. When, for instance, I hold this wine bottle in my hand, my impression is that its three-dimensionality is the very embodiment of a solid object. Philosophically, this impression may harden into direct realism, especially if, as would seem to be the case, we take moment-by-moment perceptual memory for granted almost as if it were a form of acquaintance with the immediate past. At one level this is a necessary condition of perception, but micro-analysis reveals that the clock does not stop ticking just because the concept of a continuous present has application. This brings us to another reason why the moderate sceptic takes himself to be still in play and it concerns the fact, as he sees it, that a system-based induction-problem solution is unable to show that inductive inference has logical force, rather than that it is non-demonstrative. It is true that in terms of a system the emphasis is on global extension, self-refutation, incoherence and necessary conditions; but I referred just now to its dynamics, and the notion of a necessary condition seems to involve an imperative of some kind. There is, as we know, the Kantian concept of synthetic *a priori* truth, and in the next chapter I shall contend, by means of the concept of applied mathematics, that fact and logic are not antagonistic in the way that Hume required them to be. If all this is correct, then the moderate sceptic need not cleave to a strict distinction between deduction and empirical inference, or appeal to it when attempting to rationalise his continued perplexity. He has every right to feel perplexed, but for reasons that are different from the radical sceptic's, concerning as they do the utter inscrutability of intentional concepts. Such cognitive impenetrability reveals itself in, for example, the intentionality of memory and perception, and it is to these that we now return.

7.5: Memory, Perception and Mystery

Suppose that I shut my eyes and fall backwards into childhood, my parents in my idealised representation of them always there to catch me and land me gently down. We know that this no more reduces to having mental images than writing these words equates with making marks on paper. I remember my childhood, and this is both like and unlike returning to a familiar place, which itself involves memory. It is as if I go back in time or the past surges forward into the gap; and this in itself is mysterious. But the deeper mystery is this: How can a present mental event be the memory of a past event? Well, there are dispositions; but they manifest themselves occurrently, so the question, albeit rhetorical, has not been answered; and nor can it be, one might think, for it is in the way in which memory goes, and yet does not go, beyond occurrent mental states that intentionality in connection with the past is imbued with mystery.

Turning to perception, the very notion of the intentionality involved is mysterious. I see a bottle as an independently existing physical object; and yet, my seeing of it is a subjective perceptual experience, just as it would be if, for instance, I heard a trilling sound as the song of a skylark. Moving on, let us ask again what it is to see this curved surface as a bottle. It is as if, as Wittgenstein would say, I see the whole of the object at once, or as if the curved surface projects its own continuation over the horizon of the visible. Wittgenstein, however, resorted to the obfuscatory notion of meaning, or intentionality, as use, thereby substituting one difficulty for what he took to be another. But if perceptual intentionality is problematic, it is in the sense that it occasions philosophical perplexity. Perhaps those who favour Wittgenstein would verbally agree; but what I mean by it is that such perplexity, in the form of uneasy appreciation of the mystery of intentionality, is legitimate; and that it is bound up with the philosophical problems in question and survives their dissolution.

7.6: Conclusion

Am I claiming, in all sincerity, that the problem of induction has been solved? The anti-sceptical arguments in question are their own advocates, and I do not see how the accusation of self-refutation can fail to unsaddle the sceptic. It is true that riderless the horse continues to run, but only in circles of perplexity, this being all that is left of the original problem. Has it, that said, yielded to a sceptical solution? No, not at all, for if the inductive sceptic necessarily refutes himself, then separated from his charger he is no longer a threat. Indeed, what I maintain is not only that a solution has been found but also that the underlying mystery has been exposed.

Speaking of which, it seems to me that the sceptic and his critics mistake unbreachable metaphysical limits, represented in these pages mainly by the profundities of the oceanic realm, for epistemological and conceptual difficulties that ought to be resolvable but defy resolution. These latter recede even further into the mist if a reductionist approach is taken to the analysis of intentionality; and further again if the distinction between fact and logic continues to be that between oil and water rather than water and wave. If this is correct, so that aimlessly those concerned are unable to rationalise their intellectual discontent, then the task we should assign to them is to plot a course by which the fog of confusion may be dispelled, the way then being clear to make landfall on the solid ground of a satisfactory theory of knowledge. Such a theory would give safe harbour to its own limits, perhaps by accommodating rather than confronting some quite specific mysteries, and by delving into that perplexity, so often displaced into scepticism, which the mirror of the sea in that case reflects back at us. To circumvent the sceptic, all we need do is to look into, not just at, the first layers of clarity before the darkness all the way down. This concludes the present chapter.

Chapter 8: Resolving the Sceptical Hypothesis Problem

What I now propose is to place this discussion within the contemporary debate on a particular form of epistemological scepticism, hoping thereby both to test it against sceptical arguments not yet considered and, in that arena, to confront them with the insights we have gained. There is, for instance, what has become known as the brain-in-a-vat problem, and it starts from the sceptical hypothesis that we are disembodied brains programmed with those experiences on which we base our apparent knowledge of the external world. It would seem, on the face of it, that physical theory and the sceptical hypothesis are both compatible with the experiential evidence, a question then arising as to how we can claim to know that the world exists, and in particular that our brains are housed in bodies, not vats, so that, for instance, we have hands. This is a variant of Cartesian scepticism, and schematically the argument may be set out as follows:

1. I do not know that not-H.
2. If I do not know that not-H, then I do not know that O.

So,

3. I do not know that O.

Here the sceptical hypothesis, H, might be that I am a brain in a vat; the everyday fact, O, that I have hands, which is incompatible with H. This argument seems to depend on the principle of epistemic closure, such that if I know that O, and know that O entails not-H, then I know that not-H. By contraposition, if I do not know that not-H, then I do not know that O. And the reason I do not know that not-H, where H is the brain-in-a-vat hypothesis, is that this latter is consistent with all my external world evidence, for if H is correct then the course of my experience will be just as it now is. That said, if the point of the argument is merely to demonstrate that I cannot infallibly know what I claim to know, for instance that I have hands, given that it is logically possible that I do not, then it may occur to us to concede the point without feeling that we are sacrificing our everyday certainties, which would still be justified, at least for all that has been shown to the contrary. Michael Williams (1996) agrees, and he suggests, indeed, that if the hypotheses in question are taken to support radical scepticism, then they can offer that support only if foundationalism is presupposed in the sceptical argument. Be that as it may, the assumption seems to be that the argument threatens our everyday knowledge, and then a question arises as to whether there is a general principle or counter-argument by which our practice of dismissing such deviant hypotheses may be shown to be vindicated. In search of an answer, I propose to consider a particular form of contextualist rejoinder to the sceptic, which proceeds from the view that we judge our beliefs against a background of relevant alternatives, using criteria of relevance by which alternatives that are no more than logically possible are normally, but not always, excluded. A familiar example, first given by Dretske (1999), is that of claiming to know that an animal in a cage is a zebra, in which case the sceptical hypothesis might be that the animal is a mule painted to look like one, the argument running as follows: My evidence that this is a zebra would be just the same, albeit not to another zebra, if it were a painted mule; therefore, I do not know that it is not a mule; therefore, I do not know that it is a zebra. But there seems to be a paradox here, for I *do* know that it is a zebra, despite this knowledge being underdetermined by the evidence.

Let us now see if the relevant alternatives view offers a resolution of the paradox. On that view, according to DeRose (1999), the painted mule hypothesis becomes relevant not only in easily envisaged special circumstances such as an outbreak of mule painting being reported, but also in a philosophical context in which a sceptic challenges our claims to knowledge by invoking sceptical hypotheses consistent with the evidence on which we base our everyday beliefs. In that context, it will be said, the sceptic is correct in claiming that we do not know that we have hands, or that there are zebras, and our having to agree with him may seem to us to conflict with the fact that in ordinary circumstances we *do* have this knowledge. But that, according to the contextualist, is where we go wrong, for if knowledge is context dependent then there is no conflict. Ordinarily we know that we have hands; it is just that if a sceptic raises the epistemic standards by positing that we are brains in a vat, then in that context we do not know that we have hands, or not unless we can rule out the sceptical hypothesis.

But now, this contextualist thesis seems counter-intuitive, for we are certain that we are not brains in a vat, and that conviction seems to carry over from everyday situations in which the hypothesis merits no consideration, and for the reason that there is not the slightest evidence in its favour, never mind the very strong evidence that taking it seriously would demand. Even with regard to identifying zebras, it simply is not the case that mentioning the painted mule hypothesis would be enough in itself to make it relevant, as opposed to adducing evidence that elevates it from logical possibility to serious alternative. Besides, the proposed solution, like Kripke's to a different problem, would seem to be tantamount to the scepticism it is meant to kick through the bars of the cage. Relevant here is the thesis, established earlier, that radical scepticism, if impossible to embrace when taken to mean what it says, should on that account be rejected. Thus it is that we said goodbye to the solipsist.

Still, it is worth asking whether an enquiry into the nature of reasoning might yield principles by which we take a given body of evidence to point to a particular conclusion, which it underdetermines, rather than to other conclusions to which it seems to be equally disposed. And this, as I shall now try to show, is where the thesis of evidential interdependence, previously developed, comes into its own. If I visit a zoo and identify an animal as a zebra on the basis of observing it, then this involves perceptual and cognitive processes which operate within a system, and it is one about which, in a quite peculiar sense, I know nothing. I can say that my being able to identify zoo animals depends on previous learning, details of which I may or may not be able to provide; and I can envisage epistemic circumstances in which the painted mule hypothesis should be taken seriously — but all of this is itself a matter of perceptual and cognitive processes, including those of memory, so that it occurs within a system. I know nothing of that system and have no control over it, for I feel myself swept from one belief to another by a wholly mysterious movement of forces, these being manifested only in experience itself, so that nothing counts as my peering down through the water to the source of it all. In a particular case one can say particular things, or one can generalise to some extent, as when I say that at a zoo there is never any reason to doubt one's identification of zebras. But this does not yield any general principles by which it is deemed that some alternatives are relevant and others not, or none that belong to philosophy rather than the natural sciences or the psychology of reasoning.

That said, the good news is that we can make effective use of the notion of a system in the same way as in other chapters, which is to say by enquiring into the necessary conditions of discourse and reasoning and by drawing conclusions about what it is possible to coherently assert. Suppose that I identify a zebra by its appearance and that a doubt, not philosophical but of everyday concern, intrudes when I take seriously a sceptic who points out that if the animal were a painted mule its appearance would be the same. In that case I am foolish on one count and ultimately incoherent on another. To take the hypothesis seriously is to forget that my observations are made against a background of knowing that animals in a zebra cage are almost always either zebras or keepers, easily told apart, and that it is unheard of for one species of animal in a zoo to be disguised as another in order to deceive the public. By dint of probability, then, there is every reason to think that this is a zebra and none to think that it is not. That is one answer, and another concerns the hidden incoherence of giving epistemic weight to negligible possibilities. If I allow the possibility of the animal being a painted mule to cast doubt on its being a zebra, then I commit myself to generalising this epistemic scepticism. But now, if I start from the belief that this is a zebra and then give epistemic weight to its possibly being a mule, then I am committed to weighing in the balance the contraries of all the statements to which I give assent, for all beliefs are underdetermined by the evidence, itself underdetermined, or they involve understanding, which goes beyond what is given, since nothing is just given, or they are taken, in a sense, to stand on their own. It makes no difference which it is, for the result in any case would be incoherence and cognitive paralysis. If my belief that this is a zebra is infected with doubt that feeds on logical

188

possibility, then the virus will attack the beliefs that enter into that belief or into the possibility that the animal is a painted mule, donkey or pantomime horse, or that it is a hallucination, my cup of tea in the zoo cafeteria having been doped, or that it is a zoo keeper whom I see as a zebra, the real zebra appearing as a keeper, the one brushing the other's tail. And all these possibilities in their turn would be no sooner entertained than doubted and set against their contraries, and so on.... Nothing counts as a viable proliferation of doubt if logical possibility is the vector, for the body of belief and evidence would be lifeless in a former sea of discourse from which all meaning had been eliminated. Clearly, the underdetermination of belief by evidence is *fundamental* to one's cognitive and perceptual experience of the world.

How, then, is the original problem to be solved? The sceptical argument given earlier in schematic form starts from the premiss that I do not know that I am not a brain in a vat, for if I were then my experiences would be the same. If the discussion thus far is along the right lines, then this first premiss is mistaken in what it asserts, so that the problem is thereby resolved. From the fact that any particular knowledge claim is always based on evidence with which at least one sceptical hypothesis is consistent, it follows not at all that the claim should be revised, for logical possibility cannot be a basis for legitimate doubt, and it is a fundamental condition of discourse that all empirical beliefs should have logically possible contraries. If it is now asked whether infallibility is intrinsic to the concept of knowledge, the question is, I am sure, not without interest, if only for the reason that to answer in the affirmative is to imply, rather contentiously, that the verb 'to know' is invariably misused when positively applied, for it is always possible that we are wrong when we think that we are right. In the present context, however, that question may be bypassed, for it is open to us, inconvenience apart, to speak not of knowledge but of justified belief and entitlement to certainty – or virtual certainty if one is going to be pedantic, or perhaps overly pedantic, it being arguable, after all, that logical possibility in itself has *no* epistemic weight. If that is the position taken, then it has to be squared with the fact that some of the various possibilities we have considered feel epistemically heavier than others

That we are brains in a vat is a mere logical possibility and lies at one extreme on the epistemic scale, whereas a supposed zebra being in a particular case a cleverly disguised mule is more easily accommodated in one's thoughts, for the possibility, if realised, would do far less violence to our belief system. Perhaps better, then, to place logical and negligible possibility in different categories, the second included in the first; but for present purposes it does not matter, for the brain-in-a-vat hypothesis is only a logical possibility, and the painted mule hypothesis has negligible weight and lands like a feather, not like a lion, on one's identifying of zebras.

Perhaps I may conclude this chapter by reflecting on the significance of our findings in the greater scheme of things. If necessary conditions and synthetic *a priori* truth within a system are fundamental, then this imposes constraints on understanding and explanation. The reason is that the concepts of these fundamental properties themselves belong within the system, for nothing counts as a point of view external to it. All that we can do is to acknowledge these irremovable limits by appeal to ultimate mystery, the notion of which will occupy centre stage in later chapters. In the meantime, we have work to do, for the horse or disguised zebra that we have driven through the problem of induction and through the philosophy of probability reasoning has churned up the hitherto solid ground of inductive inference itself. Time, then, to reconstruct induction on the broader basis of empirical inference, a metaphor the infelicity of which, or so I trust, will become apparent when we now turn to confirmation theory and the analysis in terms of a system of our reasoning about the world.

Chapter 9: Goodman's Paradox

In previous chapters I have tried to penetrate deep into the nature of belief and understanding in order to extract the fundamental conditions of reason. What is fundamental is not that the earth is old or that it rained yesterday but that reliance on memory is an absolute condition of knowing, believing or doubting anything at all, as is the debt we owe to expectation and prediction, together with dispositions being sacrosanct, beliefs being underdetermined, perception being inferential, and necessary conditions imposing hidden order beneath the surface of things. This is analysis in terms of a system, its enemy being empiricism and the radical scepticism to which it conduces. The sceptic about induction tells us that we stand on the solid ground of present and past observation, his target being the predictive structures built upon it, which he claims to be able to demolish by force of argument. How it is that knowledge of the past emerges intact is never explained, but nor does it matter, or not if it can be shown, in terms of a system, that past, present and future cannot be epistemically separated off into solid base and fatally flawed constructions upon it. This has, I trust, indeed been shown, and with it the self-refutation of inductive scepticism, the method used being that of a particular pattern of analysis. On that analysis the solid ground of the sceptic, given his assumptions, has been found to be full of holes, his horse having fallen into one of them. No doubt there are insights to be gained from digging even deeper now that the sceptic is lost at sea, his charger having limped over a cliff.

That being the case, one is again entitled to expect the cows to come home because they always have, a question arising only about the place of induction within the system. Accordingly, what I now propose is to bring our campaign against the sceptic to a close by re-assessing the role of induction in factual reasoning, my hidden purpose being to expose the myth of inductive inference. This will involve reaping what was sown in our treatment of intentionality in previous chapters, and perhaps being able to harvest a contribution to confirmation theory. To that end, we shall focus more on the nature of induction than on justifying it, and in particular on whether the question of the projectibility of some predicates but not others is fundamental. There is, too, a related question as to the criteria by which instances are identified and labelled, and as to the link between language and the locating of similarity and difference in the world. This is all very abstract, so perhaps we may give substance to it, as always, by fleshing it out in the form of an example, in this case one that I hope will dispel darkness in favour of light.

Suppose that upon entering a room I flick a wall switch and expect a light to come on. For my expectation to be met, it will have to be that the circuit is live, that the switch and bulb are connected, that the bulb filament is intact, ..., and so on. These are empirical conditions for the correctness of what I expect, but I need not be aware of them, or of all of them, in order for my expectation simply to obtain. Neither, it might be thought, need I have any cognisance of the deeper causes of my expectation, apart from its connection with a wall fixture. Clearly, there is room here for theorizing about the epistemic aspects of causation, except that the appeal to induction would seem to be more axiom than theory. The fact is, after all, that if I am newly arrived from a switchless land, and if I witness an object on a wall being pressed, whereupon the room is instantly illuminated, then on the basis of that single instance I may grasp the causal connection. Eventually, given the usual everyday experience of switches, I may get used to them and forget, especially if doorstepped by inductivists, that a single instance had been all the instruction that I needed. Sensing victory, the Humean proselytisers now point out, correctly if other things are equal, that if that first success with switching lights on had been followed by failure, the room now being lit by candles, then I would not have made the causal connections by which one learns to activate a light. True, one might think, but unclear in its implications.

What *is* clear is that we should target the view that the repeated instantiation of a property or event generates and justifies the expectation of further instances. This, given its lack of qualification, is narrow inductive inference, defined as being linear, epistemically separate from any background information, and based solely on repeated instances which determine the nature and strength of the resulting belief. This enumerative principle, sometimes referred to as the straight rule, is almost a caricature, but keep in mind the kind of thing that those who take Hume's arguments at face value would say; for instance, that if Hume is correct then there is no reason to predict *anything*, where this is to imply that all prediction is inductive or can be justified, if at all, only inductively. On a system-based view this is nonsense, but it does indicate a certain kind of approach to empirical inference, one which lends itself to problem and puzzle, as we shall now see when we turn to what Nelson Goodman refers to as the new riddle of induction.

9.1: The Riddle of the Philosopher's Stone

Our present concern is with a problem familiar to gemmologists in the form of Goodman's paradox or the new riddle of induction. If we enquire into the distinctive features of emeralds, taking greenness, rather perversely, to be a contingent property, then it would seem that we reason inductively when we say that all emeralds are green. This is an example of what Goodman refers to as the straight rule of induction, and what it means in the present case is that on the basis of all known emeralds being green, we take this to be true of emeralds in general, whether in a display case or still in the ground. As philosophers, however, rather than prospectors, we may prefer to be epistemically economical, perhaps by venturing to suggest only that the colour of the next emerald to be extracted will be green, an inference the modesty of which cannot save it from sceptical challenge. Goodman does not, in fact, make the sceptical case in the traditional way, preferring instead to pose a question as to what it is about properties such as colour that makes them projectible, an answer in terms of natural kinds not being found adequate. To expose the difficulty, using as an example the hypothesis — in the present context — that all emeralds are green, he constructs the rival hypothesis that they are grue, the concept of which applies to 'all things examined before *t* just in case they are green but to other things just in case they are blue'.(1983:74) They compete, one might argue, because emeralds observed before *t* to be green are also grue, so that such instances equally confirm the conflicting hypotheses

193

that they will be green after *t* and that they will be blue. We shall consider this argument as it stands, but first we need to point out that Goodman now introduces the term "bleen", such that bleenness is a property of emeralds examined before *t* and found to be blue, or after *t* and found to be green.

He now claims to be able to exhibit these new predicates as being primitive, so that "green" and "blue" are defined in terms of them and thereby become positional, an object being green if it is found before *t* to be grue, or after *t* to be bleen, and the converse for an object being blue. Goodman now asks why we should take green and blue to be the host, as it were, with grue and bleen being the parasite, the point being that no answer is readily forthcoming, where this is taken to illustrate the general difficulty of accounting for the way in which we pick out some predicates but not others as projectible. The answer that he eventually settles on is that the predicates we find it natural to project are those that burrow deep into the language, thereby becoming entrenched. But we have to analyse the problem, in which direction there be dragons, before discussing any attempt at resolution.

To begin with, if Goodman intends "grue" and "bleen" to be taken seriously as rival colour predicates to "green" and "blue", then one condition, it is commonly held, is that the new terms in relation to the old should exhibit logical symmetry, the meaning of which will depend on what one makes of Goodman's definition, that of "grue" already given, except that it very obviously requires clarificatory detail, which Goodman does not provide. This helps to explain why it is that analysing the problem will be no easy task. For there is no consensus as to meaning, or what the nature of the problem really is, or whether it is different from Hume's problem, as Goodman contends, or even whether it is a genuine problem rather than signposting others that are. That said, it seems to me that there is nothing intrinsic to the subject matter itself that renders it unamenable to clear expression.

In the interests of clarity, let us ask about the nature of the disjunction by which "grue" applies to 'all things examined before *t* just in case they are green but to other things just in case they are blue'. One possibility in terms of predicate logic is that the disjunction is formally inclusive, which is to say that if P and

194

Q are the two parts of an inclusive disjunction, written "P ∨ Q", then either P is the case, or Q is, or both are. Consider, then, an unripe fruit that looks green before nightfall on a certain day and is then placed in the dark in a heated container, ready to be opened the next morning, whereupon it has changed from green to blue. Does this qualify as an instance of grue? Seeking an answer, note first the similarity between this case and the one about to be discussed. According to Frank Jackson in an influential paper, one interpretation of "grue" runs as follows ' D_1 : x is grue iff x is green before T and blue thereafter, where T is a chosen time in the future.' This definition by temporal conjunction of terms, as he points out, entails that "grue" must satisfy both conjuncts: not just the first in the form of "green before T" but also the second in the form of "blue thereafter". Put another way, an object cannot on this account be grue before T simply by virtue of being green, for it is also required to be blue after T as opposed to being grue *if* it is blue after T. This is overlooked by some who use this definition, he says, as evidenced by their referring to an object that is green before T as being grue; and yet they treat as a contingent question that of whether the object is grue after T. Jackson does not take it further, preferring instead to maintain that "grue" thus defined, or similar such terms, do not lend themselves to paradox and are projectible. One example he gives is of tomatoes being predicted to ripen from green to red. Note, however, that this prediction is based on seasonal changes repeated every year, so perhaps we should assume that the same applies to time T. The point, anyway, is that on D_1 there is no paradox of induction. That said, it counts against any notion of induction as a simple projection from similar instances, for the inference is from an object being green to its being blue, which is to say that it does not conform to the straight rule.

What, though, of the present interpretation in terms of inclusive disjunction? We know that all interpretations are subject to the straight rule being applicable, which it is if suitable it is based on evidence presented before T, and therefore we must suppose that such evidence obtains. This is to say in the present case that all examined unripe fruits of a particular kind have been found to be green; but from this we infer to all unripe sloes, say, being green, at least if the straight rule is applied; and, too, if we have no knowledge of their turning blue as they ripen. Since, however, there seems to be no paradox involved, we need to focus on Goodman's claims as to logical symmetry.

To begin with, it has to be acknowledged that symmetry in the form of interdefinabilty clearly obtains in the sense that "green", for instance, may be defined in terms of the new predicates as "grue before T, bleen after T", but only if these latter are defined in terms of green and blue. But these conventional colour terms do not depend for their meaning on that of the constructed terms. These latter, in my view, are semantically dependent, and in particular they are temporally positional in a way that the conventional terms are not. Goodman, however, would not agree, claiming as he does that his predicates may be applied without looking at one's watch, the same as with "green" and "blue". The problem here is that of trying to conceive of such a thing: How can predicates defined in terms of earlier and later than a particular date be applied in such a way as not to be accountable to which it is?

Certainly, this is a difficulty that exercises many commentators, including S.F.Barker and Peter Achestein (1960), the authors of a much-discussed philosophy journal article. Their concern is to highlight the significant ways in which the predicate pairs may be exposed as being asymmetrical in relation to each other.The implication, if they are correct, is taken to be that there is no new problem of induction, either because the so-called "grue" paradox derives from a specious argument or because it is little more than a variant of Hume's Problem.[6] Imagine, they say, that two people, Mr Grue and Mr Green, are speakers of the grue and the green language respectively and that time T is given by 2100 AD (I have updated it from 2000 AD). Then Goodman would say that Mr Grue is able to apply "grue" and "bleen" concepts irrespective of whether he knows the date, so that for him

---

[6]Cf Simon Blackburn in *Reason and Prediction* for the view that it is the old problem in disguise

196

the predicates are non-temporal, the same as the more conventional predicates are for Mr Green. In order to expose the falsity of this claim, the two authors ask us to imagine that Mr Grue is shown two identical black and white pictures, both of a tympanum, one representing it as it is now, the other as it will be in 2100 if it does not change colour. Asked to choose from a palette the colour of the tympanum as it now is, he selects what we call blue and he calls bleen. Asked to do the same in the second case, he selects bleen from his point of view and green from ours. Thus it is that he chooses two colours for the bleen colour of the tympanum, depending on whether it was represented as existing before or after T. They point out, too, that if Grue was again asked which paint to use to represent the bleen tympanum, but without being told whether the picture would represent the tympanum as existing before or after 2100, then he would not be able to choose between, as we would say, the blue colour and the green colour. It is in this and other ways that they seek to prove that asymmetries obtain such as to expose the grue paradox as being spurious.

Whilst I do not wish to disagree with people who would agree with me, thereby creating a paradox, I think that there are simpler ways of making the point about asymmetry. Suppose that I look at a particular object for the first time, so that by conventional description I see it as blue, but that I do not know whether the time is before or after T. Then I do not know whether the object is grue or bleen, the point being that I cannot tell which it is from the way it looks; and yet the deviant terms are presented as being colour predicates. But if they were, and if conditions were ideal, I would be able to identify an object as grue simply by looking at it, rather than also having to look at my watch or calendar. And if I did look, thereby ascertaining that the time is before T, then why should it not be said that by "grue" I mean "green if before T"? And similarly for "bleen" after T. This is to take "grue" and "bleen" to be temporally constrained synonyms of "green" and "blue"; but that, for all that has been proved differently, is exactly what they are.

Taking this further, suppose that a woman retrieves a cache of emeralds just before time T, each of them hidden from view in its display box, and that she has been taught the use of "grue" and "bleen", which she knows to be time-positional. Sitting in a pub, with T only a few minutes away, she has opened all but one of the boxes, the emeralds all turning out to be green, when a man sidles up to her and asks her what the significance of time T is with regard to the new colour predicates. When she answers that it is completely arbitrary, he invites her to bet against him that the colour of the contents of the last box will be grue after T, which is to say blue. But the woman, however favourable the odds, will decline the offer, otherwise it would be impossible to explain her having survived long enough to be an emerald thief. The point, despite its denial being so widespread in the literature, is that if Goodman is correct about grue emeralds before T probabilifying their grueness after T, then the woman should expect the emeralds to change from green to blue at the stroke of T. In reality, of course, she would have no such expectation.

That being the case, perhaps we should ask the following question: by what compelling argument, which we have shown that it would need to be, does Goodman seek to convert us to the sceptical cause? The answer is that he or his followers point out that if we start with "grue" and "bleen", then it is "green" and "blue" that are defined positionality in terms of time T. But these latter are temporally positional only in relation to "grue" and "bleen", not in their normal entrenched applications. Therefore, they then announce, it must be that if the newcomers were entrenched in the same way and part of everyday colour discourse, then they, too, would be non-temporal in their normal use.

But is it really true that if "grue" had been part of the English language instead of "green" or "blue", then Anglophones would have been able to use it as a non-temporally positional colour word? It seems unlikely, to say the least of it, and for several reasons. The first is that if it were possible to use it in that way, with no need to know the time, then speakers of English would acquire that ability simply by virtue of learning the word just as they already learn new words or new languages. If this were not the case, then Goodman would suffer under the same cognitive restriction, which is to say that he would be unable to understand the meaning of his constructed predicates — and yet he claims to know that "grue" as a predicate is not positional and in that way corresponds to "blue" and "green". We are always able to extend our vocabulary, and the addition of "grue" is a case in point, for we already have the relevant colour concepts and access to a timepiece. What we cannot do is to take a time-positionally defined word and use it without knowing whether it is before or after the temporal dividing line.

Since there are several ways of making the same point, perhaps we should consider another of them. We are told that "grue" has a non-positional meaning that we cannot grasp because it is not entrenched in the language. Still, it is a colour word, the same as "green" and "blue" in being non-positional. But it does not pick out those colours, otherwise it would be positional, therefore it must pick out a new colour. The reality, however, is that there is no such colour and Goodman's terms are indeed positional. Hence the point we have been making about "green" and "blue" being pre-existing colour terms and "grue" and "bleen" being parasitic upon them. To sharpen it, I suggest that we now do some re-defining of our own, the place to start being with Goodman's definitions, except that we shall dispense with their formal disjunctive properties. Accordingly, we need four new terms defined as follows if we leave out the quotation marks:

Grebet = green when seen before T
Blaft = blue when seen after T
Blubet = blue when seen before T
Graft = green when seen after T

This gives:

Green = grebet when seen before T, graft when seen after T
Blue = blubet when seen before T, blaft when seen after T

Now suppose that our thief views all the emeralds but one before T, so that they are grebet, in other words green. Then the evidence probabilifies the last emerald being green, in other words grebet or graft, depending on whether it is seen before or after T. Since there is no paradox here, it is for Goodman to explain how it is that using formal terminology to disjoin the alternatives probabilifies the last emerald being green if examined before T and blue if examined after T. Clearly, it does no such thing, the impression of paradox evaporating when the obstacles to clear thinking are removed.

More than enough has been said, in my view, to compel the conclusion that the "grue" paradox is contrived and that the significance one attaches to it is misplaced. But how is it, in that case, that the predicates, or the claims that have been made for them, have been taken so seriously? One answer, as we are about to discover, concerns the psychological factors involved in reasoning about contentions issues widely agreed to be worth discussing. The following, I hasten to say, is not an *ad hominem* attack on those who read significance into Goodman's thesis, for I have already rebutted it. That said, my aim is partly to consolidate the gains that have been made.

If we note first the universal tendency to confuse the perplexing with the profound and imperspicuity with inability to understand, then it seems to me that this is much in evidence in the debate about grue. Since this latter is defined in terms of two colours and the concept of relative temporal position, it is governed by a principle of interpretation: that nothing should be said about grue that is not authorised by its definition. This is one of the points made, but differently expressed, by Barker and Achinstein, though not addressed by Goldman in his reply to them. By that principle, one cannot logically infer from the interdefinability of the two pairs of predicates to "grue" being non-positional in its application. If this is overlooked, it is not because the inference follows naturally in itself, for it is obvious, or should be, that "green" and "blue" are non-positional, unlike "grue" and "bleen".

An explanation is needed, and this is where psychological factors come into play, for what we are also told is that the new predicates appear to be temporally positional because they are not entrenched, unlike the predicates whose place they would have taken. In our confusion about what it is for language to be entrenched, and in our fear of betraying ignorance of the profundities we worry may be involved, we cease to think at all clearly. In particular, we do not ask whether the deductive leap is from one side of the deck to the other as opposed to plumbing any real depth.

What also militates against clarity of thought, as already implied, is the use of the formal terminology by which the predicates are defined and the fact of interdefinability expressed. It does not help, either, that Goodman makes no attempt to clarify the definition, this being left to commentators such as Jackson, whose clarification seems to undermine the problem itself. What we found earlier, indeed, is that Goodman's formal definitions may be dispensed with, the preference going to a plain-English defining of the predicates in question, which thereby become perfectly clear and unambiguous in their application. Their only drawback, ironically speaking, is that the grue paradox then turns out to be nothing of the kind.

9.2: The Myth of Inductive Inference

What I now propose is to draw upon this and previous chapters in taking a fresh look at inductive inference and the role it plays in factual belief. An assumption underlying Goodman's paradox is that empirical inference depends on intrinsic evidential relations between similar instances of a suitable kind, the task being to ascertain the principle by which some predicates, but not others, are deemed to be projectible. What I have in mind is to overturn that assumption as part of a larger attack against empiricism, in particular those aspects of it by which the notion of inductive inference and the problem of induction are buoyed up. If we return to ornithology, in particular to swans, then suppose that I open a box, glance into it and then close it, confident that I have glimpsed a swan inside. Then this is to say that from a myriad of possibilities I have embraced a single one on a very limited observational basis. One could, as always, rationalise this process by appeal to induction, for it is arguable that observational beliefs, although underdetermined by the perceptually given, are usually correct — or more particularly that what looks like a swan usually is one. We addressed this issue in the introduction, but in the meantime we have established that the underdetermination of belief by evidence is fundamental, for it is only within its framework that one may attempt to bring evidence and belief into line in any particular case. Looking more closely at what my glance seemed to reveal to be a swan, I can confirm that I was right; but I thereby go beyond the evidence again, and in all the ways explored in earlier chapters. This point is not without importance, for what it indicates is that confirmation, too, belongs within a system and is underdetermined.

As for the appeal to induction, I would no doubt claim, if asked, that my perceptual identificatory skills, whether by cursory or close observation, have improved out of all recognition since I was a baby, on which basis I am confident that the object in the box is a swan. But the rejoinder to this, as I am sure we are familiar with by now, is that the appeal to past identificatory success relies on memory, the relation between memory and expectation being that of interdependence, and with expectation being itself a form of prediction. No wonder, then, that the notion of a system has become prominent as this book has taken shape, as also that of necessary conditions within that system; and it is only in terms of these that memory and expectation, the fact of underdetermination, and indeed empirical inference itself, may be grounded. Descending at speed from the general back to the particular, it may not be without interest to note, too, that perhaps I have never before seen a swan in a box — or at least not in a telephone box on a Sunday.

All that remains to be done, in the context of this enquiry into the nature of induction within factual inference, is to bring its findings to bear on the assumptions underlying Goodman's paradox: is there such a thing as a projectible predicate or property? Well, if I glance inside a box and seem to see a swan, then *something* is being inferred on the basis of that glance, as also if I give the occupant of the box a closer look. And the epistemic reality is that my identifying it as a swan is not in doubt – or, if it is, that at least I recognise it as a bird; or at least as a living creature; or, if I have not watched any nature programmes at all, as a feathery physical object. The point is that I slot what I see into a pre-existing perceptual system or explanatory framework; and thus it is that the reason why it is difficult to ascertain the principle by which some predicates are projectible and others not is that there is no such principle. But was it not said, albeit as a joke, that one may never before have seen a swan in a telephone box on a Sunday? Here, however, the question of projectibility yields to that of epistemic relevance, so that we may ask why it is that location and day of the week are taken to be irrelevant to whether a particular object is a swan. But now, what could be *more* relevant than these two factors if, for instance, one is not initially sure whether the bird in the telephone box is a swan or a seagull, that uncertainty being dispelled when one remembers that seagulls never make telephone calls on weekends?

What I now propose is to dispel in detail the myth of inductive inference, the place to start being with the straight rule. Is there such a thing? ? Well, if I am new to tomatoes and notice them growing in a greenhouse, I may infer to green being their permanent colour, though next year I shall expect them to change from green to red—or this year if someone chooses to enlighten me. On that basis, then, I now expect the tomatoes to ripen to red, despite there being nothing inductive about the inference that I make. Should I claim that most growers of greenhouse vegetables are reliable in what they say? If I believed otherwise, it might make a difference to my expectation of colour change; but it follows not at all that induction enters into the inferences that I make. All that happens, after all, is that I hear and understand the words and expect the tomatoes to turn red.

Now consider a simple example of the straight rule: taking ninety-nine balls out of a bag, I note that they are all red, this being the colour I expect the last one to be, other things being equal. But the fact of what I expect is framed by a complex structure of beliefs, assumptions, memories and expectations, all of them connected to others, the whole forming an epistemic network in which the notion of inductive inference is just one of the many that are in play. Now take it that other things are not equal, perhaps in the sense that I have been told—the appeal being to testimony again—that the bag contains one black ball. Or, that I saw the bag being filled and noticed it myself. Then I may now expect the last ball to be black—or, there again, perhaps I am not certain as to what I seem to remember seeing or hearing, in which case the weight of the original evidence may favour the last ball being red after all.

Since this concludes our discussion of intentionality and inference as the main topics under consideration, perhaps we should review the restriction on subject matter I occasionally refer to by way of reminder. The concept of the intentional, which we have treated to illuminating effect as belonging within a system of connections and conditions, is nevertheless irreducible, a fact which, or so I have argued, does not militate against metaphysical analysis. The reference is to the theory of consciousness I have outlined but not yet developed, the positing of a nonconscious existential state being one that resonates more with some parts of the discussion than others. A paragraph or two ago, for instance, I expressed the view that we may identify an object by glancing at it; and this is informative by fitting into a perceptually explanatory framework. the pre-existence of which is evidenced by the undoubted fact of what the psychology of perception refers to as perceptual learning. Since the notion of learning things, at least among humans, connotes changes to the brain — or at any rate evokes a picture of grey matter lighting up — the first step in constructing a theory of the non-conscious is to establish that it transcends the psychophysical; and this is what I shall do after the next chapter is brought safely to shore, along with the existence of other minds. At the end of this book, the theory of consciousness in question having been fully set out, it is possible that one would wish to re-read the intentionality chapters by the light of that theory.

At present my aim is to bring this discussion to a close by condensing its conclusions into the following few lines. There is no new problem of induction, Goodman's argument showing only that homonym-based enumerative inference is invalid, which we already knew. There is, on the other hand, a problem of physical-world inference, its difficulties being those of analysis. What that analysis reveals is that such inference merges the factual and the logical into necessary conditions within a system, and it is this that is fundamental, not induction. In this connection the following may be of interest. The empiricist view is that one's beliefs about physical objects are ultimately based on direct observation; but most such objects are taken to be solid, for which in most instances there is no direct evidence at all, the gaining of which would be too destructive. How, in any case, would one directly ascertain, even if testing to destruction were practicable, that particular objects in their entirety were solid? On the other hand it is arguable, as just implied, that the assumption of solidity is a necessary condition of empirical belief. What this points to, the same as a great deal else, is that the notion of a system is in strict opposition to that of a foundation.

Intentionality belongs with that system and is a very strange creature of contrasts, mainly between consciousness and the associated intentional states. Part of that strangeness envelopes the way in which we conceive of time, as if it flows from past to future through a fixed point of awareness, hence one of the main arguments I shall advance in support of my positing of the non-conscious. It runs as follows: if I close my eyes, my conscious purview at any particular moment reduces to feelings, thoughts and sensations, and even thus restricted they go beyond that moment. The point, at any rate, is that all that makes me what I am, including my stock of knowledge, my skills and abilities, must have a presence, where this is to imply that any appeal to dispositions leaves too much unexplained, or that a disposition, too, must have a source, and in that sense a presence. Since it cannot reside in a conscious moment, any more than a stream at a physical point, or indeed in temporally unrestricted consciousness, one must conclude that a realm of the non-conscious exists, which by its very nature is mysterious.

Finally, in shooting a quiverful of anti-sceptical arrows at the induction problem and that of perception, I have turned the sceptic's arguments against themselves, and in such a way as to combat scepticism on a broader front. Thus, it should now be safe to believe not only that the sun will rise tomorrow but that it has risen in the past, long before the advent of Homo sapiens and its ancient human ancestors, perhaps those who awoke to sunlight entering an African cave, the source of that light presenting itself, even in the Pleistocene, as existing objectively and unperceived. I imagine the philosophers among them, or the poets who awoke to fingers of light on a far-distant hill, as being too dazzled by the creator of each new dawn to question its predictability or ontological status. At the end of a day's hunting, however, as they lounge in the comfort of their cave and watch their menfolk make tea, I see one of them turn to abstract reflection and perhaps fall prey to a particularly disquieting philosophical doubt; how can she be sure that these others are conscious in the way that she is? Or even that they are sentient at all? Still, such doubts did not prevent our ancestors from breeding, as we know from the existence of present-day philosophy departments, so that a question arises as to what it is that a sceptic about other minds really believes. The fact is, after all, that philosophers would not be in relationships if they genuinely believed that their partners were automatons; but also, that it is possible to conceive of an individual who is genuinely an other-mind sceptic and believes herself to be utterly alone in the world.

Accordingly, I shall argue in the next chapter that this form of scepticism is a logically valid theory of one's place in the scheme of things, or at least that it is not self-refuting, which is to say that the foregoing anti-sceptical arguments have their limitations, this being one of the points I wish to make. By way of balance, however, I would add that there is much in the approach we have taken that is transferrable to the problem of other minds, some of the arrows finding their new target, and that the other-mind sceptic can expect strong opposition when she attempts, rather inconsistently, to convert us to her point of view.

9.3: Relaxing Effect of Problem Resolution

That, as I said, is for the next chapter. To bring this one to a close, I would like to report that I now sleep easily in my bed, having resolved the induction and perception problems at least to my own satisfaction. If I wake to a yellow globe glowing in the dark, I immediately recognise it as the moon, about which I am quite relaxed, so that I am soon asleep again. Sometimes, however, I reflect for a moment on the fact, which I am again able to take it to be, that the moon has shadowed the earth for aeons, as it will continue to do, rather annoyingly, after I am dead. Beginning to feel anxious, I now clutch at a special thought: that if the other-mind sceptic is correct, in which case he, she or it is mindless and a thing, since all consciousness in the universe must reside in myself, then I have no reason to believe that I am going to die, for I stand apart from all other organisms. I now imagine myself as the ultimate Robinson Crusoe, a castaway on an island of the self surrounded by automatons, with Man Friday a comfort only in the way that a teddy bear would be. On this showing, then, one regards oneself either as living and dying among fellow human beings or as gazing for ever across a sea of empty faces. To help us to decide, let us now turn the page.

Chapter10: The Problem of Other Minds

The literature reveals that there is more than one problem and that, conveniently, they have different names. Psychological solipsism, this being one, is the theory that an individual cannot even conceive of other people as being conscious; and the epistemological problem, this being the other, impugns the commonsense view of what we know of other minds, either by rejecting such knowledge altogether or by undermining it. The argument from analogy is not, after all, a solid basis for all that epistemic weight. Might it not be said, if criteria of knowledge are really strict, that although we are well-informed about our own mental states, admittedly with ourselves as the source of that light, what we know of others' is by contrast in shadow? Indeed it might, but to not much purpose, for the stricter standards are met, or so the non-sceptic takes for granted, by our certainty that other people are conscious, even if what they are thinking is anybody's guess. The point I wish to make in the next section is relevant to both conceptual and epistemological scepticism, but it is the latter that will concern us from this point on, initially in the form of outright rejection of one's knowledge of other minds, which I shall refer to as other-mind solipsism.

10.1: Transcending the Familiar

I shall now try to render as vividly as I humanly can the presumed reality of other minds, so that we may realise how much is at stake when the sceptic challenges received wisdom in this arena. Suppose, assuming a moratorium on scepticism for present purposes, that another person and myself are looking at a uniformly blue wall, and that the similarity between our colour experiences is as great as possible. Then it is my contention that they may be exactly the same, and in the same way as my own moment-by-moment experience of that colour, so that they are qualitatively identical. To bring out the essence of what this means, let us consider objections to it, one of which concerns personal identity. The argument, or perhaps unwitting assumption, is that even if my perceptual experience is the same as the

208

other person's, what this could mean is constrained by the fact that we have separate identities, so that for each of us our unique self runs through our own experiences like a name through a stick of rock. To this it may be replied, following Hume, that I am not acquainted with myself as a subject of whom experiences are predicated, for the self is not an introspectible object. One could argue, too, that even if it *were* such an object, the experience of it could be both the same for all of us and distinguishable from other kinds of experience, for instance that of blue. There is, of course, the grammatical subject, as when one says "I am immersed in blueness", but again this reference to oneself may be exactly the same as the other person's.

And, too, a question may arise, courtesy of the work of Thomas Nagel, of what it is like to have a particular experience. Using an illustration from chiropterology, Nagel asked what it is like for a bat when it deploys its echo-location sense, his point being that the answer lies outside our cognitive purview, since we lack that particular sense. I disagree with what is implied, believing as I do that one cannot know what it is like for another person, however close to us, to be that person, let alone for a bat to be a bat; but also for oneself when younger to have been that younger self. If you think this is going too far, take out an old photo or video of yourself and ask the relevant questions. What counts for now is that this emphasis on what it is like precludes not at all the possibility of multiple slices of a single experiential cake, or actual cake, being eaten both by oneself and by others and always tasting the same. That leaves dispositional differences, but there is no reason why these, too, should not be similar. Again, then, we are back with my experience of blue being qualitatively identical with the other person's. It follows that the felt reality of that experience may be *the same for both of us*.

This is a startling result and it merits the emphasis, one indication of which, if we allow the other-mind solipsist in again, is the crashing sound as he clashes with the reality of others' mental states. Here, however, we are in danger of pre-judging the issue, the avoidance of which requires us to address the sceptic's arguments directly.

10.2: The Epistemological Problem

Let us begin with an outline of the sceptic's approach to one's claim to know that others are conscious or have particular mental states. He argues that because all that I can observe or be acquainted with in other people is behaviour, unlike in my own case, my knowledge of their inner consciousness must be indirect. If my belief is that, for instance, another person is in pain, then this has to be an inference or justified as such, so that a question arises as to the grounds for it, except that it is impossible to find any that are adequate. If we take behaviourism to be a sceptical solution, self- and other-ascriptions of mental states are semantically asymmetrical; which is to say that there cannot be any reciprocity here, for it would then be the case that each individual ascribed mental states to herself and behaviour to other people; but this is a contradiction. Behaviourism, if one teases out its implications, is tantamount to psychological solipsism— the theory that I can conceive of mental states only if I predicate them of myself. But this is not a solution in any sense, and our rejection of it should inform our treatment of the epistemological problem, given our certainty that other people exist. Thus it is that my contention in the case of the radical sceptic about other minds is that he is required to advance very strong arguments if they are to be countervailing of my conviction that other minds exist; otherwise the battleship of my certainty will smash to smithereens his little craft of radical denial.

Continuing in this vein, let us now make a crucial observation: that the traditional sceptic about other minds cannot extend that form of scepticism, whether radical or moderate, to cover induction, perception or the past – on the contrary, the thrust of his argument just is that what we believe about other minds is at best only weakly supported when compared not only with direct awareness of our own conscious states but also with our knowledge of the physical world, including the behaviour and actions of its human occupants. I know a great deal, after all, about what other people say and do, where this includes my making predictions confirmable by direct observation. But when it comes to explaining my observations by way of inference to

210

particular aspects of the inner lives of other people, or when I predict their behaviour on the basis of such inference, then nothing counts as my direct observation or awareness of their conscious states. That, at least, is the received view.

How, then, are beliefs about other minds to be justified? One possibility is to appeal to the argument from analogy, but the stock rejoinder here is that this constitutes a very feeble argument, based as it seems to be on the single instance of one's own case. There is, I believe, a decisive reason to reject any appeal to analogy, and it concerns the way in which knowledge of oneself and others forms a system. When I ascribe a mental state or sensation, say pain, to another person, I do so from within a system of interpersonal reasoning in which this other person is already recognised as such, which is to say as being similar to myself and others in having an inner life. I interpret his behaviour in terms of a limited range of alternative explanations, which in this case reduce, broadly speaking, to his being in pain or pretending to be, both of which involve his being conscious. What lends itself to my construing him as a person is that I do not see people as physical objects and infer to their mental states; rather, I see them as looking out at me from their faces, on which the play of expression seems directly linked to their inner selves, just as I see physical objects as having spatial depth.

The upshot is that psychological predicates obtain within a system in which it is rational, or at least natural, to discover connections between the consciousness and behaviour of oneself and other people, so that the question of ultimate justification is hardly ever mentioned in polite conversation. It is this question, however, with which the sceptic is concerned, so that the argument from analogy would be required not just to operate within the system but to underpin it. This would not be an easy task, for to use that argument against the sceptic I have to imagine encountering an individual without recognising him as a person, not even at close quarters when I have a clear view of his facial expression and the play of his features, to which in the normal way I might respond. If, for instance, the individual I observe is hit by a falling tree, or even by a standing one if it is provoked, then instead of saying that I see his shocked expression and hear his cry

211

of pain, I must now report that a tree crashes onto an object or swipes it with a branch, causing it to fall over. A hole appears in its top section, which is similar to my head and face, and sounds are emitted, like my own when I am in pain; therefore, this object is likely to be in pain. As an epistemological basis for our whole system of interpersonal beliefs this is not very promising.

But why, exactly? One reason is that the argument from analogy is associated with empiricism. Necessarily, we are told, my beliefs about another's mental states must be justified independently of other such beliefs, the epistemic connection being with similarities between the other's outward signs and my own, these latter manifesting the inner mental state in myself from which I infer to the other person's. If this is the best that philosophical attempts at justification can produce after all these years, then perhaps it is empiricism itself that should be thrown overboard. The fact is, after all, that very often I do not have a mental state of a particular kind at the time that I predicate it of another person. If the rejoinder is that I must have had previous such experience, then this will never do, for it brings memory and expectation into play, which in any case is unavoidable; and we know from the last chapter that these are fundamental. With regard to memory, we have seen that it obtains within a system in which its general correctness is presupposed as a necessary condition of that system and of memory itself, such that it is only particular memories that may be, or need to be, checked against fact. Since these include the memories that would enter into arguing by analogy to another's mental states, what follows is that the argument from analogy, since it depends on the notion of a self-justifying system in relation to memory, thereby endorses it; and therefore it is not needed in support of one's knowledge of other minds, which also belongs within such a system.

That apart, and needless to say, it is clearly incorrect to claim that one can other-ascribe only those mental states with which one is personally acquainted. What, in any case, would count as the required similarity between one's own outward signs and the other person's? Or the required connection between outward sign and inner mental state? One can always find similarities; and as for the connection, one cannot see one's own face or otherwise observe one's own behaviour, or not in the way that external observers can. This is less true in the age of mobile phone cameras, but it seems unlikely that interpersonal knowledge of inner mental states has improved because of modern technology and social media.

10.3: Rejection of Radical Other-Mind Scepticism

Now that the argument from analogy has been jettisoned, given that it conflicts with the notion of a system, there remains only the radical sceptic about other minds, his moderate counterpart left high and dry, the tide having gone out on the argument from analogy being weak but not completely devoid of substance. Whether the moderate thesis can be refloated via some other moderately sceptical argument remains to be seen. Meanwhile, the radical sceptic has taken command of a fleet of arguments which we are about to overhaul. Before then, however, we need to establish the rules of engagement, in particular by asking whether the radical sceptic is entitled to demand that we start from scratch when attempting to meet his challenge. This is a pivotal question, already answered in consideration of the argument from analogy, but we need to ask it again in the present context. The answer, the same as before, is that the sceptic has no such entitlement, but this time for other reasons. Note first that I cannot establish the existence of other minds if I start from scratch, whether by digging my nails into the argument from analogy or in some other way. Therefore, this demand on the part of the sceptic would necessarily be unmet and would force me into other-mind solipsism, strictly unbelievable and therefore to be rejected. This is a *reductio ad absurdum* argument involving the threat of solipsism, its target being a possible sceptical manoeuvre by which that threat would be fulfilled. Secondly, and as already indicated, the sceptic cannot consistently insist that the knowledge of other minds that is presupposed within the system should be justified externally to it. For this is impossible, as is the external justification of memory and expectation or, indeed, anything at all. There is no escape from such a system, this being one of the ways in which the sceptic about memory or expectation refutes himself.

But can it really be correct, as I seem to be implying, that radical other-mind scepticism, strictly unbelievable, should be rejected on that account. A quite peculiar difficulty here is that the sceptic would seem to surrender too easily, his particular arguments not being mobilised, so that we have yet to confront them. Why speak of rules of engagement, one might complain, if the first rule is that one's opponent surrender without a fight? We shall continue to ignore the possibility that he might withdraw into a more easily defended moderate scepticism. But now, all that we said about the insincerity and equivocation of psychological solipsism applies to radical other-mind scepticism, in other words other-mind solipsism. The fact is, after all, that the other-mind solipsist does not actually demand that we start from scratch, perhaps because he is afraid of scuppering his own thesis, and with good cause. The only way in which he manifests his belief, so-called, that he is uniquely conscious is by articulating that thesis, which he does as if he means it, perhaps because he assumes that as a philosopher, he has a special dispensation; namely, to mean what he says and yet not act on it. But this would be a dispensation to indulge one's cognitive dissonance or artificially compartmentalised belief system. We have done enough, I think, to blow the radical sceptic about one's knowledge of other minds out of the water, and it is time to let the sea close over.

To sum up: we decided that we would not instantly torpedo other-mind solipsism, preferring instead to make our own demand: that the radical sceptic produce an overwhelming display of argumentative force by which to keep it afloat. But in reality no such armada of arguments is possible, in which case our interest in other-mind solipsism is in the way in which it goes wrong and what this tells us about theory-of-mind misconceptions as they enter into the philosophical analysis of psychological concepts. On that account, much of the work of this chapter so far, and of previous chapters, has charted a new theory of knowledge, one in which the notion of a system plays a prominent part, as indeed throughout this book. It will not be too much of a wrench, that being the case, if we now turn to the sceptic's actual arguments with a view to decommissioning them on the authority of the new epistemology, a process which itself will be a voyage of discovery.

10.4: Perceptual Versus Other-Mind Knowledge

One such argument is that propositions about other minds are fatally flawed in that, unlike those about the physical world or our own mental states, they are not directly verifiable. In preparing our rejoinder to this, focussing initially on our knowledge of the physical world, we need to ask why it is that direct verifiability is thought to make physical object statements rock solid, or the lack of it to make the inference to other minds entirely unwarranted. Since a physical object is three-dimensional, I cannot observe the whole of it at once, and in many cases all I ever see of it is its external surface. What is true is that I can see the whole of it, or the whole of the outside of it, if I turn it in my hand, for instance, or walk around it, unless it is the moon, and in this way none of it need be hidden from me, whereas the mental states of other people are always hidden. This is not in dispute, but the claim as to its epistemological import needs to be brought under scrutiny. If I believe that the door behind me opens onto a landing, I believe it now, despite the absence of any direct observational evidence. Such evidence may be obtained, it is easy to assume, by the simple expedient of opening the door. But the everyday distinction between direct and indirect evidence is not such as to privilege physical-world observation over the inference to other minds, or not according to the intrinsic perceptual inference thesis, whereby even the seeing of an object is inferential. If this is intrinsic to perception, then it detracts from the sceptical import of always having to infer to other minds, for direct physical observation, for instance of another person's body, is also fundamentally inferential.

One may be tempted, faced with an epistemic equivalence claim of this kind, to object that repeating an observation, and confirming it thereby, is always possible when looking at another person as a physical object, whereas one cannot see that person's mental states even on a single occasion, let alone retrace one's observational steps. This is true but any claim as to sceptical import is misconceived, as is much more easily seen, ironically, if the sense of sight yields to that of touch. A blind woman who is also deaf may rely on touch when identifying her husband, which is to say that her tactual ascertaining of his marital status proceeds from one moment to the next, the void on one side occupied by memory and on the other by expectation, and between them the fleeting sensations, phenomenally, of the feel of him.

If this is correct, then the process of arriving at a perceptual belief and directly verifying it is wholly dependent on memory and expectation in one form or another, the point being that the past is no more directly accessible to me than the contents of another person's mind. That being the case, it is arguable that although there is a familiar sense in which physical object statements may be directly verifiable in a way that those about other minds are not, this does not yield a distinction that the sceptic about other minds can legitimately exploit. In terms of a system, the notion of direct verification commandeered by other-mind solipsism loses much of its forward thrust, the sceptic beginning to turn in a circle. He relies, after all, on memory and expectation, and in the same way as we all do.

10.5: Comparison With Introspective Knowledge

Now that the radical sceptic is all at sea with regard to knowing directly as opposed to indirectly, it is time to consider another deficiency of statements about other minds, if the sceptic is to be believed, the comparison this time being between such statements and those about the conscious phenomena of one's inner life. Again it is not in dispute that one's beliefs about the inner lives of others are evidentially indirect; but let us now turn to what passes for direct knowledge in one's own case, by way of the stock example of knowing that one is in pain. In an earlier chapter I maintained that one's authoritative self-ascribing of pain is contingent upon one's understanding of the ascription, which involves memory and being suitably disposed, so that it goes beyond what is given, which always falls short or overshoots. All this, together with an irreducible semantic or cognitive element, makes the difference between having a pain and knowing that one has it, if such knowledge is verbally expressed. Not only does knowing that one is in pain go beyond the sensation itself, but a great deal of that knowledge is indirect in more obvious ways, even with regard to pain, as with one's belief that one felt pain yesterday or an hour ago; and, too, there is all that one believes about one's intentions, one's moods and emotions, not to mention the difficulty of capturing a particular thought, which itself requires a different thought.

Recall, in this regard, the way in which in the previous chapter micro-analysis was deployed against any simple conception of knowledge by acquaintance, for instance in the case of past pain, the time interval not being an hour, as in the last paragraph, but a moment, hence the micro-analysis. The hidden fact about introspection, I claimed, is that the myth of the present, as I called it, interposes itself between us and the introspecting of, in this case, the pain we feel, which we take to be the pain we feel now, at this very instant, as if introspection were instantaneous. What becomes obvious on reflection is that on the contrary it is a temporal process, for instance if we report our findings and say that at this very moment we feel pain. But pain at any particular moment does not wait for description to catch up, the gap being bridged, rather, by memory and expectation, the necessary reliance on which is incompatible with simple certainty in any particular case. Certainty there certainly is, but of a most peculiar kind, its character bound up with memory and expectation as interdependent necessary conditions of discourse. There is much to be certain about in this peculiar sense, including the avowals to which we devoted a chapter on its own.

10.6: Moderate Other-Mind Scepticism

Setting the radical sceptic adrift, let us now ask whether a less extreme form of epistemological scepticism about other minds is worth considering or has been considered. What is often discussed, after all, is whether the credentials of the argument from analogy can be established by those who make claims for it as a defence against the sceptic, or whether it is the weak argument it seems to be, rather than no argument at all; and the indication here is that there may be a milder form of scepticism, in which it is queried whether the evidence warrants the certainty with which we attribute particular mental states to other people. There are difficulties here, apart from those arising from the obvious fact that very often we are not certain about other people in particular cases of ascribing mental states to them. There is, for instance, a difficulty attaching to the fact that the moderate sceptic, like his radical counterpart, is not entitled to insist that we start from scratch in grounding our beliefs about other minds. Rather than attempt to deny us access to the explanatory system in which such beliefs have purchase, he must show, if he can, that the inferences by which we arrive at them are less well-founded than we think. If to that end he clings to the indirectness of the evidence on which such inferences are based, then he can undermine them only if it can be shown that our rebuttal of the radical sceptic, with regard to evidence being indirect, is not effective against himself. An obstacle he faces, which perhaps is irremovable, is that the interpersonal explanatory system already accommodates the multiplicity of ways in which indirectness of evidence imposes epistemic constraints on the beliefs in question.

Suppose, for instance, that I am a research scientist doing laboratory work with a colleague, and that I form the hypothesis that hand contact with the flame of a lit Bunsen burner is painful. We now devise an experiment in which I place my hand in the flame, my colleague taking notes, whereupon she does the same, with me taking notes with my good hand. If the experiment now begins and I scream and leap into the air, my colleague reacting similarly in her turn, then I directly confirm the hypothesis in my own case but only indirectly in my colleague's. The difference this makes is that I am certain that I felt pain and still do, whereas it may be, for instance, that I have reason to suspect that my colleague suffers from congenital analgesia and pretended to feel pain because she does not wish her condition to be publicly known. And there are, of course, many cases in which a difference is made, for there are countless ways in which we are less certain about other people than we would be about ourselves. Given, then, that the system already makes allowances for evidential indirectness and uncertainty, as manifested in such differences, how is the moderate sceptic to proceed and what exactly does he wish to challenge? Would he claim that most people injudiciously compare others to themselves, for instance that there are many cases in which, unlike in the present one, we completely ignore the possibility of dissimulated congenital analgesia when someone gives every sign of being in pain? But now, such a possibility and the claim about ignoring it lie within the system, not outside it, for what is implied is that deviations from the norm are sometimes overlooked, this being a proposition which presupposes the existence of other minds and the legitimacy of the evidence thereof.

Continuing in our quest to find an epistemological niche for moderate scepticism, let us now ask whether a sceptic about other minds could mildly insist that one take more seriously the possibility of consciousness being unique to oneself. Since I have already acknowledged that no amount of evidence that other minds exist entails that existence, I have to agree, indeed claim, that such uniqueness is a logical possibility, all consciousness residing in myself; but this does not make me a sceptic, not even a moderate one, for logical possibility cannot of itself sustain any degree of doubt. It is possible, after all, with regard to the earlier laboratory experiment, that my fellow scientist not only suffers from congenital analgesia and pretended to feel pain but that she hypnotised me, unbeknown to myself, into believing that my hand was in the flame, which surreptitiously she had just switched off, and into reacting as if in pain, which I continued to believe that I felt. Her motive, perhaps, was to spare me suffering and at the same time indulge my insistence on treating as a hypothesis a glaringly obvious fact. Since, however, this possibility lacks any evidential support, I cannot coherently entertain it, and the reason is that if evidence is not required then *anything* is possible, including that the experiment never took place and that my colleague never existed. Logical possibility on its own, pace Descartes, has no sceptical significance in everyday reasoning and none in epistemology either.

If this is correct, then the sceptic is required to give reasons why the possibility in question should be taken more seriously, and again we have to ask whether in the context of a system these would be internal, in the sense that they would counter the evidence that other minds exist, the strength of which would be acknowledged. One may imagine, if the sceptic is myself, that I come to believe that it has been revealed to me in a vision that I am the only conscious human being, the others all being automatons programmed by extra-terrestrials, no expense spared, to keep me company. Such scepticism, however, would be neither moderate nor philosophical, so we need concern ourselves with it no further, neither in this chapter nor in the one about to be opened. There has been, I think, only one chance for the moderate other-mind sceptic to prevail, and to take it he had to show that our strictures against the radical sceptic do not apply to himself, so that he is justified in insisting that we take seriously, on the basis of evidential indirectness, the possibility of unique consciousness. This would entail that I, the author of these words, am the only conscious individual, since I know that I am conscious. I conclude that there is every reason to believe that other people exist, the one exception being the moderate epistemological sceptic about other minds.

Chapter 11: Mystery and Consciousness

My intention in this antepenultimate chapter and the next is to voyage in search of the mystery that attaches to that all-encompassing system the notion of which I have deployed in every chapter of this book. Within that system the mystery is that of intentionality; as such, it is distinct from the mysterianism associated with Colin McGinn, D.J.Chalmers and the Hard Problem of consciousness: that of the causal connection between brain and mind. They do, however, overlap, so that we need to deal with the Hard Problem in order to clear the decks and move on. Since the route that we take over the next two chapters will be circuitous, with several ports of call along the way, I suggest that we at least glance at the charts before setting sail. But also, the night being clear and finding ourselves on deck, that we identify some of the main constellations by which we shall navigate to journey's end. With that in mind, I shall first of all outline the considerations by which a route has been chosen and a plan of action devised, and then I shall plot the course that we should take.

If we start with the mind-body mystery, the one that Colin McGinn drapes over the Hard Problem, his thesis is that human beings are inherently unable to understand the fact of the brain causing consciousness. This thesis and the supporting arguments obtain within a framework of theory, in particular that which concerns the science of the psychophysical in its various forms, where these include neuropsychology, the study of mind-brain interaction. A salient contemporary feature of these disciplines, or so we are told, is that they are functionalist in method and lend themselves to that philosophical theory, as also to that of physicalism, including its non-reductive form. The first and last of these are associated with epiphenomenalism, the thesis by which, arguably, they are able to, or required to, dispense with the notion of mental causation, in other words causally active consciousness. This alleged redundancy fuels the Hard Problem, for we know that epiphenomenalism conflicts with our everyday intuition that the mental causes the physical, as when I cry out in pain or jerk my hand away from a hot stove. We are to take this to be folk psychology, which is meant to demean it, for the important connection, apparently, is that between physical injury and bodily reaction in one form or another, depending on the neuroscientific discipline involved and the philosophical approach. These may be such that allegiance is given to the principle of causal closure, according to which the cause of a physical event, including brain events, must always be another physical event. But surely, one might think, examination of brain processes cannot possibly reveal anything other than more of the same – indeed, we shall have some fun with this principle. For now, we note only that the Hard Problem in the present case is that of how it is that the tissue damage causes pain, a form of causation which, according to McGinn, is permanently cloaked in mystery; and, too, we may ask how it is that we feel pain if it really is the case that functionally there is no need. This leads to a further question: why is the implied redundancy of sensation counter-intuitive to such a high degree?

We shall essay an answer, but in the meantime a more detailed account of epiphenomenalism will perhaps aid perspicuity. Returning to pain, the theory is that it is physically caused but lacks all causal efficacy, which is to say that it cannot have any bodily effects or, presumably, mental ones, the same being true of all conscious phenomena that seem to contribute to mental causation. The epiphenomenal character of consciousness, as it appears to some theorists, invites a comparison with a train letting off steam. This instructs by being apposite in one way but not another, for a train lets off steam as the waste from a coal-fired steam-driven heat engine, which is to say that it is functional even if it does not itself help to push the train once free of it. This latter is the point of the analogy, but it may be misleading; for there is no explanatory gap in the theory of heat engines, whereas the steam of consciousness, according to the Hard Problem, is functional neither as cause nor as effect. The Hard Problem, on this showing, is that of explaining the particular character of different conscious phenomena, their physical causation and the fact of consciousness itself, given that on functionalist theory it is about as much use as a pram at a hen party

If the foregoing is correct, then proponents of the Hard Problem in philosophy detect a mystery in the fact of the brain as the seat of consciousness, where this represents both a narrowing down to the mind-brain problem of the traditional mind-body problem and its hardening into permanent insolubility. This is partly in reaction against the accelerating advance of the neurosciences and the freshness of so many new fields of psychophysical research, all of which is of interest to a functionalist or nonreductive physicalist in his role as neuro-researcher, philosopher or both. It may seem to such a person that a solution to the mind-brain problem will arise quite naturally when the neurosciences ripen and start to bear fruit. McGinn does not doubt that such a crop will be reaped, but he thinks that any buds that might hold out a solution will always fail to open. Hence his mysterianism, which we shall have occasion to reject, but not because we share the bright outlook that is characteristic of a new science and fully justified, I am sure, in the case of our future understanding of the neurosciences. Mysterianism is to be rejected because McGinn's notion of the mysterious is misplaced. It is naturalistic and depends on the premiss that the limitations of human cognition are such that we cannot understand the causal connection between brain and consciousness. This is to imply that we would, if differently intelligent, be able to understand it. I shall argue against this theory and in favour of the following: that there is indeed an irresolvable mystery, which is that of intentional consciousness, and that it transcends the neurosciences and their attendant problems. The mystery, in other words, is not naturalistic but metaphysical. This is a distinction that very likely will be flattened by future combine harvesters working in what I am sure will be a vast field of neuroscientific knowledge – one in which all the hedges between the different disciplines have been removed. If they spring back up, this will occur not in science but in philosophy.

Clearly, we are dealing with a complex of problems; and there are others, not yet featured, that compound it. These concern the epistemology and conceptual analysis of causation itself. It is undeniable that Hume's causal and inductive scepticism is germane to the brain-mind problem; for if causal relations are reductively explicable in terms of constant conjunction suitably

223

circumscribed, as Hume insists, then defenders of the Hard Problem, obliged to defer to the fact that the mental and the physical are constantly conjoined, should now attack Hume's thesis that causation equates with constant correlation, as we would call it. This is because Hume would disavow any notion of cause compelling effect, whereas McGinn and others would seem to require it. For if Hume is correct then the brain does not generate consciousness if this implies causal necessity as usually understood; but the question of whether it does or not is by no means easy of answer, and it is arguable that Hume's position is not so much that natural causal necessity does not obtain as that the notion of it is incoherent. Another possibility is that of taking a deflationary approach to this causal notion, such that it is taken to be compatible with constant conjunction. This is all of a piece with the widely recognised difficulty of coherently interpreting Hume's inductive or causal scepticism. The problem is partly that of reconciling it with everyday empirical inference or belief and with scientific method. McGinn, however, must believe that natural causal necessity exists, if we set aside some of the previous considerations, and this commits him to the rejection of Hume on causation; for otherwise the mysterian thesis would be that we cannot understand what it is for correlations to obtain between brain and consciousness. But that would be absurd—for clearly we can.

Now note, with regard to those who reject epiphenomenalism, that they, too, may be concerned with mental causation in the strong sense that implies causal necessity, if one may speak of such a thing; and that in this respect they side with common wisdom — or, if you like, with folk psychology. This would explain why the epiphenominalist thesis gives every impression of being strictly unbelievable. But another possibility is that the thesis should be dismissed because it entails the repudiation of a whole system of interpersonal discourse and psychological explanation; and of the very notion of each individual at the centre of his or her conscious world. This whole issue is, indeed, a tightly spun web of conflicting intuitions that will break if stretched beyond its limits, all of which militates against easy resolution or the acquiring of a coherent philosophy of mind. As regards this latter, if it just is a fact, however mysterious, that the brain causes consciousness, why should the converse not also hold, complete with mystery, so that psychophysical interaction is taken as fact in philosophy as in everyday life? The main reason concerns causal closure, one hears, but I have hinted that when this tugs at the web it is easily immobilised; and in any case it would, if it escaped into the field, have to negotiate the muddy furrows of the problem of causation. This may be possible, but the point is that any position one takes is open to challenge, therefore the argument from causal closure cannot be clearcut in the way that some commentators take it to be, and neither can epiphenomenalism.

If psychophysical interaction, by which I mean two-way causation, was deemed by philosophers to be seaworthy, as in any case it is in everyday life, its coming under scrutiny at the captain's table, as it were, would still be enough to drag perplexity in its wake; for if the fact of mental causation just seems so odd, then how can the ghost in the engine room possibly operate the physical controls? But it does, and the point about a ghost, with apologies to Gilbert Ryle, is not that it partakes of the insubstantial but that its essential nature is hotly debated, as befits an engine room, as is that of causal concepts in general. This is, in my view, a point about which one's reasoning turns, and it is pivotal because it necessitates a change of course.

In what does that necessity consist? If acceptance of mental causation is imposed on the crew, there will be mutterings among them about the difficulty of incorporating full psychophysical interaction into their theory of cause and effect. Very likely it will not be long before a schism opens up, with one half of the ship heading for the South Pole of natural causal necessity, the other for the North Pole of qualified constant correlation, and in each case the destination will not be reached. The reason, apart from a ship cut in half immediately sinking, is that this polarised treatment of the problem of causation in relation to consciousness contributes to its apparent intractability, and what this indicates is the necessity of seeking a solution midway between the two extremes, in fact by following the line of, as it were, the equator itself. In circumnavigating it, we shall describe a circle – that of the system to the centre of which all problems treated so far have gravitated. Our aim will be to show that thus located our present problems will also attract a solution; or at least that a resolution will be arrived at insofar as this is possible, given the mystery at the centre of the world.

Apropos of that aim, it may be recalled that in the chapters on the problem of induction and empirical inference in general we circumvented rather than confronted Hume's critique of inductive inference and causation, which is to say that the issue of causal necessity versus qualified correlation was referred to the notion of a system of conditions and connections. It was in this way that we neutralised some of the difficulties by which the problem of causation is constituted. For instance, natural causal necessity exhibits itself within a system as a relation between cause and effect that is necessarily subject to other things being equal. Speaking of which, such considerations led to the view that the distinction between inductive and deductive is not fundamental; but that the ceteris paribus condition is both fundamental and universal across all inference. Already, then, the causal aspects of psychophysical interaction seem to be more amenable to treatment, and there are other reasons, too, for seeking a system-based solution to the mind-body problem. For it was by means of the notion of a system that previous problems were solved and that we gained insight into the analysis of intention, perception, empirical inference in general, memory, expectation, causal concepts and much else, all of it relevant to the present set of problems.

Where, to return to it, does this leave mysterianism? If we do as I suggest, one of our aims will be to show that despite the perplexity we may feel, which I now suggest is genuine but misplaced, no mystery naturalistically construed attaches to the fact of psychophysical interaction. It is true that there are vast swathes of unexplored ocean, as befits the relative infancy of technology-assisted neuroscience and neuropsychological research; but this points not to mystery but to discoveries waiting to be made if the world of the psychophysical is to be fully mapped out. The mystery, if that is what one wishes to call it, is cartographical, whereas the mystery of intentional consciousness goes beyond the terrestrial into metaphysics and fills the whole of conceptual and cognitive space. Since it is to this that one's perplexity should be attached, one of my aims will be to demystify the fields of research just mentioned, all the better to demolish the pretentions of those who claim, or give the impression, that a full knowledge of the mental and its connection with the physical is over the horizon. One day, they seem to suggest, though without specifying the particular millennium, it will rise with the sun and reveal the character of consciousness itself. It will do nothing of the kind, or so I try to prove by detailed argument; but this returns us to a point already made and here emphasised: that the advance of the sciences in question, with their functionalist bias, will make it harder to keep consciousness in place between brain event and bodily reaction, or to stop it slipping below eye level and becoming invisible. But it will always remain, one trusts, just behind the foreheads of philosophers, who will continue to debate whether such localisation is at all significant in the context of a metaphysical treatment of the mind-body problem. This, to repeat, will involve the notion of the non-conscious in connection with intentionality.

But just because, one might think, the sciences cannot resolve the mystery of intentional consciousness, it does not follow that we are justified in positing a realm of the non-conscious as part of our theory of mind; for it might be, for all that we can tell, that consciousness and its brain-based aetiology are all that constitutes human mentality. This is the next leg of the voyage, that by which I seek to demonstrate that on the contrary we can be certain that the non-conscious exists, as also that it is the hiding place of the intentional, just as we know that the ship is upon the water, even if we have no idea what lies beneath.

11.1: Functionalism and the Hard Problem

Turning now from the preliminaries to the actual discussion, let us weigh anchor and make for the churning waters where the Hard Problem rocks in the waves. We shall creep up on it, oars muffled, the place to board being where the name itself implies an obvious comparison; and a distinction between the Hard Problem and easier problems of the psychophysical has indeed been made by McGinn, Chalmers and others, who think that there are obstacles to the understanding of human mentality that, even when hard in the ordinary sense, at least in principle admit of circumvention. With regard to psychology, for example, an inherent difficulty is that of combining the first- and third-person point of view. Such difficulties are said to be resolvable in mainly functionalist terms, the methodology involved being centred on observation rather than introspection, on the objective rather than the subjective, and on the functional rather than the phenomenal.

This is the approach by which the psychology of perception and of much else becomes a science with matching terminology, so that one speaks of sensory stimuli and information-processing in connection with the perceiving of a particular object, and of goal-directed response if the perceiver is actively interested in the object in any of a number of ways. An obvious objection here, in the context of a first-person point of view, is that the approach in question conflicts with it, the scientist overlooking, as always, that her knowledge of an independently existing objectively describable reality is mediated by her senses and the inescapably subjective character of their deliverances, all of which applies to perception of the sense organs themselves. Thus it is that methodology morphs into a theory that lends itself to the epiphenomenalistic approach.

That said, functionalism in philosophy, psychology or the neurosciences is, up to a point, in line with common sense, and we saw in the other-minds chapter that very often our everyday concern is with the overt behaviour and performance of other people, which clearly must also be of interest to the philosopher and the neuropsychologist. If this latter records brainwaves from a wired-up subject while he works out a mathematics problem, then quite possibly her concern is with the connections between brain processes and problem solving, not with conscious reasoning, provided that the subject actually is conscious. It does not follow, however, that particular conscious phenomena elsewhere are of no research interest or that they are inaccessible to the researcher, who perhaps is especially fascinated by, for instance, not just the physiology but also the actual experience of pain or sensation in general. Why is it, she might ask of the functionalist, that he barely glances at the pain itself, in line with which he rejects the everyday view of the explanatory efficacy of the consciousness involved in sensation, perception, memory, reading, writing and arithmetic? To begin with, I hear him reply, one should speak of causal, not explanatory, efficacy; but in that case, she counters, it is for him to clarify the distinction, and in such a way as to pay due deference to Hume. This brings us to the point at which the functionalist approach extends beyond methodology into theory.

For on one interpretation of the functionalist theory, which I shall refer to as being radical, the study of sensation, say, lays claim to being scientific when it focuses on function rather than phenomenology. What function might that be? is an obvious question, but in some cases, such as that of pain, the answer is clear enough on the everyday view of it. With physical pain, one feels it when, roughly speaking, bodily injury occurs and causes it, the effect of which is that one seeks to minimize the pain and concomitantly the damage, or to work towards repair. This is interesting, and perhaps a mental image of Darwin springs to mind; but any thought of the Hard Problem need not, for there seems to be no connection. What connects them, we are told, the everyday view being for peasants and their feral cousins escaped into the woods and high mountains, is that the causal processes involved are purely physical all the way from initial bodily trauma, if it occurs, to changes in the nervous system and, an instant later, one's very often involuntary reaction, perhaps in the form of snatching one's hand away from a hot stove. In this narrative one is permitted to feel pain, but it is reflected, as it were, off the physically observable, so that it becomes whatever sensation it is that is caused by injury and manifested in or leads to pain behaviour, where this includes that by which pain is avoided or relieved, the theory thereby being distinguished from that of behaviourism – but not, one might think, by much.

What one might think, indeed, is that the radical functionalist, like the behaviourist, feigns anaesthesia – that supremely quotable expression again. If pain is whatever sensation is caused by injury or manifested in pain behaviour, then it need not be a sensation at all. If this is acknowledged but not taken to be fatal to the theory, then perhaps the reason is one already familiar to us;

namely, that we are invited to focus on a particular case in considering a theory, and in order to make sense of the theory thus applied we follow the theorist in failing to apply it to similarly suitable cases. It is on some of these, because they have been overlooked by the theory, that the support this latter gains from the particular case depends. That support falls away when the theory is more consistently applied or when the attempt is made and the theory thereby exposed as being incoherent. Thus exhibited, it may not even hold for the particular case as an exception to the rule; or, if it does, then it is only as an exception. In the present case, that of a person injured and in pain, the functionalist account is very likely presented to us in third-person terms, so that we think of another person, not ourselves, as being in pain. Our stance is observational, the focus being on pain behaviour, and perhaps we tell ourselves that we cannot, after all, feel the victim's pain, so how do we know ...? And so on.

But at the same time, and quite unconsciously, as it were, we take the injured man to be conscious, and in any of the usual other ways, so that he is perceptually aware of his injury, or is in shock or anxiously waiting for the ambulance, or is astonished, almost, at the serenity that he now feels, all of which requires him to be awake and aware. But radical functionalism is consistent with a complete lack of consciousness in others, which is to say that it equates with psychological solipsism. We may be unaware or oblivious of continuing to use the whole of our interpersonal conceptual and epistemic scheme, proof of which is that we can be dissuaded from the theory if its implications for solipsism are pointed out. If that fails, then all that is needed is to gently turn us until we are facing a mirror, followed by the magic words about feigning anaesthesia, perhaps with the clarification that it would have to be the effects of a general anaesthetic, in other words unconsciousness, that we feign. The obvious truth, with a nod to Descartes, is that we believe that we are conscious; therefore, we are conscious and we know that we are, and the same in the particular case of pain. A theory of mind that applies only in the third person, if at all, but not in the first, is incoherent and absurd. Since radical functionalism thus characterised renders redundant the question of whether it leads to epiphenomenalism or solves

230

the problem of consciousness by eliminating it, we need no longer concern ourselves with it, at least for the moment, apart from some explanatory remarks as to the ways in which it gains purchase.

Turning to these, there is a well-known paper by Chalmers (1995) in which he is a radical functionalist in the stance he takes on the Hard Problem. Reading it, one may be struck by his inappropriate objectivity of style, as illustrated, for instance, in his list of conscious phenomena amenable to functionalist explanation, the fourth one of which consists of 'the ability of a system to access its own internal states'. This is computer-speak, behind which the hidden reference is, presumably, to an actual person being able to introspect his inner life or engage with his memory of past events. Comparing this translation into plain English with the original, it is easy to see why the latter is preferred, for it hides the fact, in the present case, that the "system" is a human being, to whom the distinction between subjective and objective applies.

Again, then, we have to ask how it is that the obvious can be overlooked; and one reason, in addition to that already given, is that Chalmers now distinguishes between consciousness and awareness, for instance in connection with a further distinction: that between wakefulness and being asleep. He says that 'Often, we say that an organism is conscious as another way of saying that it is awake.' Note the use of "organism" rather than "person". Reading the quoted sentence, we now think of being conscious as being awake, and any further statements about being awake we now unwittingly apply to being conscious. What are such statements? Turning to Chalmers again, 'For an account of sleep and wakefulness, an appropriate neurophysiological account of the processes responsible for organisms' contrasting behaviour in those states will suffice.' And now we think of the use of brain-imagery in ascertaining whether a person is awake, which the setting up of all that equipment would, one might think, guarantee. Perhaps the idea is that its use is consonant with wakefulness being a state of awareness rather than consciousness. The reality is that we closely associate being awake and being aware with being conscious, so that we assimilate them at the same time as

231

Chalmers wishes us to contrast them. I think I have done enough to be able to say that the theory of radical functionalism need detain us no longer.

11.2: Mental Efficacy and Causal Closure

We are left with moderate functionalism, which we may characterise as the theory by which methodological functionalism is intellectualized, given that no attempt is made to eliminate consciousness as opposed to sidelining it, this latter by appeal to epiphenomenalism. Witness the earlier reference to research into the connection between brain processes and mathematical problem solving, the conscious reasoning involved being ignored but not denied. Even here, however, the functionalist would seem to encounter a difficulty in adducing such a case, for what exactly would be the theory thereby supported? It would be epiphenomenalism itself, one presumes, against which one might argue that it is perfectly possible to conduct research into the connection between brain processes and conscious mathematical reasoning. The point to be made is that this would be different from the original research project, and with very different objectives or experimental aims. The functionalist's rejoinder would have to be that such an experiment would be pointless, because the conscious phenomena involved would be devoid of causal agency. One might ask why this would make them uninteresting; but for the moment our own interest is in moderate functionalism only insofar as it implies epiphenomenalism, which again makes its entrance and demands our attention.

What exactly is the case against mental causation? Note first that nothing in our theory of the non-conscious will conflict with the following: that if I strive to work out a maths problem in my head, then it is obvious to me, setting metaphysis aside, that it is by conscious reasoning that I may effect a solution; and, concomitantly, that the mental effort involved is also conscious. If this apparent causal process can be shown to be illusory, then the sceptical argument by which this is achieved must be very powerful indeed. The reason, as already pointed out, is that to cleave to that sceptical conclusion is to renounce the entire personal and interpersonal explanatory and conceptual scheme by which discourse about the mental, the physical and their interrelations is made possible. What we actually find, however, is that the theorist invokes considerations that are very general, their application far from obvious, such as that conscious causal efficacy violates the principle of causal closure, whereby physical events may have conscious effects but are themselves purely physical in their aetiology. Now, a difficulty with appealing to this principle is that one thereby pre-judges the question of whether mental events may generate physical effects. But surely, it will be said, the principle must already have proved itself in order to gain its credentials; and it does, after all, have glowing references from the hard sciences, including those for which the brain is an object of interest. No reputable researcher would claim that mental causation reaches beyond the individual human body, and even if the claims for telepathy or telekinesis could be substantiated, the mechanism involved would no doubt reveal itself as being physical, especially in the case of telekinetically willing a physical object, perhaps a pedestrian, to move out of the way. What the principle shows is that a conscious event cannot have a physical effect, for that would involve a physical force, and such a thing is completely alien to our conception of consciousness.

That, at least, is what one imagines being said, but it will never do, and for two related reasons. The first is that some of the argumentation just detailed would apply equally to brain processes causing conscious ones: how can a brain event, involving physical energy or force, cause a non-physical event? This, one may recall, is a source of bafflement to McGinn, Chalmers and other mysterians. Secondly, the charge that the use of the principle is question-begging still stands. For the point about the brain is that it is wholly unlike other physical objects in that it is the seat of consciousness; hence my saying that the two reasons are connected. One cannot extrapolate from causal relations in the purely physical realm to those in the psychophysical. One has to look and see, and what is found is that clearly the physical causes the mental, as with injury causing pain; and also, one might think, that clearly the mental causes the physical, as with pain and its overt expression and associated avoidance behaviour. Since, if this is correct, one should be able to put it to the test and show that it is, I suggest that we join a scientist of the psychophysical in her laboratory.

Suppose that she is conducting research into the seeing of ambiguous figures, to which end a subject is shown a Rubin's face-vase figure and instructed to press and hold the button with a "V" on it when he sees a vase and the other, button F, when he sees two faces, the hypothesis being that he will increasingly see the figure as a vase rather than as faces. This may be tested if the button-pressing information is fed into a computer, which at the end of the session will display the processed data in graphical form. It is possible that the terminology by which experiments of this kind are written up will favour observation over subjective account, for instance if the researcher in the present case reports that by way of preparation the subject was trained to press and hold button V when he described seeing a vase and button F when his description was of seeing two faces. The researcher is being objective, or so she believes, when she refers to the subject's report of his visual experience rather than to the experience itself. It hardly matters, for the experiment is understood to be about changeable visual experience of a certain fascinating kind, testimony to which is that an observer who was unfamiliar with such experiences and wanted to understand the experiment would be shown the ambiguous figure and told to stare at it, not at the subject staring at an identical figure.

Since it seems clear that the subject presses a particular button because of what he sees, one must ask how anyone might think to disagree. One answer, on behalf of the Hard Problem, is that the references to the visually phenomenal may be omitted, given that nothing turns on them, as in the following account of the sequence of events, Light from the ambiguous figure impinges on the subject's retina and triggers a physiological response encompassing events in the brain, such as to cause either the pressing of button V or the pressing of button F. An observer, looking slightly puzzled, will ask what it is that decides between the one action and the other on the subject's part, only to be told that this latter believes mistakenly that his decision depends on seeing the figure as a vase or as two faces; whereas the reality is that it depends on his brain states, as does the experience of "seeing as", which serves no purpose. Suppose that the observer now maintains, speaking as a folk psychologist, that an explanation in terms of "seeing as" makes perfect sense, whereas on the physicalist account nothing is explained. But that, he is now told, is because the experiment is basic and makes no use of neuroscientific techniques, this being a reference to modern technology in connection with research into the psychophysical. To see the difference this is claimed to make, and whether it does, consider the following high-tech extension into neuroscience by which the experiment becomes more sophisticated.

Suppose, then, that beforehand the subject was not only trained, as previously, but was wired up to the computer via electronic sensors attached to his head, such that the visual cortex activity data associated with processes of "seeing as would be fed into the computer and synchronised with the button-pushing data. Suppose further that the visual cortex neural events associated with seeing a vase, and with seeing two faces, are clearly differentiated and that their relative frequency matches that of the pressing of the buttons V and F, and in such a way as to again confirm the hypothesis. The researcher is now able, in other words, to ascertain from data about neural processes in the visual cortex whether the subject is having a visual experience as of a vase or as of two faces. This is impressive and very promising as a party trick but in what way has neuropsychological enrichment of such experiments lent additional credibility to functionalism and the Hard Problem? It is not as if we now realise, by virtue of technologically sophisticated research and in general of the progress being made in the relevant fields of enquiry, that the brain is the seat of consciousness; for this has been common knowledge since the very first Neanderthal symposium on the philosophy of mind, with particular reference to recently arrived Homo sapiens illegal immigrants, the question being that of whether they could be said to have one.

Whatever the answer, our own question is that of whether the accumulating wealth of neuroscientific knowledge, no matter how great, can lift out of poverty the functionalist purchase on such a case as that of a subject staring at an ambiguous figure and choosing which button to press on the basis of what he sees. In the enriched experiment just discussed the functionalist will have access to such correlations as that between neural state F and the pressing of button F, and the same with state and button V, and he may mention those that relate to the two "seeing as" images, but not as part of any explanation, except perhaps of the subject's misguided folk view as to why he presses one button rather than the other. The problem here, however, is that the functionalist account is of a different experiment, one that is neurophysical and concerns neural states and physical action; but the actual experiment concerns phenomenal experience in the form of seeing the ambiguous figure as a vase or as two faces. This may be shown as follows.

Imagine this time that a strong correlation between button choice and particular neural state has been established over numerous trials and that the hypothesis under test by the researcher, of no interest to the steam-averse functionalist, has been confirmed, and to such a degree that the subject always sees the figure as a vase, or, as the functionalist would have it, the neural state and button-choice V now prevails. But suppose further that although the subject continues to press button V, the vase being what he sees at every trial, the brain imaging unaccountably switches to showing not the V neural state but the F state. Then the researcher will say, if he believes the subject to be reliable, without which there could be no third-party phenomenological research, that the hypothesis continues to be confirmed at every trial, the subject agreeing with him; but the functionalist will say that the frequency link between neural state V and button choice V has been broken, so that his own hypothesis, that the latter invariably partners the former, as also with neural state F and button choice F, has, other things being equal, been falsified. This is interesting, and on several counts. Firstly, it contrasts the functionalist approach with that by which the focus of research is on the connections between cerebral and conscious processes as objects of study. Secondly, it helps to explain why it is that the functionalist approach prevails, given the difficulty of turning subjective answers into objective data or the findings based on them. Thirdly, it raises a question about explanatory schemes, and it is to this that we now turn.

It is likely, with regard to the present experiment, that for the functionalist the failure of his hypothesis indicates only that the causal connections between the F and V states and the face- and vase-visual perception responses are complex, so that they involve other neural states, whereas for the experimenter there is no such complication. From this one might conclude that the disagreement, really, can be traced to opposing explanatory or conceptual schemes. No doubt there is that opposition, but this should not imply that they already seriously compete, or not according to certain philosophically-minded neuroscientists, for example Raymond Tallis (2016). Known to be a sceptic about what in its multifarious extremes he refers to as neuromania, Tallis argues that advances in the field are grossly exaggerated by the media and by researchers themselves. The relatively modest reality, he says, is that correlations obtain only between brain structure and very general psychological functions, such as cognition; or, between brain processes according to type or location and psychological features again falling into very broad categories. Even with regard to location, he claims, mental items do not map onto specific areas of the brain, which instead is an integrated system, rather tellingly, in which particular memories correspond to distributed processes, which in practice equate with scattered areas of the brain lighting up on a screen; and even this, we are told, is very much a construction of the instrumentation employed. Thus it is that our experiment involving neural states F and V and very particular visual states is not yet possible and waits upon future developments.

11.3: Progress Report

What do these findings indicate? Perhaps that in one's inflated claims about present achievements one is prescient about future triumphs; or perhaps that only a shallow grave awaits the neuroscientific researcher. I prefer the former, not only because I believe it to be true but also because one should assume it when addressing points of view that depend on it. The main one of these, as we know, is the thesis, yet to be directly confronted, that future developments will turn the key by which consciousness is unlocked, in opposition to which I shall counter that no key can possibly fit, since there is no lock and no gate, or only into a unified field of the neurosciences. But it may be, despite the doubts I have expressed, that the future will belong not to the radical functionalist, or not only, but to the non-political, as it were, researcher into the psychophysical in all its aspects, including its two-way causal correlations between brain and consciousness. This prospect makes no difference to our negative prophecy: that the day will never come when the sun rises in the east on a world of darkness about what it is to be conscious and dispels it by the time it sets in the west. I have given my reasons and we shall, of course, return to them when our own theory of mind is on the horizon. What is already clear is that the theory of epiphenomenalism, a pernicious weed at present, ought not to survive any future agricultural advances and ruin the crop. Bringing the science of the psychophysical into line with everyday psychology will eradicate this unwanted plant, as would adherence to radical functionalism. Since we have rejected this latter, we need to prove conclusively that our faith in mental causation may be rationally grounded.

11.4: Epiphenomenalism Grubbed Out

So far, we have tugged at the theory and loosened its roots, mainly by emphasising the obvious: that it challenges our whole system of personal and interpersonal discourse at every level and in all ways. Actually, the obvious is in some respects hidden, for it is very often the case, as pointed out in the other-minds chapter, that our concern is with the demeanour, performance, function or role of ourselves and others, so that we overlook the fact that this necessarily obtains within a framework of consciousness, without which these outward features of an individual could not be exhibited. Also emphasised, and indeed made much of, was the fact, which not many people seem to know, that epiphenomenalism presupposes a clarity of causal concept that even without Hume would not reveal itself to philosophical reflection. In order to drive this point home, the epiphenomenalist not seeming to be in control of the vehicle, suppose that I am taking balls out of a bag, all of them so far being either black or white, so that I have two boxes, one black, one white, into which I place them according to colour. Then we are expected to believe what exactly? That it is not on the phenomenal basis of seeing a ball as white that I place it in the white box? If that is what it was, after all, then it would be by virtue of the conscious content of that experience, or because of it, or explicable in terms of it, that I chose the white box, which itself would be accounted for in the same way. Any of these locutions would do, and for a reason already established: that the analysis of causal concepts is attended by a great deal of controversy, as would the question of how to distinguish between such expressions if the aim was to separate out those that betoken mere explanation or correlation as opposed to causation. No easy task, but a similar difficulty attaches to the use of "cause" itself. Is it conceivable, even, that one could define that word in such a way as to accommodate not only very specific physical effects, as with one ball impacting another, but also the assassination of archduke Ferdinand as a cause of the first world war? Of course it is, for one of these variants could be substituted for "caused", say "brought about"; or, there again, one could construct a theory of causation complete with counterfactuals, categoricals and dispositions. But now, the same point as before still stands, if such a thing is physically possible, for there is no theory of causation that is not contentious or clearly unsatisfactory in one way or another. If analysis in terms of counterfactuals is considered, so that from "A causes B" one derives "If A had not occurred, then B would not have occurred", then this shifts the question to that of what the counterfactual means. But also, the analysis fails, for within a system, as we have seen, there are always necessary ceteris paribus conditions. And yet, we are expected to jettison an entire system of psychological explanation and discourse on the basis of the lights and bells of a highly artificial representation of the brain as it appears on a monitor attached to the electrodes that are sticking out of somebody's head. This is mad.

To bring that madness into further relief, we need to trace out the full implications of the point being made. To begin with, I referred just now to the phenomenal basis of sorting the colours, but we know from previous chapters that perception is intrinsically inferential, so that the phenomenal basis broadens out into perceptual inference and therefore into the perceptually intentional.

But the phenomenal, as we found, cannot be separated out from this wider basis, and this in itself is enough to refute epiphenomenalism. For convenience, however, we shall continue to refer to just the phenomenal and reserve the analysis of consciousness, by which all these issues will assume a very different complexion, for the next chapter.

The second point is as follows: if it does not matter what colour phenomenally obtains, then its complete absence dos not matter either. But now, by the same token we may suppose that nothing is felt, seen, tasted or smelled, the sensory blackout being complete. What follows, or would follow, this being a *reductio ad absurdum* argument, is that any experience whatsoever is consistent with my sorting the balls by colour, including any perceptual experience, such as that by which I would normally be described as recognising each ball as white and placing it in the white box. What we are invited to believe, then, is that I could have this experience while correctly sorting both black and white balls. This is condemnation enough, but a more decisive argument is about to shift its weight.

Let it be the case that a mental causation sceptic is looking at a screen connected to electrodes in my head, so that he notes that the colour detection part of my brain is showing the W state when I draw a white ball and place it is the white box, and the same for the B state when the ball is black. According to this epiphenomenalist researcher I correctly place the ball by colour because light of a particular wavelength impinges on my eye and initiates a purely physical causal process by which my body places the right ball in a box. Now suppose, imagination being free, that the sceptic places a device behind my eyes that interferes not at all with the neural causal chain by which my body with its brain sorts the colours. What it does do, however, is to trip the switch by which cerebral processes of perception generate the corresponding sensory experience, the gap in my consciousness being filled by a visual experience as of seeing a teddy bear on a windowsill. This is not the same, one might think, as perceiving such a thing, or thinking that one does, but if the sceptic, which is to say the epiphenomenalist, is correct, then it should be conceivable, with no contradiction involved, that I seem to see one thing when in fact I

240

see another. That this is refutation enough is a point I have already made, but it is not the proof I at present have in mind, which concerns the necessary conditions of confirming, while I am having the window sill experience, that I am sorting the balls by colour. Since I cannot do it by sight, I cannot do it at all; therefore, I have to do it at some other time. But this will necessarily involve my visually identifying the balls by colour. It might be, for instance, that the experiment was filmed, so that I could look at the video after the device had been switched off; but I then identify the balls and the box by colour in order to confirm that I had correctly placed one inside the other. But wait a moment, it will be said: are we not permitted to assume, in time-traveller mode, that neuropsychology is in the ascendant and has mapped out all possible correspondences, whether causal or not, between conscious processes and those in the brain? Indeed we are, but we cannot match brain state to sense-experience without relying on its deliverances into consciousness, including those by which events in the brain and the various instruments of its examination are themselves observed. And this, as we are familiar with by now, betokens a system at work, in terms of which our experiment would be possible only as a special case of non-conscious perceptually-based action framed by conscious perception as a necessary condition. The closest we can come to it in present-day ordinary life is by sleepwalking. According to the sceptic we never wake up, in which case neither we nor the sceptic could know it.

11.5: Conclusions

What this discussion suggests very strongly, in my view, is that the theory of the psychophysical that constitutes folk psychology is indispensable to the understanding of the inner life and outward actions of oneself and others. They are interactive and interdependent, hence the fact that the theory belongs within a system, within which it competes not at all with the neurosciences. The mistake made by the epiphenomenalists, in their philosophising about the sciences in question, is that from the astonishing discovery that the study of the brain reveals only facts about the brain they conclude that folk psychology must be misconceived.

But I have shown, I trust, that this absolutely cannot be correct. Where does this leave the Hard Problem? Just because we are back with the epistemic and conceptual status quo, it does not follow that it goes away, and we have seen that both Chalmers and McGinn are perplexed as to how it is that consciousness, which is non-physical, can arise from the physical. Since this question is predicated upon, or at least made more acute by, the assumed redundancy of conscious phenomena, we need to ask whether it survives the reinstatement of consciousness as playing a causal or explanatory role. We know that mysterianism is promoted as being naturalistic, against which I have argued that it just is a fact that the brain is the seat of the conscious, so that its factual status should negate, or re-direct, any perplexity one is tempted to feel. Otherwise, the seekers after perplexity would be spoilt for choice. How, for instance, can touching a piece of copper wire, even if it has no sharp edges, be fatal? How can pressing a button make moving pictures appear on a screen? How is it that the moon does not come crashing down? It is all so perplexing – except that the perplexity would thereby depreciate rather steeply. This is to deny not that it obtains but that it is naturalistic in character as opposed to being metaphysical. That this is where the mystery truly belongs is a thesis I hope to be able to establish in the next chapter.

Chapter 12: A New Theory of Mind

If we start with intention, let us consider again the possibility of reductively explaining the intentional in terms of dispositions. Our thesis has been as follows: the dispositions associated with intentional concepts are such that intentionality enters into their realisation, so that the analysis involved is not reductive. Also, that if intentionality, for instance understanding, is considered in a social context, then one has to distinguish between individual understanding and interpersonal communication. This distinction was brought into play in our critique of Wittgenstein in the first chapter, but by then we had already broken free of him, and in a way that the distinction itself serves to illustrate. For Wittgenstein what counts is agreement in group use, the notion of which we found problematic, but clearly it places emphasis on the third-person point of view, in contradistinction to our first-person approach. On this latter the interpersonal communication between teacher and pupil separates out into their individual understanding of the instruction, or in the pupil's case his misunderstanding, ultimately Wittgenstein's, there being no such sequence as the one that is written for the pupil. This would have become apparent very quickly, the pupil realising his mistake, and what this indicates is that there is no deep insight to be gained from contemplation of a particular instance of understanding, in the present case that of pupil and teacher, to the exclusion of the wider understanding in which the particular instance is embedded.

If this is correct, then we need to ask what it is that a deeper analysis will reveal, the answer to which is to some degree disappointing, for the deeper the darker, as we discovered in the form of the irreducibility thesis, at least until it led us to a new theory of consciousness. That theory is very striking indeed, which is why I have gone into argumentative detail, and in the hope that the force of argument will be felt as an epiphany. The essential first step is to establish that the theory cannot be naturalistic, for then the source of human consciousness would be cerebral, my aim being to show that on the contrary it is metaphysical, as will now be made clear.

12:1 Intentionality and the Brain

Consider again the problem of the link between brain and mind. The two are quite separate, and in interesting ways. For instance, the brain may be the seat of consciousness, but it would be a category mistake to speak of sitting on one's mind. If we view them as belonging within a system, there need be no conflict between distinguishing them and insisting that the intentional transcends that distinction. To show that this is the case, let us look again at the way in which intentionality enters into perception; for it is only through subjective perceptual experience that we gain admittance to the physical world. This is perplexing enough to radically polarise opinion into physicalism at the one extreme and ontological idealism at the other, this latter being the theory that only mind exists. To bring this perplexity into focus, imagine I look at my brain, perhaps in a mirror after a craniotomy, my visual experience being of an independently existing physical object. But the experience is a wholly subjective, there being no other kind, conscious process that could not possibly contrast more starkly with what it is to be my brain or any other physical object. Given that this is a defining dual characteristic of my perceptual experience, it would seem to be both fundamental and to lend itself to paradox.

But in what exactly does the paradox consist? Since a particular example would not come amiss, consider this brown rectangular table in front of me: it presents itself as being objectively subjective or vice-versa, by which I mean, with regard to colour, that the phenomenal quality of brown appears to inhere in the table itself. But colour defines shape, the two properties being associated with spatial depth, and before we know it the whole table becomes a projection of my visual experience. Except, of course, that it is nothing of the kind, for the existence of the table depends not at all on mine. But I paint the table, as it were, with colour and shape, or that is how it seems. Hence the paradox, but also the perplexity, for I see the brown rectangular table as existing independently and unperceived, a fact which no argument, however ingenious, can overturn without upsetting the applecart of coherence and consistency. Phenomenalism is tantamount to solipsism, perceptual idealism takes leave of the senses, quite literally, so to speak, and naive realism is not really the theory of common sense that it seems to be.

We are left with direct realism within a system, which has its difficulties but at least preserves the everyday distinction between mind and matter. But it still is the case that the qualities of visual experience by which I pick out the table and its particular features appear to inhere in the table itself. Indeed, the very fact that we are driven to such extremes of apparent descriptive paradox betrays the profound character of the mystery of perceptual intentionality. Note, too, that this is all in terms of the sense of sight, but our perplexity deepens even more if the other senses, say touch and hearing, are considered; for it is very easy to focus on the subjective quality of auditory and tactile experience and to think of it as a form of sensation at the same time as we know that it reveals an externally existing physical world.

We now come to the crux of the matter, for if direct realism within a system is the only coherent theory of perception, and yet the relation between perception and its object is wholly mysterious, and in the same way as with intentionality in general, then what is mysterious about the brain on the one hand and consciousness on the other is the distinction itself, the causal connection being subservient to it. I suggest, that being the case, that we work towards dispensing with our brains, and in favour of the transcendent metaphysics of the muddle of it all. This resides in the intentional, not in the causal interface between brain and consciousness, which depends on it; and the actual mystery is not resolved by appeal to processes in the brain or to this latter as the seat of the mental. We have said enough to show that a theory of mind needs to transcend the distinction between the brain and consciousness, as ours will do. Since this is an important point, we shall reinforce it as much as possible; and one way to do this is to return to the topic of perception, memory and expectation, this time going even deeper than before.

12.2: Memory and Perception Misconceived

Analysis reveals, it may be recalled, that perception is Janus-faced, turning outwards to the physical and inwards to the mental.

But can we say, with at least a semblance of certainty, that there is a something out there, an existent in which the physical and the mental in here? But "out there" in what sense? We can be certain that the physical world is out there, but clearly this is not the sense intended, which is not naturalistic but metaphysical. The fact, as just mentioned, is that the distinction between the two faces itself depends on perception, which we have just shown to be Janus-faced, and it depends, too, on reasoning in philosophy, which clearly is intentional, just as perception is. It is a cognitive and epistemic merry-go-round, the trick being not to try to get off, or not if one wishes to keep one's balance. Keeping a firm grip, what is it that we have learned on this metaphysical carousel? That perception is representational, where this is very similar to saying that it is intentional, but perhaps a little more revealing. A portrait may represent a person, who is independently identifiable, so that the two may be compared. But a perceptual object does not invite a comparison with anything independently identifiable that is not a perceptual object. Perception is, after all, irreducibly intentional.

Is there more to come? Indeed there is, for we have yet to revisit the topic of memory and expectation, the former being explicit and the latter understood. This will be interesting, for memory is not at all as it appears, the same as with perception and with reflecting on it, to which it is also similar in being representational; and, too, in being subversive, metaphysically, of one's everyday acquaintance with the world. In what way, then, is memory representational? Here we find that one's view of it is obscured by one's confused misconceptions about the relation between memory and its object. To see what these are, suppose again that I actively remember a childhood picnic, including my mother opening a hamper basket, and that my recollections lasts only a few minutes, whereas the picnic lasted two hours. Now consider an assumption that is, although it conflicts with temporal discrepancies of the kind just illustrated, so deeply entrenched that an effort is needed to retrieve it; namely, that a past event — one that we have experienced — is in some sense a direct objet of awareness. One's feeling is that to remember it is to access it, as if to observe it from another galaxy and see it as it used to be.

The impression we have is both conceptual and epistemic, this latter in the sense of memory-knowledge being direct, which in fact it is not; hence the anomaly of inductive scepticism taking the deliverances of memory for granted or, which comes to the same thing, the sceptic deferring scrutiny of them until it is their turn. That said, they are at least in the epistemological queue; but the conceptual question of what it is to be a past event would seem to be overlooked. And yet, there is no straightforward answer but only confusion if the question is asked. For if we take memory to open a window directly onto the past, this being the muddled picture we may have, the glass being too crazed to qualify clearly as a belief, then our view of what it is to be a past event may be obscured, and the picture of memory as observation through time's window misrepresents it. For instance, it implies recollective accuracy, but this is belied by such facts as that to remember an experienced event is very often to see oneself as if externally observed, even when one's memory is not of looking in a mirror. The psychologists follow this track over long distances, and their findings indicate that the act of remembering is that of reconstruction; but they do not pursue it across the border into philosophy. If they did, they would perhaps be receptive to the thesis, which we mentioned earlier, that to remember an event or one's experience of it, whether or not it is to reconstruct it, is fundamentally to represent it, and that to represent it as a past event is to manifest continuity with representing it as a present event. In any case, this is one of the areas I now propose to explore in greater detail, in part because it corroborates the brain-transcendence thesis. Again, then, around we go.

Note first that if we think of memory as directly accessing the past, then this loosens our grip on an otherwise obvious fact: that after an event has occurred there is literally nothing left of it, exactly as if it had never been. That said, we may remember it; hence the intentionality of memory and the need to do justice to it. With regard to the picnic, we have seen that my active recollection may last a few minutes and the picnic much longer, so we should have to say, if the access is direct, that it is temporally selective with only a few scenes being recalled. But this is not what happens, and even if it were, in the sense that I recollect for a few minutes the events of a few minutes, the notion of direct access would still be very highly suspect. Does it mean, for instance, that my memory image is a copy of its object? Well, I now have a memory image, if you insist, of my mother opening the basket; but that image simply is not something that is like or unlike a physical object or feature. For a start, I cannot hold it steady, or not as a purely phenomenal item, in which guise it in any case lacks identity; for nothing counts as yesterday's being numerically the same as or different from today's. Not that it matters, or not in relation to the following thesis: that quite simply nothing in my mind now can afford or constitute direct access to something that does not exist. The conclusion to be drawn is that my memory of the picnic represents it, this being the form that recollective intentionality takes. As for what this implies, it is that the past, metaphysically but also as an object of everyday informed reflection, is not just another country but one to which, paradoxically, we have never been and have no access. That is, it is not a country at all but a wholly mysterious realm, a tropical atoll illuminated at night by a miner's lamp; and the full implication is that no-one has any idea what it is that the past consists in, the cage becalmed at the bottom of the shaft.

Now that perception and memory and expectation have been shown to be representational in their intentionality, keeping in mind the absence of any independently identifiable represented object, let us ask where we should go from here. My over-arching aim, already specified, is to bring together the intentional and the non-conscious within a system, thereby proposing for consideration the theory of mind to which all this argumentation tends. My present aim, it may be recalled, has been to show that the intentional cannot be analysed or explained in terms of brain processes: rather, it transcends them. I think that I have shown that indeed it does, but in any case we know from the previous chapter that there can be no question of the mental being explained in terms of brain processes in any sense other than causing or being correlated with them. We have one more piece to fit into the puzzle, namely the centrepiece in the form of the non-conscious; but manoeuvring it into place will wrest us away from the familiar and transform the picture of the theory of mind by which the jigsaw will be completed.

12.3: The Non-Conscious as the Last Piece of the Puzzle

In what does the concept of the non-conscious consist? Since the defining contrast is with the concept of the conscious, we need to consider each in relation to the other, relevant to which is the everyday notion of unconscious processes at work, which owes much to Freud but in one way or another pre-dates him. It must always have been the case, after all, that correlations are noticed between sleeping on a problem and awaking to the answer already up and about. My concern, whilst I acknowledge the similarity between unconscious and non-conscious, is to show that this latter is fundamental to consciousness, not just a proxy for it when, in more than one sense, we switch off the light. My aim, then, is to go deeper, and in order to show that the non-conscious enters into the conscious at all points, an intimacy by which they go hand in glove across the whole range of the intentional in all its aspects. That accomplished, we shall indulge in speculation as to why it is that theorists and inquisitive everyday folk overlook an entire realm of existence, a plausible answer to which is that the non-conscious connects at every point with the conscious and uses it as cover.

Perhaps we may begin by recalling previous findings, mainly that dispositions, metaphysically speaking, do not belong to consciousness, nor to brain states, therefore the only suitable habitat is the realm of the non-conscious. Then there is intentionality itself, which is irreducible and belongs within a system of conditions and connections. If that system enjoys any form of existence, it must repose in the non-conscious, or the converse, or we could say that the system is non-conscious – at the present level of enquiry it hardly seems to matter; hence our needing to go deeper. Our concern will be with conscious awareness or intentional consciousness: for instance with memory or expectation or reasoning rather than with sensation, which is not intentional, unlike sensation concepts, which are; and our aim, to repeat, is to show in more depth that the conscious is umbilically linked to the non-conscious. To that end I shall advance three arguments.

Suppose with regard to the first argument that I read the following: If a>b and b>c, then what further inequality statement using the same symbol is thereby deducible? And now I write "a>c". Then the target to be toppled is the unthinking assumption, in my view so ingrained that it requires considerable mental effort for us to realise that we cleave to it, that intentional consciousness, in this case of the reasoning and reading kind, is a sufficiency unto itself, with no need for the non-conscious. Our target, then, is the assumption of conscious adequacy, to give it a name, and we know that my reading of the first inequality, and then the second, has fallen away into the past when I write "a>c". Even if I repeat them to myself in my mind, the first does not exist by the time of the second; yet the inequality that I deduce is truth-conditional upon both of them. Might it be that my experience of them as conscious objects a moment ago informs my experience of reading "a>c"? But this is to presuppose, via "informs", that the meaning or the understanding of the inequality is capable of being constituted by pure consciousness: that involved in reading the inequality sentences. If in reading them I had a twinge in my arm followed by another in my leg, nothing would count as the one sensation informing the other; hence the presupposition.

Very well, it might be said, but in favour of the pure consciousness thesis is the fact, acknowledged in the first chapter, that reading with and without understanding are different, the difference being at least in part phenomenal. Against this, however, the qualification was made that the experience as of understanding might be the same if one believed wrongly that one understood, and that in any case there must be more to understanding and to the intentional in general than purely conscious processes. The missing gears, this being the thesis at present being established, engage one another in the non-conscious, even if we have no idea what the drive or the driven is, or how it connects with mental awareness.

But in that case are we not ourselves begging the question? We are presupposing, after all, a notion of consciousness that is purely phenomenal, and then it follows that intentionality must lie elsewhere. This is a thesis that I have already attempted to establish in previous chapters, in particular the first, but in itself I acknowledge that it is counter-intuitive. Taking a ball out of a bag, I know that it is red because I *see* it, and I see it as red. This, however, is not in dispute, the point being that seeing red is purely phenomenal, whereas knowing that it is red is intentional, for it involves meaning and understanding— and these cannot be phenomenologically defined. Perhaps, though, we need to be more nuanced, for is it not possible that there is more to the conscious than the phenomenal? We speak, after all, of being conscious that an object is red. Even so, this is not a counterargument, for we know already that the conscious adequacy thesis is very solidly entrenched. This latter does carry weight, I have to say, but note that counterarguments may be outweighed, as in the present case if we now move on

The second argument concerns memory and dispositions. Since we know that memory is intentional, we need to ask whether it is to be accounted for in terms of pure consciousness. Not if the first argument is correct but set it aside for the moment. What is it, in the present case, for me to remember the two inequality statements when I write down the third? Keep in mind that it need not involve active recollection or recall, for perhaps I infer immediately from premises to conclusion. But I must be suitably disposed, for instance to refer to the premises or to re-read them, all of which involves intentionality, and I previously argued that a disposition must have a categorical source, which I suggest is located in the non-conscious. Recall, too, the thesis by which recollective memory represents the past, but with the crucial caveat that the represented object and the representing of it are not distinct. Thus it is that the intentionality of memory transcends consciousness, not only in the sense in which memory is dispositional but also because it is irreducible and cannot be equated with its conscious deliverances.

Thirdly, we have treated our registering of each inequality statement as if it occupied a continuous present, in line with our subjective impression of the flow of time with ourselves, or our selves, somehow detached from it as if stationary on the bank. But all that we have said about inter-temporal relations between the three statements also holds intra-temporally for each of them.

If I deduce that a>c, by the time I write "c" the "a" has gone as if it never existed. One of the reasons why I have the subjective impression just noted is that I can still see the "a" when I write the "c", the psychology of the subjectively temporal being a topic to which we shall return. In the meantime, I wish to present the fourth argument as a continuation of the third, to the effect that consciousness connects with the non-conscious at all points, the apparent unconvincingness of which is at its most pronounced in relation to its main corollary: that consciousness is *momentary.*

Since the fourth argument involves a very shocking thesis indeed, with ramifications into much that we have already written, one may be forgiven for wishing to condemn it before the case for it has been fully set out. It cannot be correct, one will say, because reasoning, as in the present case, is a conscious process if one is conscious throughout as opposed to falling asleep. The process, far from being momentary, unfolds over a period of time. But now, none of this is in contention, in particular that we may be continuously conscious when solving a problem. My point is that the fact of the conscious and the temporal both being continuous misleads us as to their differences; for there is only the conscious content of each moment, previous content having come and gone as if it had never been,

To hasten the recovery from intellectual trauma, I shall now argue from the obvious to the less obvious, hoping thereby to carry conviction and render my thesis more evidently true, this to be achieved by focussing on the measurement of time. Take it that I am listening to a pendulum clock tick-tocking from one second to the next, so that for each auditory second it is as if the previous one had never existed. And now it is the next second, about which the same is true, and so on. But my attention, it will very likely be said, spans more than one second, so that I have two beats of the clock in my conscious awareness, not just the one. No doubt this may be true, but why stop at two seconds? This is not, after all, a boxing ring, and I myself am perfectly able to keep five beats in mind before boredom sets in. But the conscious content of my auditory awareness five seconds ago is as if it had never been, and therefore three seconds ago, and therefore one second ago. It may well be true that what I heard one second ago is fresher in my mind than the sound of the clock five seconds ago; but that fresh feeling obtains now, as part of the conscious content of the present moment, as does my recollection, however vivid, of the sound of the clock five seconds ago. It is not as if that sound, or my hearing of it, somehow forges a link to the present moment; for such a link would itself have to be a conscious item, according to the conscious adequacy assumption, and would therefore be part of my present, not my past, consciousness, in which case it would not be a link at all.

A similar point to be made is that these references of mine to the present are misleading, for it cannot be the case that the continuous conscious present literally exists, and this may be shown if we treat of the temporal separately from the conscious, noting first that each second that passes can in theory be timestamped. The time and date now is 13:28:09 on 17/02/2021, or it was, and what this shows is that each tick of the clock is unique and can never be repeated, for no two events can be both successive and simultaneous. But think of Christmas lights draped around a conifer, each bulb in succession momentarily flashing, the speed of the sequence being controlled with a handheld device. When the setting is on "slow" each flash occurs in isolation from the previous one, as if it had never been. It is in this way that consciousness would flash if the occurrence rate was the same. Now suppose that the setting is on "fast", so that the scene is transformed, with a snake of light appearing to slither up the tree. This is a nice analogical image but slightly misleading; for it is to the intentional that the snake owes its existence, not to increase of flash rate. More accurately, we may compare a moment of consciousness to a single flash of light, the point being that each flash occurs in temporal isolation from the others and in its own moment, so that there cannot be any conscious link between the flashes, since this itself would be another flash in its own moment. The links between flashes belong to the non-conscious, as do the objects linked, but this is where our improved analogy is nevertheless liable to mislead us, for the connection between flash of light, cable and electric current is ascertainable, unlike that between the conscious and the non-conscious.

12.4: The Conscious and the Non-Conscious Again

If I close my eyes after making myself comfortable, all the better to ignore external nuisance calls on my attention, then the world shrinks dramatically – or, rather, my inward glance reveals very little connection with it. A faint reddish glow behind my eyelids; a shriek of laughter which I know to be my partner's granddaughter downstairs; a slight feeling of unease at doing this when I should be writing – oh, I am writing. And that, really, is it. But it is a sparseness that indicates, in conjunction with the thesis of momentary consciousness, that the world, or my knowledge of it, is nothing without the intentional. This latter defies neuroscientific explanation and must therefore, since the brain projects no light on it, reside in the non-conscious, which cloaks it in a different kind of darkness. That, in outline, is the account that we have given, our present aim being to use it to explanatory effect.

Starting, as always, with memory, we have already brought the notion of the non-conscious to bear on its paradoxical character, the gist of which runs as follows. If there exists a non-conscious realm with consciousness at the surface, then the non-conscious processes underlying conscious recollection, perhaps of a childhood picnic, belong to the same non-conscious realm as the non-conscious processes underlying past conscious experience of the picnic itself. The question of how these processes are linked is, of course, incapable of answer, as also that of the link between the non-conscious and the conscious. But also, to recollect is to be in memory mode, just as to read is to be in reading mode, a locution which derives its meaning from our theory of consciousness. Thus it is that the appeal to a non-conscious realm has explanatory value, both in the present case and in others.

With regard to these latter, and in the particular case of perception, note again that when I see an object only particular parts of it occupy my field of view at any one time, the other parts being inferred. This is the starting point for the argument by which the intrinsic perceptual inference thesis is established. But it also sets in motion the distinguishing of the conscious from the non-conscious with regard to the sense of sight. For what it shows is that perception is explicable partly in terms of perceptual processes involving memory, expectation and inference, all of which are rooted in the non-conscious. Not only that but there is, too, a strictly perceptual intentionality, as when I look at an object and see it as being three-dimensional, as if I see it from different angles all at the same time. This itself is the non-conscious manifesting itself in my perceptual awareness of the table. I am aware, that is, of seeing a three-dimensional, perception-independent physical object, where this constitutes what is distinctive about visual intentionality. What it also indicates is that the nature of time is itself mysterious.

12.5: Language and the Non-Conscious

Consider its being said to a very short-sighted monolingual French person "Your glasses are upside down", which she registers as a non-francophone would if the sentence was "Vos lunettes sont à l'envers." In each case it would at best be a sequence of uncomprehended words; but in fact it would more likely be heard as a jumble of sounds, repeatable as distinct word-units only after training. Now switch the speakers, the effect being that each hears the sentence in his or her native tongue, as opposed to a foreign tongue, perhaps in connection with French kissing. Each speaker understands the statement being made and is better able to explain the frequency with which the glasses keep falling off. Now suppose that her interlocutor asks whether she understands what he said, perhaps taking her idiosyncratic spectacles positioning to be a sign of, well, idiocy. However that may be, the fact is that she is sure that she understands, and that she understands at that very moment; hence my suggestion that her cognitive confidence derives from the non-conscious processes by virtue of which she does indeed understand, these also being explanatory of the experiential difference between the interlocutor speaking her own language as opposed to some   other. Again, then, we find that the appeal to non-conscious processes, which permeate conscious ones, has explanatory value. Finally, and with our theory of the mental now in place, let us ask again about the limits of knowledge and the mystery to which it surrenders, thereby bringing to an end our circumnavigations.

Picking up on the earlier comments about cases in which representation and object are not distinct, perhaps we may start with the observation that if one thing represents another, it is within a system, as is the present statement to that effect. To show that this is the case, note first that if there is a sense in which to remember an event is to represent it, then we need to draw parallels with representation elsewhere. Language comes to mind, in particular the sentence "I saw a flash of lightning a moment ago", which represents the fact it conveys. Now try to focus on the utter dissimilarity between sentence and fact, this being none too easy, given that words are like windows onto meaning, the glass being perfectly clear in its non-metaphysical use. Still, practice makes for proficiency, and once we attune ourselves to the dissimilarity at issue, it resonates whenever we reflect on linguistic use. If, on the other hand, we fail the proficiency test, we can always imagine exposure to a foreign language.

Returning now to the sample sentence, and keeping in mind the dissimilarity thesis, my memory of seeing the lightning is conveyed by the sentence in its descriptive role. But this is not to imply that memory is one thing and description another; rather, it is in describing the event that I remember it on this occasion. We have said that the descriptive sentence is utterly different from the description as having semantic content, this being a reference to non-conscious processes or states, those that manifest themselves in one's experience of uttering the sentence. But also, in recalling the event by describing it we represent it, this being easier to accept than the claim that memory per se represents past events. But still, it does, and this is now easier to show as applying elsewhere, for instance in the case of memory images, perhaps of a flash of lightning during a picnic. Remembering it, I see the flash and hear the thunder in my mind as the plastic plates and cups are hastily packed back into the basket. This is explicable, in all its intentionality, only in terms of non-conscious processes buoying up those images, such that all those years ago one's conscious experience of the picnic and the suddenly darkened sky was also kept at the surface by the forces of the non-conscious. Hence the reference to a hidden realm of the non-conscious in which connections are made and conditions obtain,

256

in this case between present and past non-conscious processes. Really, then, we are dealing with a system, characteristic of which is that it is hidden except for its conscious manifestations.

And now for a rather startling metaphysical consequence of some of these arguments. If memory represents the past, and in the way that language represents its object, and if the past is represented not only when memory expresses itself through language but in all cases of recall or recollection, then the least that should be said is that conscious items of memory need not resemble the object remembered, any more than description resembles the object described. Going further, is it possible at all for memory to resemble its object in any way that throws light on the relation between them? I remember my mother securing the picnic-basket lid, which is to say that I have a memory-image of her tightening the straps; but what I wish to do, knowing that it is not possible, is to detach that image from the memory, so that it becomes an intentionally inert mental image. Pretending that my mind can play host to such an item, I now contend, if that is not too strong a word, that the image bears no resemblance to the memory object: the sight of my mother kneeling in front of the basket. It has about as much substance, after all, as the shadow of a ghost; and this is to say that phenomenally-speaking it resembles nothing at all — or would do if it could be detached in that way. If, on the other hand, I cease the pretence and fall back into fully-intentional memory mode, then the question of resemblance lapses. This is interesting, for the difference between memory and image is the same as that between reading this page and trying to see it as a sheet of paper covered in squiggles. They are not the same objects, hence the impossibility just highlighted: that of trying to do both at the same time.

In recollective memory, then, to remember an object or event is to represent it, this being the point at which one should prepare to be startled, for it has far-reaching consequences. Memory is intentional, and intentionality is tied up with the non-conscious, but equally with consciousness itself; and just as my memory-image of my mother is not the same as an inert mental image, the intentional interposing itself between them, so it is that conscious memory cannot be separated out from the non-conscious; and yet, there is a sense in which up to a point it can, just as one may speak of an inert mental image as opposed to a memory-image. Memory as intentional consciousness, insofar as we may speak of such a thing, gives no indication in itself of what it is to be a past event, or past experienced event, or the memory of one. 'But in my mind, I see my mother as she was on that day!' I exclaim against myself, and then I am reminded of what this means: that my image of her is nebulous, and that even if its outlines were sharper it would represent my mother only insofar as it involved the non-conscious. Indeed, it makes no difference, in this respect, if I give myself over to recalling the picnic while gazing at a photograph taken at the time, perhaps showing my mother closing the basket while I, or the little boy I used to be, looked on. The photo helps me to recall details or confirm them, but at the conscious level, with the usual caveat, this consists, perhaps, in my looking at the photo and saying to myself or aloud some such words as 'Oh, yes, I'd forgotten about that.' And now we are back to flat word-sounds having meaning only if semantically inflated by connection with the non-conscious, which at the same time breathes living memory into the conscious content of my looking at the photo. It now follows, this being the startling result, that a sense exists in which what I mean by my words is a mystery even to myself, their intentionality being non-conscious; and if it is through them that I remember the picnic, then this, too, is mysterious, as is also the case if I remember by way of memory-images or in any other way.

This is very startling indeed, for the clear implication is that the past is not what it was and will never be the same again. I refer to our conception of it and its change of complexion in the light of the present analysis. And yet, the past being mysterious and unknowable makes a perfect fit with the familiar strangeness of the passing of time in the everyday experience of many of us. Much will be made of this when, at the final horizon, we tack into purpler waters.

But can this analysis really be correct? If it is, then the present moment is also representational in its intentionality, since it instantly slips back into the past. Note, too, that with language my command of it involves cognizance of meaning one thing ra-

258

ther than another. When, for example, I state that I placed a pen in this desk drawer just now, where this is to imply that I know what I mean, I can demonstrate that knowledge, and in a variety of ways. I mean that I placed, (repeating the action) in this compartment that slides in and out (opening the drawer), this writing implement (taking out the pen).

If we now reflect on the previous paragraph, my claim to know what I mean by my words need not conflict with intentionality being unknowable and mysterious; rather, it is opposed to my not knowing what I mean, the mystery at the level of metaphysics being such as to transcend the distinction. Similarly, the mystery of recollective memory as being representational transcends the distinction we make between its being correct and its being incorrect. We are back, then, with intentionality as mystery, one that resides in the realm of the non-conscious and its relation to consciousness, that relation itself being wholly outside our cognitive purview.

Re-reading these paragraphs, it seems to me that the desired startling effect derives from the familiar transformed into the very strange indeed; but we can take this further if we now focus on what it is to represent a thing. "pain" in French represents what in English is represented by "bread": and now we align these words with that Anglo-French dietary staple and announce that the word represents the object. This is very familiar, just as its link with ostensive definition in the case of concrete nouns is unsurprising. And yet, it is even more strange than it is familiar; for what is it that the word "represent" represents? And with what, exactly, is it aligned? We said that recollective memory represents the remembered event, and clearly the memory is one thing and the event another; but it is only via the deliverances of memory that we have any knowledge of it as a past event, and also any conception of the past. The representation enters into the comparison between memory and event by which the representative relation is established; and yet we know that the event did occur and was real at the time. If we say that the representation represents itself, this at least captures the degree of perplexity and how strange it all is. It is the notion of irreducible intentionality that enables us to make sense of it: but only by obliging us to substitute mystery for explanation.

Even so, it is possible to go further again, perhaps deeper into Plato's cave, albeit fancifully, the shadows taking form as follows. Let it be pointed out, perhaps by way of expressing reservations about our present thesis, that on my own showing the concept of the past belongs within a system in which relations of interdependence obtain between the concepts of the past, present and future, for instance by way of confirmation, as with my opening a drawer to check my memory of placing the pen. This is not in dispute, but it reinforces rather than detracts from the thesis. For what is true of memory is true of intentionality in general. One may ask about the intentional content of the word "intentional" or about what it represents, and then about the intentional content of "represents". Reference to intentionality is itself intentional, but this is not at all to deny that such concepts have no legitimate application at the everyday linguistic level. In the realm of the metaphysical, however, one has to be mindful of concepts that reference themselves. If intentionality is mysterious in that realm, and in some ultimate sense, then so is the meaning of the present sentence or of the proposition it conveys. As for memory in particular, in connection with which the signal from that realm is necessarily encrypted and deciphered only at the level of the non-conscious, I can still say that in the present context I have no idea what the concept of the past consists in, provided I do not say it with sceptical intent.

But now we have a problem, one approach to which would be to bypass it before the navel-gazing results in cognitive paralysis. This would be viable, however, only if I removed all reference to it, which I do not seem to be doing. The problem is that the appeal to metaphysical mystery does not exempt me from tracing out its implications, for instance with regard to claiming that I do not know what the concept of the past consists in. Since in the ordinary sense I do know it, I must think that some other sense is also on the horizon. But my imperspicacity extends to intentionality in general, not only as a logical extension but as indicated in particular cases. If I do not know, metaphysically speaking, what the concept of the past consists in, then that of memory, too, must also be implicated. Indeed it is, and this is easily shown by treating of the particular case. Suppose I remember placing a pen in this drawer yesterday. But that event, the highlight of my day, has no presence in consciousness, exactly as would be the case if it had never occurred. At that level, then, my memory reduces to my belief that I placed a pen in this drawer, irrespective of whether I can "see" myself carrying out that action. Expectation, too, would be thus reduced, and recognition, this latter being another key term. As for belief itself, the concept of that, too, is beginning to lose its bearings, never having regained them after I said that we just *have* a belief. But if I can say it, the italics conveying what I mean, then I do mean something, and I do think it goes deep, in which case I can also say that I do not know what certain concepts consist in, despite at another level knowing perfectly well how to use them. I just *have* a sense of the complete unknowability of what there is— but no sense at all of a hidden reality. I *do* think that the intentional, for instance that by which these words are imbued with meaning, resides in the nonconscious, about which I am quite relaxed when it is pointed out that I have not defined it; and this despite the fact that it is a neologistic term expressing a new conception of the mental and a new theory of mind. A great deal has been said about it, thereby accruing semantic content to it, and this will have to suffice.

12.6: The Notion of a Closed System

Since this is the section before the transition to a fittingly lyrical closing of this chapter, followed by the chapter on meaning and mystery by which the book is concluded, I shall rectify what seems to be our relative neglect of a central feature of the notion of a system: that it is epistemically and conceptually closed, the degree of which will depend on the scope of our enquiries. If we start with probability concepts belonging within a system, or perhaps a sub-system, this is to imply that it is partially closed in relation to evidence and confirmation. Consider what is known as the problem of the priors when Bayesian probability methods come under scrutiny. If, for instance, a bag contains five black or white balls, one of which is drawn and found to be black, the aim being to estimate on that evidence the colour proportion of the balls in the bag, then there are five possible hypotheses, for instance that the bag contains four black balls and a white ball, given by $(b_4 w_1)$. A Bayesian may posit equal priors, each hypothesis assigned a probability of a fifth, thereby raising a question as to how this is to be justified. Initially, however, one should ask about truth-conditions, for we know that a one-fifth probability implies that in a series of suitably configured trials the bag should turn out to contain four black balls and a white ball with a frequency of about one in five, such frequency, as already explained, being itself a probability construct. But now, the methods used to interpret the experimental data are themselves probabilistic, relying as they do on sets of alternatives being treated as equiprobable simply because there is nothing to choose between them. But this is to say that they are equipossible, the same as in the case in question; that in which the five colour proportion alternatives are deemed to be equiprobable. What follows is that Bayesians cannot be criticised purely for positing equal prior probabilities on the basis of equipossibility, which is to say that a legitimate criticism would have to be internal to the system—perhaps it would exploit the truth-conditional connection between equiprobability and equal relative frequency. Again, then, we find that underdetermination is a necessary condition. If space permitted I would now argue in detail that probability theory in action is very often such that particular cases of doubting, checking, confirming or disconfirming rely on the probability calculus itself. Thus it is that the system is partially closed.

What, though, of the notion of a closed system as applied to knowledge and reasoning in general? This, really, is a central consideration in the present work, and much has been written already that is of relevance to it in one way or another. Addressing it directly, I shall have to be selective and narrow the discussion down to a particular issue: that of the use of the no-miracles argument to demonstrate that established scientific theory cannot be correct by chance. A stock example derives from quantum electrodynamics and concerns the much-trumpeted fact that the theory is accurate to several significant figures in the value it yields for the magnetic moment of the electron. From this fact the proponents of the no-miracles argument (NMA) as justificatory of science infer that the probability of such a chance matching of theory and observation is extremely low, just as the consequent presumption in favour of the truth of the theory is correspondingly high. This, if we pursued it, would be puzzling, for why should it be thought that support of that kind is needed, and what, in any case might it consist in? Would the null hypothesis be such as to set calculations derived from the theory against random number sequences?

The point, in the present context, is quite simply that the very idea of a magnetic moment is theory-saturated and relies for its buoyancy on other such entities that rise to the surface only within a densely esoteric explanatory system. Theoretical predictions in this field are measured not against observation, unless a monitor screen display qualifies, but against laboratory experiments that register within the system and in terms of its abstract entitles, their existence itself owing much to interpretation. One may speak, of course, of magnetic moments, perhaps after posing with one's favourite film star; but to know what it means within the stellar orbit of particle physics, one would also need the concepts of spin and electric charge and electron. These in their turn would have to intersect with other circles, and the same for them if one's understanding is to form by cognitive accretion and thereby present itself as grasp of theory.

The difference this makes is that any appeal to the NMA as vindicating quantum theory via the accuracy of magnetic moment estimates, the puzzling implication being that external support is needed, must thereby extend to the whole of science; hence the claim that scientific realism in general stands or falls if the NMA thesis is called into question. But the notion of magnetic moment belongs within a system in which the validity of quantum theory is presupposed, the existence of electrons and other sub-atomic particles being subsumed under the theory itself. Moreover, and again in line with the notion of a system, if the sciences need external underpinning, then so does empirical knowledge in general. There is no demarcation line by which everyday reasoning may be distinguished from scientific inference, such that the latter but not the former needs bolstering by the NMA. If this is correct, then a difficulty for the NMA thesis is not just that physical-world scientific theories are interconnected but also that they belong within the same system as that of everyday knowledge. But this, too, is where the NMA itself belongs, both as probability theory and as having physical-world application, for instance via perception and the observations that are made. It follows that such knowledge would itself require an epistemic licence to be issued by the NMA. Thus it is that a fully comprehensive sweep of reasoning and knowledge would reveal that the system is closed.

12.7: Mystery, Reality and the Purple Plains

Time, at last and with all finality, to relax the arguments and set a course for the open ocean with its purple plains, all the better, this being my intention, to dramatize the mystery of it all. Perhaps our first destination should be not ultimate mystery but ultimate reality, in particular the metaphysical or perhaps mystical theory that what exists is ultimately a unity, one which in some sense is timeless, so that the distinction between mind and body, or between consciousness and its objects, loses all purchase, along with the philosophical problems arising from it. All that I need say is that when I consider such a theory I see the terrain in all directions as littered with a variety of obstacles as I speed down the motorway; and that others, too, such as the digits of the car clock marking the minutes, as if counting ominously down, conspire to blind me to the unreality of time.

Since I see no point in speculating about the nature of ultimate reality, I now suggest that we voyage, metaphorically, to Polynesia, this being the only way in which I am ever likely to travel there. The purpose of our visit is to seek out a conceptual atoll, with its volcanic origins, within which the notion of ultimate mystery derives from something deeper, enriched as it is by a sense of the world's incomprehensible beauty, this latter exhibited in the sparkling silver sands and scintillating colours of the enclosed lagoon. Divesting ourselves of academic restraint and craving immersion in turquoise, the same as in a previous chapter, let us relax the arguments even further and give recognition to the elemental intellectual forces by which epistemological dynamics upthrusts into philosophical perplexity. These forces, after all, do not become quiescent just because the sceptic, who inhabits each of us, has lost command of the ship. There is a reason for this, and it concerns the hidden metaphysics of the submarine origins of concepts, which manifests itself as the unanswerability of certain questions over aeons of philosophical time. How can an event now occurring, the snap of a camera shutter or a moment in the birth of a baby or a star, fall away into nothingness in the very act of its occurrence?

This is a rhetorical question and yet it concerns, along with similar questions, a genuine mystery that manifests itself in various ways. How, for instance, can the intentionality of the senses, at least on first approach, be so easily overlooked in favour of perceptual sensation? But also overlooked is the mysterious interface between subjective and objective — and, too, between past and present, or between using temporal and perceptual concepts and grasping them at a deeper level: that at which coral islands form from emerging seamounts over millions of years.

Speaking of which, one must not forget the past, however unpredictable it may be. We cannot hope to appreciate the temporal ordering of events if the discontinuities in the concept of the past are ignored, for instance those implicit in my vivid memories of the rock-strewn glacial moraine in the hills above my childhood home. One rock in particular, which towered over me and still does when I go back, stands upright by a spring-fed stream, a scene which I can describe in detail, photo-assisted, down to the shape and colour of the lichen on the stone. Such knowledge, according to some, is the kind of thing that memory consists in; but the memory of an event cannot be equated with its epistemic effects, which on the contrary may be explained by appeal to it; and in any case they obtain within a system in which memory seems to acquaint us with the past but in fact represents it, just as perception represents the physically present, not only insofar as it involves memory but in its own right. But the notion of representation, as we have seen, fails to explain anything at a certain level. Memory being irreducible within a system, I now remember sitting at the base of that rock on a hot summer's day, my arm rapidly drying from being very slowly immersed, at the sensuously optimal millimetre rate, in the deliciously cool water of the stream, the thrill of it constantly renewed as the lick of the cold met the heat of my skin. I do indeed remember this, and the description I now give, adjusted only for tense, would be the same as the one I could have given then, had I harboured such a wish. But the non-conscious is all-pervasive in connection with consciousness, including conscious memory, and we seek in vain the past that we have lost, just as we mistake for substance the surface of the present.

And yet, the rock recalled is decades adrift of the present, and I am sitting not against it but in an office chair in my study, the events of that day recurring only in my memory. But in reality the past cannot recur; and still I remember, though I do not understand what it is that I do, a fact my grasp of which is itself at the mercy of the moon and the tides, as is my cognizance of the intentionality intrinsic to my describing the remembered landscape of my childhood. I am perplexed about what it is for me to write about the rock and the brook, the sheep-mown patch of grass between them; the hollow where we picnicked just a little way downstream, the village below the foothills and across the river; the tiny puff of black dust each time the buckets gliding above the coal-waste tip across the valley empty their contents; the tinkling of the stream cascading over accidental weirs a few inches in height; and the trilling of skylarks in the blue auditorium of the summer sky.

I am adrift, too, of the familiarity that passes for my more recent memories, perhaps of yesterday, and of the strangeness that passes for my memory of yesterday and of a moment ago. I typed these words, which is to say the last sentence, and yet I do not know what it means. How can perplexity be so saddening, an ominous telegram from a metaphysical front? I have a vivid memory—there is no other way to put it, as if a thesaurus could make any difference—of a windy day when I sat on a glacier-deposited rock, as I now know it to be, in the hills above the house, and of seeing my mother, a slight figure easily missed, pegging clothes on the garden line. And I remember thinking, as she struggled with flailing work shirts, and with sheets billowing into her face as if slapped, that one day the line would snap and the washing bulge and ripple over the vegetable garden, like the parachute that crashed its rider during the war, I recalled her say-

266

ing; and I hurry home.

A previous question was that of how it is that an event now occurring can fall away into nothingness in the very act of its coming and going. How is it that physical events appear to have only a continuously changing present existence? The answer, one might say, is that the essence of events is to strike sparks off the leading edge of time, some of them emitting memories, all of them extinguished in the space between successive instants. This is perhaps to assume a significant difference between object and event; and yet, how can solid rock — Earth itself — with its towering superstructure of permanence, insidiously combust in the tiny ignitions of the solar sub-atomic? Millions of years hence, they say, the earth will surely catch fire and the whole edifice will topple into the interplanetary sea, which itself will be engulfed along with the other planets, each with its doomed museums of the pioneering space age. And the ashes drifting like snowflakes in the silence of the interstellar void, with no footprints this time to mark the final extinction of the myriad creatures of human thought. And not a single word, not even from the vast chronicles of human history or from interplanetary philosophy conventions, will survive transcription from light into heat, the final utterance melting, perhaps, on the lips of the last descendant of the human species.

I see her in the few moments that remain, her hand on her swollen belly, her face like the Munch painting from unimaginably ancient art forms but framed by one of the cockpit ports of the escape vehicle still on its launch pad at the Kuiper station on Makemake beyond Pluto. And she watches as the terra-forming machines catch fire, the distant habitation dome of Kuiper itself, the solar system city farthest from the Sun, already reduced to smoke and rubble. What are almost her last words begin a question: 'Why...?' and both hands are protective now, her fingers listening for a signal — one that reaches back to the beginning, to initial contact with the alien life of infinite uterine space and the first cry of recognition. Yet here it ends, her fingers urgently attempting communication against her taut skin, their message belying her intention, which is to soothe and reassure. But the waters of the human spirit cannot always hold, and their breaking completes the question: 'Why? Why?' she cries out. And the only answer, now and forever, is that there is none that we will ever discover, not even in the birth and death of a baby and a star.

But also, and to cap it all, there are *other people* and the philosophical problems they pose, these latter to some degree a recapitulation of interpersonal difficulties in everyday life. How can I be so *unreconciled* in my encounters with them, caught between staring at bodies and looking at fellow human beings, except that their bodies are all that I can see? It is not as if I have any realistic prospect of resolving them into purely physical objects, to be approached with extreme caution but free from any feeling of awkwardness. Once I quit my study, as Hume once again would perhaps agree, I abandon all hope of unique consciousness, other people being too insistently *there*, pressed hard against the windows of their eyes, for me to risk taking them to be automatons. Immortality is, I dare say, a consoling feature of other-mind solipsism, albeit short-lived, but the reality is that other people are always with us. This brings its own consolation, not least when we seek them out if we need to huddle alone together, rather than scan the singular horizon at the rift between earth and sky. Other people are, truth to tell, necessary, as is easily shown if we turn one last time to the teddy bear, that indispensable companion to the philosopher of mind. For the wisdom that this cuddly toy imparts as we soothe it anxiously and scan its face for any sense of its own insentience, turning it this way and that in the morning light, is that were it not for other people we should have to invent them; and that this in any case is what we do, just as, even before it rises into consciousness, we hallucinate the Sun.

Chapter 13: The Meaning and the Mystery of Life

Let us begin with the familiar view that life has a meaning only insofar as we make it meaningful in the way that we live.[7] This is to focus on the value of each individual life, in which respect it may be contrasted with human destiny as being part of a greater scheme of things, as when we look to religion to give significance to our lives beyond our earthly pursuits. What is implied, then, is that human life is devoid of any transcendent meaning, so that we are not the protagonists in a cosmic drama starring Christian or other deities, the final act being that in which we depart this life and set sail for another. On the contrary, when we die we sink into oblivion, and that is all there is to it.

If humanists argue that life is what we make it, then they have to reconcile this thesis with the facts of mortality, misery and change, and here one's adherence to the argument is at the mercy of storm and shipwreck, the sun always rising on an uncertain sea. When we are bereaved, or when at the end of our own lives our struggle to stay afloat is of no avail, then it may be hard not to feel, as a symptom of powerlessness, that life has no point and that self-deception and transience are the only constants in this world. We say when a loved one dies that only last week she was making plans and full of hope, which has now been so cruelly dashed, and that it reminds us once again that we are as nothing in this universe, there being no other, or that nothing exists except by accident and happenstance.

It is hard to decipher the subtext to such reasoning, except that it clearly includes the idea that mortality and suffering detract from the meaning of life. And yet, one can imagine an individual who lives for ever, despite which he is troubled in the

[7] Revised version of article in THINK / Volume 12 / Issue 33 / March 2013, pp 53 - 63.Permission to reprint the article here has been granted by Stephen Law, the editor of THINK, and by the Royal Institute of Philosophy (copyright holder) and Cambridge University Press.

same way as the rest of us by the possibility that his actions are ultimately pointless. If his longevity is such that the narrative of his life unfolds on historical timescales, his childhood being as distant as the Stone Age and beyond, though still vividly recalled, then this may affect his sense of what is real and important. Perhaps a feeling of emptiness, of events having the reality leached out of them by the flow of time, would be more acute in him than in mere mortals with their thin biographies, and with their delusions of stability more or less intact. And, of course, he could look forward to more misery than is in store for other people – in fact, to an eternity of suffering, not to mention the boredom of never doing anything new, the high point of each day being the change of date.

If this is what the passage into an endless future would be like, then it shows that immortality does not guarantee meaningfulness, or not if one's life continues on the same course in every other way. But suppose that in addition to immortality, or even instead of it, human life underwent significant change, such as to revolutionise the view we have of our place in the cosmos. It could be, for instance, that the gods vouchsafed to us compelling evidence of their existence, or that scientific discoveries, whilst falling short of religious revelation, nevertheless satisfied the same need in us for meaning and transcendence. It is, after all, a familiar refrain among exobiologists that if extra-terrestrial life, be it ever so humble, were to be discovered, then it would have a transformative effect on human consciousness. This, it has to be said, is clearly untrue as it stands, for it is unlikely that the harassed parent or the professional hit man, the stooped peasant or the porn star, would be transported into a higher realm of being by the discovery of a Martian worm.

Suppose, however, that we learnt of the existence not of alien invertebrates but of advanced civilisations, the emissaries of which presented themselves to us here on Earth as the saviours of our planet, bearing reasonably priced climate-stabilising tools, or as ambassadors from the Milky Way Confederation of Developed Worlds, united against the forces of darkness lurking in the Andromeda galaxy. Or, again in the realm of science fiction, think of the film "Close Encounters of the Third Kind", with its quasi-religious theme of a visitation in the form of a musical mother ship, one which bathes in a celestial light the chosen few who are about to ascend into its bosom. Imagining such events, we may easily come to believe that contact with an alien intelligence protective of the human race would elevate its status as it stepped from planet to star; but what we now have to ask is whether this is to imply that our lives would acquire meaning in a deeper sense.

It would, after all, be a small step compared with that which the devout Christian expects to take from this life to the hereafter; and yet, such people tend to drink from the same well of unhappiness as those without faith. That said, some among them achieve serenity in this world, which they regard as a proving ground for entry into a realm of eternal bliss and ultimate meaning. Of course, the non-believer need not agree that secular life is devoid of significance, if that is implied, or that human life on Earth is valid only as a means to a supernatural end. It seems to be generally assumed, however, that the Christian hereafter is quintessentially meaningful, so let us now ask what the idea of heaven can tell us about the concept of the meaning of life.

If we think of heaven as representing the ultimate in eternal bliss, then by that definition it is free from suffering, as also from the annoyances and frustrations which reduce us to the level of horses tormented by flies. It is regarded, indeed, as a higher state of spiritual being from which not only insects but also all forms of negativity are absent, no ripples of envy or malice being allowed to ruffle that oceanic feeling of being at one with the Almighty. What must be absent, too, or so it is assumed, is any feeling of doubt about the meaning of life, since God in his immanence is in all things. Clearly, this numinous quality of the divine landscape is one that the architects of Christianity strive to capture in stone and stained glass and in its rituals of worship, whether those of the parishioner in a quiet church or the congregant whose voice resonates to the sound of the organ in a grand cathedral. The feelings thus induced are informed by the story of Christ, but when lacking that structure they may occur quite separately from any religious narrative, as when evoked by meditation or recreational drugs or by dancing to the point of frenzy.

271

In my own case, for instance, I used various means of waking my senses to the world, and I vividly recall a clear summer night on a remote beach in the Gower peninsula. The full moon in a sparkling sky shone a silver swathe of light on the sea, and at the water's edge a sighing sound as the long fingers of the surf caressed the swell of sand. Touched by beauty, we desired its exalted embrace, and to the thunder of drums we gyrated ever faster around a driftwood fire until abruptly a crescendo reached its climax. And when the giddy whirl of flames and shadows came to rest, my eyes opened on sky and sea transformed. The moon's reflection on the water was now the glowing wake of unseen space-bound ships; and beyond Earth's edge the black ocean of the interstellar void; and on its far shore the glittering cities of the Milky Way. Enraptured, I opened my arms to the diamantine stillness of the sky, immensity of yearning measured by infinitude of space. And for a moment, touched by eternity, the ego to which I was in thrall relented, self and its objects melding into the one consciousness, and within it a cathedral dome of stars, the only sound the ebb and flow of sighing at the fingertips of the tides.

A characteristic feature of such elevated perceptual states is that events unfold without, as it were, a backward glance, no regret being felt as one experience yields to the next. Like a child I delighted in the wonders I beheld, and I clutched at the fingers of the present as my eyes brightened with stars, my gaze voyaging beyond them to the myriad constellations of the galactic disc, which for exquisite moments filled my world. There is, indeed, a childlike quality to being thus enthralled, and in the same way, if less magically, Christian believers place their hand in God's on the steps of cathedral or church. Such comparisons may help us to conjure up eternal bliss, even if earthly delights are always limited in duration, in view of which it helps, too, if we are able to imagine these experiences of the sublime as being indefinitely prolonged, which in my case would have meant that I continued to inhabit that enchanted universe of light and space.

The point, anyway, is that parts of the wealth of human experience may be used as capital for conceiving of eternal bliss, which we may picture not as a constant state but as variations on a blissful theme, much as we pursue different sources of fulfilment here on earth. Speaking of capital, the return will be even greater if, as I now suggest, we relax the requirement of perfection and allow into heaven the kind of flawed happiness with which we are all familiar, as when eating ice cream when plagued by flies, or when dancing frenziedly but never quite breaking the bonds of self.

Let us now consider the following objection to this approach, namely that however closely we assimilate heavenly bliss to the best that human life has to offer, the fact remains that the idea of a hereafter is incoherent, for to be alive is to be corporeal in a physical world, and it is part of Christian doctrine that the soul, not the body, ascends to heaven, which is not a physical place but a state of being. To this it may be replied that although the objection seems valid, it leaves open the possibility that heaven exists in a form that is immune to it. Perhaps when we sink into what seems to be the oblivion of death we surface in a different body on a parallel planet, one in which God reveals his presence and bathes us in the warm glow of his beneficence, so that we know that we are in heaven, even if the way in which it was depicted in scripture turns out to be incorrect. Such a world seems conceivable, provided we do not interrogate it too closely, just as I portrayed with very wide strokes of the brush an individual who is immortal here on earth. It could not be a perfect world, since it occupies a physical realm, but we have just seen that perfection may be dispensed with.

That being the case, we may now ask whether ultimate meaning is necessarily realised in heaven. If certain objective conditions must obtain before heaven may be said to exist, then it would seem that the link with particular states of mind, namely blissful ones, is causal, so that it could be different. Perhaps in some cases a newcomer to heaven is initially very happy until doubt begins to intrude, so that eventually she comes to believe that heavenly pursuits are pointless and that her life on earth had more meaning. Such a belief is heretical, but the concept of the meaning of life straddles fact and value, so that she cannot be accused of misapplying it by rejecting a particular view of what it consists in. This, it seems to me, is a pivotal point, for it undermines the mystique of heaven as the crucible of all meaningfulness, the atheist having to be content with her life being what she makes of it. It is true that if there is a heaven then God is in it, but in principle our newcomer could fail to be impressed even by him, especially in view of his appalling human rights record, and it is imaginable, indeed, that hell is populated by disillusioned Christians who have had enough of heaven.

If we resist the temptation to speculate further on the demographics of the hereafter, then there remains little to be said about the notion that once we have passed through the gates of heaven the question of life's meaning is settled. Clearly it is not, even given the fact that heaven is by definition for ever, whereas on Earth one has only a short-term lease. As before, then, we may ask whether a finite human life can have meaning, one response to which is to point out that people vary in their attitude to death, which some of them seem able to accept with equanimity. The fact remains, however, that the fear of death weighs heavily on the bones of many of us, the pressure not being eased when we are told, as is often the case, that our fear is not of death itself but of dying. I would say, on the contrary, that the mortal enemy we dread is non-existence, our own and that of the people we love; and I imagine a returning time-traveller showing me footage from a hundred years into the future. Here is my house, and gazing through the windows I see only strangers, for I am dead and long forgotten. Here are the clubs and discos of Cardiff and the Rhondda Valleys, the dance floors crowded with other people but empty of me, always and for ever. And here, finally, is the cemetery and my sunken grave, the headstone listing, my ship having foundered on the rock of old age or accident.

Where, then, does this leave us? One answer, in view of the earlier remark about fact and value, is that we are free to decide whether or not the spectre of death renders human life meaningless. For myself, however, I am not so much free as engaged in a struggle, one which perhaps this act of writing will help to resolve. I have no doubt but that I would love to play a central role in the Ultimate Cosmic Scheme and would wish above all else to be a god, so that I could impress people with my supernatural powers. Failing that, I would settle for the kind of communion

274

with a reality transcending misery and death which, by some accounts, is possible not only through drugs but also by listening to music and in other ways. Indeed, I am stirred and moved by, for instance, the James Horner film score from "Titanic", my difficulty being not with emotion but with attaching it to thought, with forming a coherent idea of the deeper meaning which such music is claimed to unlock. That idea is always a distant speck on my cognitive horizon, one which is in peril and needing to be saved; but when in the film the iceberg plants itself in the ship's path, I behold it as an ominous marauder from a melting Greenland and Arctic Circle, even though I am aware of the anachronism; and then the music serves only to remind me of the freezing waters awaiting the passengers and the global warming afflicting us.

There are those, of course, who claim to have more insight, and they would appeal to mysticism and one's feel for what is beautiful, in this way hoping to replace or augment the consolations of religion. They believe that they intuit a hidden reality revealed by drugs or meditation, or in music and art, such that the turbulence in our lives is washed out into an ocean of stillness. In *The Doors of Perception* (1954), Aldous Huxley described his experience when taking mescaline, a psychedelic drug similar in its effects to magic mushrooms. His aim was to probe beneath the surface of his mind in search of spiritual enlightenment; but not having studied the book I do not know whether he succeeded. All I can say is that my own excursions into semi-mystical perceptual states, illustrated earlier, were more modest in what they revealed, and they gifted me with the key not to a hidden reality but to an experiential world of heightened sensation and aesthetic delight. That night in the Gower I had no impression of cosmic doors opening onto ultimate truth, and in any case they would, as it were, have closed again as the fire went out, for instance if the truth apparently revealed was that all change is illusory. What, after all, could this *mean*? If reality is timeless and unchanging, one might as well put one's hand in boiling water, since what seems to be an important effect – one's excruciating pain – is just an illusion. Not only that, but if mysticism opens a porthole onto the meaning of life, then the seascape thereby revealed must have personal significance – but why should that be the case?

Time, perhaps, to go deeper into the link between change, mortality and life being meaningless, to which end we should start not with death but with impermanence in general, some instances of which are more significant than others. When I eat an ice cream as it melts in the sun, I do not weep and say that it has gone for ever, as if it had never been, thereby relating it to the ultimate perishability of all things, for I do not feel it as a loss of that kind. On the other hand, and in a more personal vein, I vividly recall that on a stile on a footpath from Corntown, just by Ewenny Priory, I shared an ice cream with my first love one summer's day, both of us in our teens, and we licked each other's lips and vowed that we would always be true. Decades later, on the anniversary of that day, I returned, the stile being the same and yet forlorn, and as I sat there I tried to reconcile my tantalising memory of her with my present awareness of an empty space beside me. It is mysterious indeed that we experience the present moment as charged with reality in the very process of its falling away into the past, to which it is connected only by remembering, which itself is a process in the same way. But also, it is arguable that memory depends on the illusion that the past continues into the present. I can speak of making that pilgrimage only because I recognised the place and its apparently enduring features, an essential framework of stability and identity in which the transient events of that lovers' tryst, gone for ever, could be located. And yet, one could argue that this is to appeal to a superficial distinction, for the stone of which the stile, the ancient priory and the village were built was no more composed of unchanging substance than were the leaves in the trees, which as I sat there seemed to look the same as on that other summer's day. This adds to the mystery, and all the more so if we note the part played by personal identity. When I sat there on my own, conflicting impressions assailed me only because I took myself and my first love to have identity through time, just as the stile and the priory seemed to be the same as before. But this should remind us of Hume on personal identity and on what it is for a village church to be the same from one year to the next.

What I suggest, then, is that such mysteries underpin the

question of whether life has a deeper meaning, which we may doubt partly because of the all-pervasive nature of change and decay, some of which we feel as loss or anticipate with dread. This returns us to the subject of dying and of being dead, neither of which, in my opinion, is to be recommended, given the way in which they crash the party and upset the guests. In writing this essay, I have tried very hard to believe that life has meaning in some profound sense, however elusive and hard to grasp. At one point, when listening to the music of Mahler from the film "Death in Venice", I almost succeeded, except that I noticed a butterfly in difficulties above a windowsill, and as it clawed at the empty air, an invisible instrument frantically played, I heard only the drum-roll of it landing and breaking up, a solitary figure waiting on a white beach for death, from which not even the most delicate beauty can hope for a reprieve. It is all very well to say, as people do, that the claim that life has no meaning is self-indulgent, for we would give the lie to it if we were starving or waiting to be killed. If this means that each individual is fully engaged with her life, which is charged with her needs and desires, her seeking and striving, her primal instinct to stay alive, unless she actually *feels* that her life is empty and of no consequence, in which case she is depressed and needs help, then I agree. But I would add that it is *because* one is fully alive, each moment so real, the expectation of survival intrinsic to so many of one's mental states, that death makes a mockery of it all. The horror of one's own mortality is not only personal oblivion but also the absolute severing of self from this life of joy and suffering and from those that we share it with. Death forces us to abandon those we love at the very time when they need us most; and we die in such bitter sorrow: knowing that we cannot be there to hold them and to kiss away their tears.

What it all means, then, is that the human race matters only to itself and that we are mortal, these being facts that not even the humanist can face broadside on, reduced like the rest of us to keeping busy and the ship in good shape. We pretend that the world is round, but we know, really, that ahead of us the onward curve of the horizon will flatten to a final edge, the heartbeat of the engine stopped, and that the ocean and all those at sea will plunge into nothingness. And, too, that the very stars will spiral into that void, from which not even the light of the heavens can escape.

Finally, perhaps mention could be made of a local area of archaeological and scenic interest. On Garth Hill, a few miles to the north of Cardiff, the path connecting the main 4000-year-old Bronze Age round barrows ends abruptly at the edge of a rocky crag, which juts out above the valley of the Taff. It is a natural lookout point, in profile like the prow of a ship, conspicuous from the road when I drive to the weekly Taff's Well dance on a clear night. Peering up at it, I try to make sense of what I know to be true: that since the end of the last ice age, more than 10000 years ago, numerous human beings must have stood there, just as I have done. In my imagination, as it takes me back four millennia, I see a young couple in the heat of summer slip away from the busy construction site of the latest burial mound and follow the path leading to the crag. Poised at its edge, they gaze out across the forest, smoke drifting from the clearing by the river where they live, perhaps on the site where now I dance, and in the distance the silver strip of the sea, now the Bristol Channel, shimmering on the horizon. Presently they move back from the edge but more urgently now, the dead hand of a forgotten chieftain pointing the way, and in a hollow in the lee of the crags they embrace, fingers fluttering over skin. Each sensation is exquisite but yields to the next until there are no more, each kiss gone for ever until the next and then the last. I see them stroll away, perhaps after vowing to each other always to be true, back to where the adults of the tribe toil at the monumental task of immortalising the dead. They all help to pat the mound into place, the equivalent in geological time of making sandcastles, and then they fade from view and I continue to my own destination.

Each of us will one day have all that we have built of our lives swept away, for we cannot stem the tide – unless, that is, we seek salvation in the miraculous powers of a personal god. But there is no god and there is no heaven, except in the delusions of those who feel that otherwise life has no meaning. And they are right, except that, as we have seen, not even a god can guarantee that life is meaningful.

Humanists, too, deceive themselves when they claim that life has the meaning we give to it, for we give it none, being much too preoccupied with all the important projects that each of us crams into it. If we look up from all this work, or if we press the off switch, we see only the blank face of the sky or the screen; and in interplanetary space there are no extra-terrestrials heading our way – except in the form of asteroids with enough destructive power to shatter all our dreams. But if, instead, we lower our gaze and look around us, then we may notice the haunted looks of our fellow passengers on this voyage to nowhere, those who are adult, and the fragile space occupied at the deck rails by children, with their capacity for enchantment, and we may feel moved to respond. This, together with clasping one's lover's belly from behind as she kneels by a cold mountain pool on a hot summer day, her naked breasts reflected as she leans out and sinks down, and thrills to the limpid shock of twin kiss and cupped caress, is the most that one should expect of the meaning of life.

Bibliography

Ayer, A.J. 1959. *Philosophical Essays*
   (London: Macmillan)
——1972. *Probability and Evidence*
   (London and Basingstoke: Macmillan)
——1973. *The Concept of a Person*
   (London and Basingstoke: Macmillan)
——1973a. *The Central Questions of Philosophy*
   (London: Weidenfield and Nicolson)
——1985. Wittgenstein
   (London: Weidenfield and Nicolson)
Barker, S.F. and Peter Achestein. Oct 1960. 'On the New Riddle
   of Induction' in The Philosophical Review, Vol. 69
Bar-On, Dorit and Douglas C.Long. March 2001. 'Avowals and
   First-Person Privilege' in Philosophy and Phenomenological
   Research, Vol. 62
Blackburn, Simon. 1973. *Reason and Prediction*
   (London: Cambridge University Press)
Baker, G.P. and P.M.S. Hacker. 1984. *Scepticism, Rules and
   Language* (Oxford: Basil Blackwell)
—— 1985. *Wittgenstein Rules, Grammar and Necessity* (Oxford:
   Basil Blackwell)
Carnap, Rudolph. 2013. *The Unity of Science* (Routledge)
Cassam, Quassim. 2007. *The Possibility of Knowledge*
   (Oxford University Press)
Chalmers, David J. 1995. 'Facing up to the Problem of Con-
   sciousness' in Journal of Consciousness Studies, No. 3
DeRose, Keith. 1999. 'Solving the Sceptical Problem', in *Scepti-
   cism: A Contemporary Reader*, ed. by DeRose, Keith and
   Ted A. Warfield (Oxford: Oxford University Press)
Dretske, Fred. 1999. 'Epistemic Operators', in *Scepticism*, ed. by
   DeRose and Warfield
Fisher, Ronald A. 1947. *The Design of Experiments*
   (Edinburgh: Oliver& Boyd)
——1956. *Statistical Methods and Scientific Inference*
   (Edinburgh: Oliver& Boyd)

Gelman, Andrew. 2008. 'Objections to Bayesian Statistics', in Bayesian Analysis

Gelman, Andrew and C.P. Robert. 2013. 'Not Only Defended But Also Applied: The Perceived Absurdity of Bayesian Inference' in The American Statistician, Vol.67

Goodman, Nelson. 1983. *Fact, Fiction and Forecast* (Harvard University Press)

Grayling, A.C. 2008. *Scepticism and the Possibility of Knowledge* (London; New York: Continuum)

Grice, H.P. 1957. 'Meaning', in Philosophical Review

Harrod, R. 1974. *Foundations of Inductive Logic* (Macmillan)

Hattiangadi, Anandi. 2007. *Oughts and Thoughts* (Oxford; Oxford University Press)

Howson, Colin. 2000. *Hume's Problem* (Oxford: Clarendon Press)

Hume, David. 1975. *An Enquiry concerning Human Understanding*, ed. Nidditch (Oxford University Press)

——2003. *A Treatise of Human Nature*, edited and abridged by Wright, John P, Robert Stecker and Gary Fuller (London: Everyman)

Huxley, Aldous. 1972. *The Doors of Perception* (Chatto & Windus)

Jackson, Frank. March 1975. 'Grue' in The Journal of Philosophy, Vol. 72

James, William. 1950. *The Principles of Psychology* (Dover Publications)

Jones, O.R. ed. 1971. *The Private Language Argument* (Toronto: Macmillan)

Keynes, J.M. 1973. *A Treatise On Probability* (London and Basingstoke: Macmillan)

Kripke, Saul A. 1982. *Wittgenstein on Rules and Private Language* (Oxford: Basil Blackwell)

Kuhn, T.S. 2012. *The Structure of Scientific Revolutions* (University of Chicago Press)

Lange, Mark. 2002. 'Okasha On Inductive Scepticism' in The Philosophical Quarterly, Vol.52. No. 207

Law, Stephen. 2004. 'Five Private Language Arguments', in International Journal of   Philosophical Studies 12, no.2

Locke, John. 1997. *An Essay Concerning Human Understanding* (Penguin Classics)

Macdonald, Cynthia. 1998. 'Externalism and Authoritative Self-Knowledge' in *Knowing Our Own Minds* (Oxford: Oxford University Press)

Martin, C.B. and J.Heil. 1998. ' Rules and Powers' in Philosophical Perspectives, Vol. 12 Language, Mind and Ontology, 283-312

McDowell, John. 1998. *Mind, Value and Reality* (Cambridge, Mass.; Harvard University Press)

—— 1998. 'Response to Crispin Wright' in: Smith, B.C, C. Wright and C. Macdonald eds *Knowing Our Own Minds* (Oxford; Oxford University Press)

McGinn, Colin. 1987. *Wittgenstein* (Oxford: Basil Blackwell)

——1991. *The Problem of Consciousness* (Cambridge Mass.: Blackwell)

McGinn, Marie. 2007. *Routledge Philosophy Guidebook to Wittgenstein and the Philosophical Investigations* (United Kingdom: Taylor and Francis Ltd)

Mellor, D.H. 2004. *Probability: A Philosophical Introduction* (Routledge)

Miller, Alexander 1998. *Philosophy of Language* (London: UCL Press)

Moore, G.E. 1959. *Philosophical Papers* (New York: Collier Books)

Nickerson, R.S. 2004. *Cognition and Chance: The Psychology of Probabilistic Reasoning* (Psychology Press)

Nagel, Thomas. 1979. *Mortal Questions* (Cambridge: Cambridge University Press)

Ogden, Charles K. and I.A. Richards. 1989. *The Meaning of Meaning* (Mariner Books)

Okasha, Samir. 2001. 'What Did Hume Really Show About Induction?' The Philosophical Quarterly, Vol. 51. No. 204.

Peacocke, Christopher and Colin McGinn. 1984. 'Consciousness and Other Minds', in Proceedings of the Aristotelian Society, Supplementary Volumes, vol. 58, 97–137.

Pears, David. 1988. *The False Prison: A Study of the Development of Wittgenstein's Philosophy*

(Oxford: Oxford University Press)

Quine, W.V.O. 1953. *From a Logical Point of View* (Cambridge, Mass.: Harvard University Press)

Russell, Bertrand. 1995. *Portraits From Memory* (Spokesman Books)

Shoemaker, Sydney. June 1994. 'Self Knowledge and "Inner Sense"' in Philosophy and Phenomenological Research, Vol. 54

Smith, A.D. 2002. *The Problem of Perception* (Cambridge: Harvard University Press)

Smith, Barry C. 1998. 'On Knowing One's Own Language' in *Knowing Our Own Minds* (Oxford: Oxford University Press)

Steup, M. and E. Sosa. 2005. *Contemporary Debates in Epistemology* (Blackwell Publishing Ltd)

Stern, Robert. 2000. *Transcendental Arguments and Scepticism* (New York: Oxford University Press)

Stone, James V. 2013. *Bayes Rule: A Tutorial Introduction to Bayesian Analysis* (Sebtel Press)

Stove, D.C. 1986. *The Rationality of Induction* (Oxford: Clarendon Press)

Strawson, P.F. 1952. *Individuals: An Essay in Descriptive Metaphysics* (London: Methuen)

Stroud, Barry. 2000. *Meaning, Understanding, and Practice* (Oxford: Oxford University Press)

Tallis, Raymond. 2016. *Aping Mankind* (Routledge Classics)

Weatherford, Roy. 1982. *Philosophical Foundations of Probability Theory* (London, Boston, Melbourne and Henley: Routledge and Kegan Paul)

Williams, D.C. 1947. *The Ground of Induction* (Cambridge, Mass.: Harvard University Press)

Williams, Michael. 1996. *Unnatural Doubts: Epistemological Realism and the Basis of Scepticism* (Princeton, New Jersey: Princeton University Press)

Wittgenstein, Ludwig. 1969. *On Certainty* (Oxford: Basil Blackwell)

——1976. *Philosophical Investigations* (Oxford: Basil Blackwell)

CPSIA information can be obtained
at www.ICGtesting.com
Printed in the USA
BVHW050842020622
638737BV00014B/267